ETYMA

An Introduction to Vocabulary-Building from Latin & Greek

C.A.E. Luschnig

with

L.J. Luschnig

UNIVERSITY
PRESS OF
AMERICA

LANHAM • NEW YORK • LONDON

Copyright © 1982 by

University Press of America,™ Inc.

4720 Boston Way
Lanham, MD 20706

3 Henrietta Street
London WC2E 8LU England

Printed in the United States of America

Library of Congress Cataloging in Publication Data

Luschnig, C. A. E.
    Etyma, an introduction to vocabulary-building
Latin & Greek.

    Includes bibliographical references.
    1. English language--Foreign elements--Latin.
2. English language--Foreign elements--Greek. 3.
Vocabulary. 4. English language--Word formation.
I. Luschnig, L. J. II. Title.
PE1582.L3L8   1982   422'.471   82-45038
ISBN 0-8191-2570-9
ISBN 0-8191-2571-7 (pbk.)

CARIS PARENTIBUS

Acknowledgements

The authors wish to take this opportunity to express their appreciation to those who helped with the preparation of the manuscript, expecially Barbara Hisel, Cindy McIntosh, Cindi Thornburg, Gretchen Giles, and Agnes Weeks; and to the College of Letters and Science of the University of Idaho for funding the typing of the text. To many friends for encouragement and help at various stages of the project, expecially Robyn M. Champagne, Thomas R. Loughran, Connie McQuillen, and Joan and Dennis West, and to several generations of undergraduates in English Word Origins at the University of Idaho, _gratias_ _maximas_ _agimus_.

TABLE OF CONTENTS

TABLE OF CONTENTS (continued)

PREFACE

The purpose of this book is to aid students who have not had the opportunity and pleasure of studying Latin and Greek in organizing the vast word stock of English (over eighty per cent of which is derived whether directly or indirectly from the classical tongues) by introducing to its readers the tools of vocabulary building as well as the fascinating study of word origins. In order to offer variety, we divide attention between the practical aspects of word formation and the interesting histories of words and groups of words. The first of the three parts of the book deals with the history of foreign influence on English: this section can be treated in class or, in a short course, used for students' projects as a holiday from the drier, more practical exercises. The second part begins with a short description of the Latin language and explains how Latin words are Englished and how Latin compounds are formed. Finally the third part introduces the readers to Greek words and procedures for compounding Greek elements used in both everyday and technical English. Throughout there are exercises concerned with interesting word origins, words derived from the names of people and places, words relating to Greek and Roman history, culture, literature, or mythology, so that the book is suitable for general humanities courses.

It has been our experience that students enjoy writing papers on the vocabularies of their fields, compiling word diaries, and looking up interesting words and phrases. The books which the authors found most useful and which we think should be made available to the students are:

The Oxford English Dictionary
Webster's Unabridged
The American Heritage Dictionary
Funk and Wagnall's Standard Dictionary of the English Language
Eric Partridge's Origins
R. F. Schaeffer, Latin-English Derivative Dictionary and Greek-English Derivative Dictionary (American Classical League, Oxford, Ohio)
Bergman, The Concise Dictionary of Twenty-Six Languages (Signet Books)
Mary S. Serjeantson, A History of Foreign Words in English (NY, 1936)

Some other books which we found helpful are:

Donald Ayers, English Words from Latin and Greek Elements (Tucson, 1965)
Henry Bradley, The Making of Modern English (New York, 1931)

William C. Grummel, <u>English</u> <u>Word-Building</u> <u>from</u> <u>Latin</u> <u>and</u> <u>Greek</u> (Palo Alto, 1961)
Edwin Lee Johnson, <u>Latin</u> <u>Words</u> <u>of</u> <u>Common</u> <u>English</u> (Boston, 1931)
Roland Kent, <u>Language</u> <u>and</u> <u>Philology</u> (Boston, 1923)
L. M. Myers and Richard L. Hoffman, <u>The</u> <u>Roots</u> <u>of</u> <u>Modern</u> <u>English</u> (Boston, 1979)

Moscow, Idaho   C. A. E. L.
Palm Sunday, 1982   L. J. L.

x

SECTION ONE: Chapter One

FAMILIES OF LANGUAGES

Definition: <u>FAMILY</u>:   a language group derived from the same
parent.

Over four thousand languages are spoken in the world. These,
along with their ancient ancestors, have been classified into several hundred families of languages, each family descended from a
common ancestor, which--even if it can no longer be known--is assumed to have once existed from the common roots and structures
that exist in known languages: that is, by comparing the words
and grammars of known languages, family relationship is discovered. Descent from a common ancestor is, then, the criterion that
is used in saying that languages belong to a given family.

The families of languages vary in size from a mere two distinct member languages to over a hundred. The group to which our
own language belongs is one of the largest (both in speakers and
in number of languages), the prolific <u>Indo-European</u> (I-E) family.
It has been so named for geographical reasons, since it extends
over Europe in the west (though there are some languages in Europe
that do not belong to it) all the way to India in the east.
<u>Aryan</u>--derived from a Sanskrit word meaning 'noble'--has been used
as a name for this language group, (and is also sometimes used as
a synonym for "Indo-Iranian," one of the branches of I-E, see
Chapter II), but for obvious political reasons, that designation
is not commonly used any longer but may be seen in older books on
I-E philology. Not only does the I-E family include most of the
languages in the territory of India, Persia, and Europe, extending
from Iceland, Ireland, and the Hispanic peninsula to Ceylon, but
also through colonization it covers the Americas, Australia, and
parts of Africa. Furthermore most non-Indo-European speakers who
study a second language, learn one of the I-E tongues.

Of the hundreds of other families of languages, let it suffice to name only a few and in the process to remark on some of
their contributions to English.

1. The AFRO-ASIATIC Family (also called Hamito-Semitic and
Semito-Hamitic) has two sub-families:

    1. SEMITIC (Semite: 'a descendant of Shem' [the first son
    of Noah]) includes Arabic, Hebrew, Ethiopic, Amharic (the
    official language of Ethiopia), Aramaic; ancient Phoenician
    and Syriac.

    2. HAMITIC (Hamite: 'one descended from Ham' [Noah's second

1

son]) includes the Berber dialects (of North Africa), the Cushitic dialects of Ethiopia, ancient Egyptian and its descendant Coptic.

From this family, English has borrowed a number of words: for example, from Hebrew, amen, shibboleth, manna, rabbi, seraphim; from Arabic, admiral (= emir), saffron, mattress, hazard, zero, alcohol; from Aramaic (or Hebrew), Messiah, mammon (through Latin and Greek from Aramaic māmōnā 'riches'); from ancient Egyptian, (through Greek and Latin), ebony, barge, elephant, ibis; Pharaoh (through a transcription into Hebrew); from Coptic, oasis (from Coptic ouah, 'to dwell'). [Additional words will be found at the end of this chapter in the exercises.]

Most of the words from Hebrew that have been taken into English come from the Bible, though there are some that were first borrowed by Greek or Latin, and by English only at second hand. Many Arabic words begin with al-, which is the word the (the article) in Arabic: e.g. alfalfa, algebra, alcove, alchemy (originally Greek), alkali, elixir (from al-iksir), artichoke (from alkharshuf), albacore. A large number of the entries from Arabic recall the exotic splendor of classical Arabic culture and the contribution of Arabic scientific and mathematical discovery: of the latter, zero, cipher, algebra: of the former, sofa, mattress, harem.

An example of a Semitic word that has come into English:

The stories behind words are often fascinating, revealing aspects of history, culture, religion.

SHIBBOLETH is such a word. It is a word from Biblical Hebrew that first came into English as a transliteration of its Hebrew original in Wyclif's translation of the Bible of 1382.

The modern meaning of shibboleth is "a password, test or watchword of a party or faction," or " a password, phrase, custom, usage, slogan, catchword that is distinctive of a particular group" [Scribner's dictionary]. Its meaning in Hebrew is "an ear of corn" or "a stream in flood." How did the word for "an ear of corn" or "a stream in flood" come to mean a "password"? The answer can be found by reading the Biblical passage in which the word occurs [Judges xii. 4-6]:

Then Jephthah gathered all the men of Gilead and fought with Ephraim; and the men of Gilead smote Ephraim, because they said, "You are fugitives of Ephraim, you Gileadites, in the midst of Ephraim

2

and Manasseh." And the Gileadites took the fords
of the Jordan against the Ephraimites. And when
any of the fugitives of Ephraim said, "Let me go
over," the men of Gilead said to him, "Are you an
Ephraimite?" When he said, "No," they said to him,
"Then say Shibboleth," and he said "Sibboleth," for
he could not pronounce it right; then they seized
him and slew him at the fords of the Jordan. And
there fell at that time forty-two thousand of the
Ephramites. [RSV]

The word Shibboleth was, as you see from this context,
used by Jephthah, king of the Gileadites, to distinguish the
fleeing Ephraimites, who could not pronounce the sh sound,
from his own men. For want of proficiency in their enemy's
tongue, 42,000 men died: can you think of a better argument
than that for bilingualism? The word passed into English,
first to refer to this passage of Judges, but was gradually
extended by a people well-versed in the Sacred Scripture to a
more general use, to mean any word or sound which a person
has trouble pronouncing or which can be used as a test to detect foreigners: for example, "They had a Shibboleth to discover them, he who pronounced Brot and Cawse for Bread and
Cheese hat his head lopt off" [John Cleveland, 1658]. Later
it extended to an even looser use: a custom, habit, mode of
dress or mode of speech which distinguishes a class or set of
persons; and a password or formula adopted by a group for
discerning its members and excluding others.

2.   URAL-ALTAIC (a hypothetical group including Uralic and
Altaic): this group is spread over a surprisingly wide geographical area.

URALIC language group:

1. Finno-Ugric includes Magyar (Hungarian), Estonian,
Finnish, Lapp.

2. Samoyedic: the languages of the Samoyeds who live in the
tundra lands of Northeastern European Soviet Union and
Northwestern Siberia.

ALTAIC group: Turkic (e.g. Turkish, Turkoman, Tatar, Uzbek),
Tungus (a language spoken in Eastern Siberia), Mongolian, and
possibly Korean.

English has borrowed some words from several of these languages including, from the Uralic group: hussar, coach (from the
place name Kocs), goulash, paprika (from Magyar) and lemming (from
Lapp). From the Turkic group of the Altaic sub-family we have

3

borrowed such words as <u>khan</u>, <u>horde</u>, <u>tulip</u>, <u>odalisque</u>, <u>turban</u>, <u>caftan</u>, <u>coffee</u>, <u>caviar</u>, <u>pasha</u>, <u>fez</u>, <u>macrame</u>, <u>latakia</u>.

An example of a word from the Uralic group:

COACH in all its meanings comes to us from Magyar, the language of Hungary. It is derived from <u>kocsi</u> meaning 'of Kocs,' a place near Buda, in Hungary. Forms of the word, which came into use in Hungary in the late 15th century when the new kind of vehicle (i.e. 'coach') was first built at Kocs, appear throughout Europe from the sixteenth century (in England by 1556). Its original name was <u>kocsi</u> <u>szeker</u> in Hungarian ("Kocs-cart," rendered in Latin <u>cocius</u> <u>currus</u> or <u>currus</u> <u>kotsi</u>). The first meaning was a large closed carriage, usually a state carriage for royalty or officials of the government (as "the Lord Mayor's coach"), or a public carriage (stage-coach). Its use has since been extended to a railroad car, a bus, and the economy section of an airplane. The use of the word COACH to apply to a private tutor who helps students prepare for an examination begins as University slang in the 19th century: "Besides the regular college tutor, I secured the assistance of what, in the slang of the day, we irreverently termed 'a coach'" (1850). Some years later, COACH began to be used to mean an athletic trainer.

3. SINO-TIBETAN (A far-Eastern language family):

SINITIC includes the various dialects of Chinese (e.g. Mandarin, Cantonese, Fukien, Amoy, Shanghai).

TIBETO-BURMAN includes Tibetan, Burmese, Lolo, Balti. English words from these languages mostly describe (as do the foregoing words from Semito-Hamitic and Ural-Altaic) things peculiar to the culture of the speakers.

From Chinese, we have borrowed such words as: <u>ginseng</u>, <u>tea</u> (from the Amoy dialect: the Mandarin word is <u>ch'a</u>) and several of its varieties: <u>pekoe</u>, <u>souchong</u>, <u>oolong</u>; as well as <u>tong</u>, <u>ketchup</u>, <u>japan</u> (a kind of varnish, from the Chinese name for Japan [<u>Jihpun</u>, 'Sunrise']). And from Tibetan: <u>lama</u> (a Buddhist monk), <u>dalai-lama</u>, <u>yak</u>. The Japanese language does not belong to this oriental group, and in fact has no proven affinities to any other language, although it does use many words borrowed from Chinese. Among the words English has taken from Japanese are the familiar: <u>kimono</u>, <u>kamikaze</u> ('divine wind' from <u>kami-</u> 'God' and <u>kaze</u> 'wind'), <u>sakē</u>, <u>samurai</u>, <u>hara-kiri</u>, <u>ginkgo</u>, <u>sen</u>, <u>geisha</u>; as well as a number of Chinese words that Japanese borrowed before lending to us (e.g. <u>soy</u>, <u>tycoon</u>, <u>yen</u>, <u>jujitsu</u>).

Our earliest borrowing from Chinese is the word silk which shows numerous permutations in its wanderings from language to language. SILK comes to us via Latin sericum from the Latin word Seres or from the Greek Sēres, respectively the Latinized and Hellenized names for the oriental people (perhaps the Chinese) from whom silk was first obtained. Other words were borrowed from Chinese first through translations of foreign works and then, starting in the 16th c. were introduced by English traders and travellers. Japanese loan-words on the other hand are very scarce in English until the opening of Japan to the West in the 19th c. The study of the foreign words in English can provide to the thoughtful student a guide for the cultural, literary, political, and commerical history of English-speaking peoples.

4. Other Language Groups from which English has borrowed:

AUSTRONESIAN (also called Malayo-Polynesian).

This group includes Indonesian, Melanesian, Micronesian, Polynesian (Hawaiian among others) [note: -nesian is from Greek nēsos, 'island'].

Although there are no very early loan-words from this group and most have entered English since the latter part of the 16th c., some have become very familiar. As with many of the loan-words that have come to us through commerce, colonization, and travel, most of the words from this group describe plants, animals, and products made from them that are characteristic of the area: for example, among the earliest loan-words from Malay are, sago, bamboo, gong, gingham, cockatoo, launch, bantam, caddy (for tea, from kati, 'a weight'), junk, orangoutang (from Malay ōrang ūtan, 'man of the woods'); amok (from Malay amuk, 'rushing in a frenzy to murder'), rattan, raffia.

In the late eighteenth c., as a result of Captain Cook's explorations and discoveries, the first Polynesian words begin to enter English. Besides the various names for plants and parrots, some of the words that have found a place in everyday English speech are: tattoo, taboo (also spelled tabu), poi, ukelele, luau, lanai. The first word borrowed from Australian aborigines was kangaroo (used by Captain Cook in his Journals for 4 August 1770). Others from the 18th and early 19th c. are koala, boomerang, wombat, and a number of words describing native animals, birds, and trees.

KANGAROO

Attached to the word kangaroo is an amusing if apocryphal story. Captain Cook writes (1770), "The animals which I

5

have before mentioned, called by the Natives Kangooroo or Kanguru." Obviously the worthy captain believed that this was the name given it by the natives of Queensland, Australia, but other explorers did not find the word in use. Thus the story grew up that when Captain Cook pointed at the remarkable marsupial and inquired "What is that?", the bewildered native responded "Kangooroo," meaning "I don't know!" The debate over the origin of the word and the native name of the creature can be seen in these passages from the diaries of later travellers:

1770 The largest was called by the natives kangooroo. [Banks]

1787 We found that the animal called kangooroo, at Endeavour River, was known under the same name here [in Tasmania]. [Anderson]

1792 The animal...called the kangaroo (but by the natives patagorong) we found in great numbers. [Hunter]

1793 The large, or grey kanguroo, to which the natives (of Port Jackson) give the name of Pat-ag-a-ran. Note, Kanguroo was a name unknown to them for any animal, until we introduced it. [Teuch]

1834 Kong-go-rong, the Emu...likely the origin of the barbarism, kangaroo, used by the English, as the name of an animal called Mo-a-ne. [Threlkeld]

1835 They [the natives of the Darling Range, W.A.] distinctly pronounced 'kangaroo' without having heard any of us utter the sound. [Wilson]

1850 (Kangaroo) It is very remarkable that this word, supposed to be Australian, is not found as the name of this singular marsupial animal in any language of Australia. [Wilson]

Such is the intriguing information to be found in the Oxford English Dictionary (s.v. kangaroo). Whatever the origin of the word, whatever the aboriginal name for the beast, it is now called kangaroo by all the Australian tribes, thanks to the English explorers Captain James Cook & Sir Joseph Banks and their anonymous knowing or inventive native informant.

NORTH AMERICAN

From the Americas, too, a number of words has entered the

English language. Those from North American Indian dialects began to be adopted after 1607, the date of the refounding of the colony of Virginia; later settlements brought the English into contact with the dialects farther up the coast. Some of the Amerind words remain as resident aliens even in their native American land, used only to describe customs and objects of Indian culture: such as wigwam (from the Ojibwa language), wampum (Algonquin), squaw, papoose (also Algonquin), tepee (Sioux), tomahawk (Algonquin); but others are in general use, especially the names of animals, plants and foods, and things that have been adopted for general use by English speakers: racoon, opossum, persimmon, moose, hominy, hickory, woodchuck, catalpa, pecan, caribou, succotash, tamarack, chipmunk, catawba, toboggan, moccasin; and from Eskimo: kayak, umiak, igloo. Some native American words have been genuinely naturalized by English, their meanings extended to apply to the culture of the English-speakers: among these are mugwump (from Natick mugquomp, 'great chief'), pow-wow (from an Algonquin word that originally meant 'medicine man' but later was used for 'conference').

SOUTH AND CENTRAL AMERICAN

From South and Central America, once again we have many plant and animal names, and the names of some very important foods, as well as some imported objects of everyday use:
Plants and Animals: iguana, yucca, petunia, tobacco, llama, condor, jaguar, coca, vicuna, ocelot.
Foods: cocoa, cayenne, quinine, mescal, potato, maize, chocolate, tomato, chili, avocado, cashew, tapioca.
Objects, etc.: canoe, hammock, poncho, barbecue, buccaneer.

AFRICAN

Few words have entered English from the languages of Africa (other than from the Semito-Hamitic group). From the large Bantu family [Bantu in Bantu means 'people': ba plural prefix + ntu 'man'] which includes Congo, Swahili, Zulu, Luba, Kikuyu, Luganda, Nyanja, we have the word zebra. Other common words from Africa are gnu, gumbo, voodoo, banana, okra, yam, cola, gorilla (which was borrowed by Greek through the Carthaginian geographer Hanno who used it as the alleged native name of an African tribe of hairy men, though the word is actually used in Greek only in the feminine; the word was first used in English in 1847 for the largest of the anthropoid apes).

EXERCISES

Exercise I. Non-Indo-European Words Adopted into English

7

Choose one or more of the words in the list below and find the story behind it, trying to answer the following questions:

1. What language does it come from? What family does that language belong to ?

2. What does the word mean in its original language?

3. What does it mean as an English word?

4. If it has changed significantly in meaning, try to find out how it got from 2 to 3. Notice any change in part of speech.

5. When did we adopt this word? Write down the date of and the quotation given for the first citation in the Oxford English Dictionary.

6. Consider, if possible, the significance of the date of this word's entry into English: was it borrowed during a period of commericalism, exploration, imperialism, war? Was its first English-speaking user a merchant, explorer, naturalist, military or governmental official? Or is it a religious or literary word?

7. Would you say that this word is a 'naturalized citizen' in English (extended and used for something in our everyday lives), or is it a 'resident alien' (still used only to apply to an aspect of its native culture)? Did we borrow an object with this word or have we applied it to something we already had? [For example: burnous (or burnoose) remains foreign, an Arabic article of clothing, but sash (also an Arabic word) is much more at home in English, used to describe a variety of cloth belts. Or when we eat couscous, we know that we are having foreign food, but sherbet is right at home in our freezer and can be bought at any supermarket.

List of non-I-E words for consideration:

barge   admiral   hazard   mammon   sirocco   assassin   kosher
ghoul   safari   azimuth   nadir   zenith   minaret   jar   tunic
arsenal   calibre   mufti   alfalfa   alchemy   hegira   muezzin
harem   syrup   sherbet   couscous mattress artichoke candy
burnoose mohair   elixir   fakir   Messiah   elephant   Pharaoh
oasis   amen   rabbi   kimono   soy   mikado   tycoon   magazine
cinnamon jubilee   japan   ketchup   lama   tong   cabal   sash
shekel   babel   behemoth gingham   caddy (as in tea-caddy)
launch   orangutang voodoo   gumbo   cola   tobacco   macrame
gorilla   odalisque tulip   amok   mugwump   powwow   succotash
hammock   poncho   buccaneer tomato   tapioca   horde   pariah

8

Exercise II. Word Games

1. Match the words in column A to those in column B that are derived from the same Arabic root.

	A		B
1.	admiral	a.	Alcatraz
2.	albatross	b.	azimuth
3.	assassin	c.	cipher
4.	syrup	d.	emir
5.	zenith	e.	hashish
6.	zero	f.	sherbet

2. Match each word in column A with a word or phrase in column B that translates its original meaning:

	A		B
1.	algebra	a.	hereditary drummer
2.	amok	b.	striped
3.	arsenal	c.	the brine of pickled fish
4.	assassin	d.	great lord or chief (use twice)
5.	bantu	e.	a die for coining
6.	fakir	f.	I do not know
7.	gingham	g.	ear of corn/stream in flood
8.	japan	h.	dwelling place
9.	kamikaze	i.	the people
10.	kangaroo	j.	man of the woods
11.	ketchup	k.	sun's origin
12.	macrame	l.	divine wind
13.	magazine	m.	a turban
14.	mattress	n.	the annointed
15.	Messiah	o.	a towel
16.	mufti	p.	medicine-man
17.	mugwump	q.	a storehouse
18.	oasis	r.	wine or other drink
19.	orangutang	s.	place where something is thrown
20.	pariah	t.	the putting together of broken parts
21.	pow-wow	u.	eater of hashish
22.	sequin	v.	workshop
23.	shibboleth	w.	a Mohammedan priest
24.	syrup	x.	a poor man
25.	tulip	y.	rushing in a frenzy to murder
26.	tycoon		

ANSWERS:

1: 1-d; 2-a; 3-e; 4-f; 5-b; 6-c

2: 1-t; 2-y; 3-v; 4-u; 5-i; 6-x; 7-b; 8-k; 9-l; 10-f; 11-c; 12-o;
13-q; 14-s; 15-n; 16-w; 17-d; 18-h; 19-j; 20-a; 21-p; 22-e;
23-g; 24-r; 25-m; 26-d

THE INDO-EUROPEAN FAMILY OF LANGUAGES

The Indo-European family tree has eight main branches (as are shown in the chart below). English belongs to the <u>Teutonic</u>, or <u>Germanic</u>, branch in its basic vocabulary and grammatical structure, but has elements of vocabulary from all the others as well as from many languages that do not belong to the I-E family at all, as has been demonstrated in the previous chapter. Of the other branches, two will be especially considered in this book: <u>Italic</u> which survives in Latin and the modern Romance languages (Italian, French, Spanish, Portuguese, Rumanian, etc.); and <u>Hellenic</u> which is known from Ancient Greek texts and Modern Greek. Languages from these groups, notably Latin, Greek, and French, have greatly influenced and enlarged the vocabulary of English.

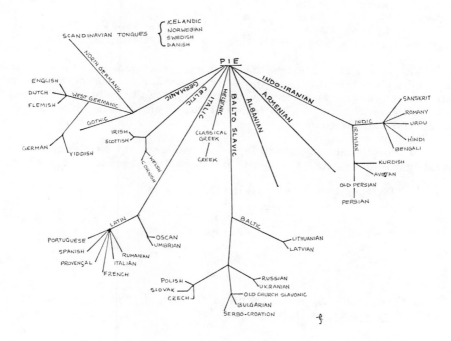

Chart showing branches of I-E

11

ENGLISH AND THE OTHER GERMANIC LANGUAGES

That English belongs to the Germanic family is clear from a comparison of native words in some of the languages in the branch. To take a few examples:

English	German	Dutch	Swedish	Norwegian	Icelandic	Yiddish
good	gut	goed	god	god	goðr	gut
thirst	Durst	dorst	törst	tørst	þorsti	darscht
book	Buch	boek	bok	bok	bók	buch
flask	Flasche	fles	flaska	flaske	flaska	flasch
arm	Arm	arm	arm	arm	armr	orm
and	und	en	och	og	og	un
kiss	Kuss	kus	kyss	kyss	kyssa	kisch
life	Leben	leven	liv	liv	lif	leben
knee	Knie	knie	knä	kne	kné	knie
learn	lernen	leren	lära	laere	laera	lernen
milk	Milch	melk	mjölk	melk	mjólk	milch
warm	warm	warm	varm	varm	varmr	varim
glass	Glas	glas	glass	glas	glas	glos
son	Sohn	zoon	son	sønn	sonr	suhn
daughter	Tochter	dochter	dotter	datter	dóttir	tochter

These words would--with a little practice--sound familiar to an English speaker because they are so similar to common words in our own language. Many more German words can become understandable to those who know a few rules of consonant correspondence between the two languages.

1. English t, for example, usually shows up as German z at the beginning or end of a word, or as ss in the middle of a word.

ENGLISH	GERMAN
to	zu
tongue	Zunge
heart	Herz
(to) let	lassen
street	Strasse

2. English p appears as pf in German at the beginning of a word, as f, ff, or pf in other positions.

ENGLISH	GERMAN
pepper	Pfeffer
harp	Harfe
plum	Pflaume
ape	Affe

3. Where English shows <u>k</u>, German often has <u>ch</u>:

ENGLISH	GERMAN
(to) seek	suchen
cake	Kuchen
break	brechen
week	Woche

4. Where English had <u>d</u>, German shows <u>t</u> (or <u>tt</u>) and where English shows <u>th</u>, German has <u>d</u>.

ENGLISH	GERMAN
(to) do	tun
deed	Tat
death	Tod
bed	Bett
bread	Brot
thumb	Daumen
then	dann

Words of the type in these lists are called COGNATES ('born together', from Latin <u>co</u>-, 'with, together' + (g)<u>natus</u>, 'born'). DEFINITION: <u>Cognates</u> are words in different languages that are derived from a common ancestor. It is possible to show such correspondences not only between words in the various Germanic languages, but among all the languages in the Indo-European family. The discovery of the laws of consonant correspondence was the heroic feat of linguists of the last century, notably Jacob Grimm, a German philologist (of the brothers Grimm who collected the familiar fairy tales), and Karl Verner, a Danish philologist, who gave us, respectively, Grimm's Law and Verner's Law. These laws show how words in the language groups of the I-E family are related according to a regular pattern of change in consonants that are (generally speaking) produced in the same part of the mouth. Most often, for example, labials will correspond to labials, dentals to dentals, palatals to palatals. DEFINITION: <u>Labials</u> are those sounds formed by closing the lips, as <u>p</u>, <u>b</u>, <u>f</u>, <u>v</u>, <u>ph</u> (from Latin LABIUM, 'lip'). <u>Dentals</u> are those sounds formed with the tongue in the region of the teeth, as <u>d</u>, <u>t</u>, <u>th</u> (from Latin, DENS, stem DENT-, 'tooth'). <u>Palatals</u> are formed in the region of the hard or soft palate as k, g, ch, y (from Latin PALATUM, 'palate').

For example: I-E p, which remains p in most of the other groups, changes to f in most of the Germanic tongues (in German, the f-sound is represented by the letter v) and v in Dutch. English: FATHER

> German: Vater; Dutch vadar; Swedish & Danish, fadar;
>   Norwegian, far; Yiddish, foter
> Latin: pater [cf. French père, Spanish & Italian, pad-
>   re; Portuguese, pai]
> Greek: patēr
> Sanskrit: pita

I-E s which remains s in most of the languages sometimes changes to h in Greek [s becomes h also in Avestan, Old Persian, and Armenian].

English: STAND

> German: stehen
> Latin: stare
> Ancient Greek: histanai
> Sanskrit: stha
> Russian: stoyat; Czech: stati; Serbo-Croatian: stajati;
>   Polish: stać

I-E bh remains bh in Sanskrit, but changes to ph in Greek, to f (or b) in Latin and to b in the Germanic languages (and to p or b in the other branches).

English: BEAR (vb. meaning 'to carry') and BRING

> German: bringen
> Old Irish: in(d)ber
> Latin: ferre
> Greek: pherein
> Sanskrit: bhri

Or, from the I-E root BHA- 'to speak'

> Old English: bannan ('to proclaim') which yields Modern
>   English ban, banns
> Latin: fari, fatus ('speak') which gives us fate, fa-
>   ble, preface
> Greek: phanai ('speak'), phēmē ('sound'), phōnē
>   ('voice') which give us phone, telephone,
>   phonetics, euphemism, cacophony, and many
>   others.

14

I-E i/y appears variously as y, j in most of the groups, but in Greek as h or z and in Old English and Middle Dutch as g. From the I-E root YEUG- (meaning 'to join'):

Old English: geog (meaning 'yoke')
Modern English: yoke
Latin: jugum, jungere [which give us such words as jugular, conjugate, subjugate, join, junction, adjunct]
Greek: zugon ('yoke') [which gives Modern English zygo-, syzygy, zeugma]
Sanskrit: Yoga

SOME THINGS THAT ARE KNOWN ABOUT THE INDO-EUROPEANS

Indo-European may be defined as the relationship of these languages--both ancient and modern--to each other: a relationship that indicates a common ancestor called Proto-Indo-European. Proto-Indo-European (PIE) was spoken long before the advent of writing and so left no direct trace. Writing has preserved for us some of the ancient languages: Latin, Greek, Sanskrit among them, ancient tongues of which knowledge was never lost, but which were passed on from generation to generation in the natural way; and when they ceased to be spoken in their classical form, they continued to be preserved in the schools much as they are today. Nor is it correct to say that they are dead languages. The death of languages comes hard and twinges of life appear again and again. Ancient Greek may not be--indeed it certainly is not--spoken now just as it was two and a half millennia ago: but its direct descendant, Modern Greek, closely preserves its words and roots and its grammar, in a simplified form, just as the Hellenic people proudly protect their great and enduring classical heritage. So, too, Sanskrit is preserved and read by all educated Hindus in their ancient religious texts, the Vedas (Veda, meaning 'knowledge', itself preserves the ancient PIE root weid- 'to see', related to our word wise, to Latin videre, to Greek idea and historia) and is preserved too in the spoken language of millions of people in such languages as Hindi, Urdu, Punjabi, Bengali, and Romany.

Finally, Latin has left its mark through the classical texts, the basis for all humanistic education, and through its linguistic impact not only on its direct descendants (the Romance languages) but on English and many another language as well.

From the relationship of words in the various languages in the I-E family, linguists have come up with basic I-E roots, a dictionary, as it were, of the roots that are known or

15

conjectured. The reconstruction of I-E roots is a tricky business that is not undertaken lightly. I-E linguistics (formerly called Comparative Philology) is a game with complex rules: the rules of sound correspondences between the scattered children of the Proto-Indo- European language, the rules of vowel gradation, the complex histories of the languages that have survived in spoken and written form, and the histories of the people who spoke or speak them. The study of linguistics is the study of change: all languages change constantly, though the changes are largely imperceptible to their speakers: this is why a sudden change, such as a neologism (or newly coined word or phrase), is so often greeted with disgust as a barbarous use of language. By studying the changes in languages that are known, linguists are able to work back to those that are no longer known.

But, a word of caution is in order: PIE cannot now be known in its entirety: it cannot be spoken, though we use its roots--changed and built upon in the various member languages--constantly in our daily conversations. The early comparative linguists did believe that it was possible to find the basic language and they sought for it religiously in the hope of finding the origin of all languages, the pre-Babel mother-tongue of the human race. Some believed it was Sanskrit. And Sanskrit did play a crucial role in the discovery of the parent of all I-E groups. An English judge and philologist, Sir William Jones, noticed the similarities among Sanskrit, Greek and Latin, Gothic, Celtic, and Old Persian and realized that they "have sprung from some common source, which, perhaps, no longer exists." The linguistic connection of East and West had been noticed before, but Jones' work with Sanskrit was a new starting point which--in the hands of a series of brilliant scholars--has shown the language branches to be sisters, rather than descendants of Sanskrit, their related native words to be cognates rather than derivatives.

It should be noticed that when we apply the term family and other words implying family relationships--kinship, mother-tongue, sister-tongue, cognate, descendant--to languages, we are using a metaphor, with the purpose (as is the nature of metaphor) of making a strange and distant concept clear and familiar and even homely. But the family is indeed an ancient institution known to the Indo-Europeans; and the transference of family relationships to other aspects of life and thought is an ancient Indo-European metaphor. For the study of the common words in the various languages has not only made it possible for us to know I-E roots but it has also told us some things about the nature of I-E society and environment. Language is the most important and the most enduring aspect of culture. And the aspect of a language that offers the clearest, most cogent guide to what its users thought about and how they lived and perceived the world is its vocabulary. The vocabulary of a language is for a linguist what potsherds and soil samples are for an archaeologist. By examining the vocabulary of a language, we find out what foods a people eats, what kinds of trees they distinguish, what seasons they recognize, what kind of climate they have, whether or not they are an agricultural society, what clothing they wear, what degrees of kinship they recognize as integral to the family unit, what God or gods they worship. Word study is, as it were, the archaeology of a language. But of equal importance--where archaeology is left behind--from the words a people uses, we can learn something about their minds, how they perceive and think and feel about the world and how they define knowledge itself, and even how they perceive language.

For example:

1.   The Indo-European word for God has been reconstructed as *deiw-os [note that * beside a word indicates that the word is not actually known from written or spoken records, but that it is postulated from the available evidence] and the name of the chief god as *dyeupter. In Latin he is called Juppiter, in Greek Zeus pater ('father Zeus'), in Sanskrit Dyaus pitar. The pater element in these names for the highest god means 'father' and indicates a patriarchal society. It shows further the transference of an aspect of human society to the Divine. It indicates too that the idea of God the Father is very old indeed even among our non-Semitic ancestors and that it pervades even the preliterate, pagan Indo-European culture.

The meaning of the root *deiw- (of the word *deiw-os, 'god') is 'to shine'; and it shows up in many words meaning 'sky', 'heaven', or 'god', indicating that the chief god in the I-E pantheon was a sky and weather god, one who was to be propitiated by an agricultural people, dependent upon nature and the weather.

Some other words from this root, with their English descendants are:

Germanic: *Tiwaz which shows up in Old English Tiw, Tig, Tiu, the god of war and sky, whose name is preserved in the word Tuesday.

Latin: deus, 'god' which survives in many English words; among them: deity, Deism, adieu, joss, deification, deify, deific.

And in Latin, divus, 'divine', which appears in English in divine, diva, divinity, divination, divinize.

The name of the Latin goddess Diana ("the luminous one" or

moon goddess) is from this root too, as well as the Latin word
dies, 'day', from which English gets many derivatives, including:
dial, diary, dismal, (possibly from dies mali [bad or unlucky
days]), diurnal, meridian, a.m., p.m., adjourn, journal, journey,
sojourn, quotidian.

From the name of Juppiter (Latin spelling), besides the planet Jupiter, we get the name Julius and its variants (meaning 'descendant of Jupiter') and the name of the month July (named after
Julius Caesar). And from the variant Jove is derived jovial('born
under the sign of Jupiter', the planet regarded as the source of
happiness).

The word *deiw-os itself and its association with brightness
and day tells us more about the Indo-European view of deity than
the discovery of temples or other artifacts ever could.

2.   Other roots give strong evidence that the Indo-Europeans were
a patriarchal society: the word pater (Lat. pater, Gk. patēr Skt.
pitar, Gm. Vater) means 'father' in the sense of 'adult male head
of the household' as in the Latin expression pater familias, a social institution of great antiquity as is seen from the evidence
of I-E vocabulary. There are names for the -in-laws of the bride
but not for those of the husband, indicating that she entered his
home and became part of his family. The social unit was probably
the extended family: the root *bhrater- [English brother, Latin
frater] seems to mean 'fellow member of the clan or group' and so
would extend to male relatives in the group, beyond those with
common parents, as the Greek cognate phratēr 'fellow clansman'
indicates. Likewise *swesor- [Latin soror, Gm. Schwester, English
sister] seems to mean a 'female member of one's own group' and
very likely stems from the root *seu-, reflexive pronoun referring
to the members of a social group as distinct from outsiders:
-self: from this root, a number of English derivatives, both
native and borrowed will show its social significance: self, sib,
gossip, swain (originally meaning 'servant'), suicide (from Latin
sui 'of oneself' + cide 'killing'), per se ('through itself', from
Latin); the Latin prefix se- 'without, apart' (i.e. 'by oneself')
as in secede, secret, secure; possibly the Latin word solus
('alone', as in sole, soliloquy, solitude, etc.); sodality (from
Latin sodalis 'companion' < 'one's own, relative'); suescere
(Latin, 'to become accustomed' < 'make one's own'; cf. custom,
consuetude, mansuetude).   Related to this root are Greek ēthos
('custom': ethic) and ethnos ('people, nation' < 'people of one's
own kind': ethnic) and Sanskrit Swami ('prince, owner' < 'one's
own master'). [Note: the sign < means "from"]

Words for the community are *dem-, both the 'house' and the
'household': Latin domus, dominus: 'house', 'master: head of

18

the house': cf. English derivatives from the Latin, domicile, dominion, dominate, domain; Greek despotēs 'master of the house' with its English derivative despot; and possibly the native English word timber [i.e. 'material for building a house']. *weik- represents the next unit, the village or clan: Latin vicus 'quarter of a town or neighborhood', villa, 'country house, farm' whence come English vicinity, villa, village, villain, wick; in Greek, oikos, oikia, 'house, dwelling': whence English ecology, economy, diocese, parish, ecumenical; in Sanskrit, vaisya 'settler'; and perhaps *da-mo 'division of society: in Greek dēmos 'the people' (cf. English derivatives: deme, demos, democracy, demagogue).

3. Economy: The Indo-Europeans were an agricultural society: they practiced stock-breeding and the cultivation of cereals. Several types of grain are distinguished in the I-E word- stock: corn, wheat, spelt, barley, rye [*grano-, *yewo-, *puro, *bhares-, *wrughyo-]. There are words for ploughing, sowing, gathering, grinding and for pasture land. Further, we know what animals they bred: pigs (*su- and *porko; cf. pork and swine); sheep and lambs (*owi- and *agwhno-; cf. ovine and Agnus Dei); goats (*aig- and *ghaido-), kine (*gwou-). The dog (*kwon-; cf. cynic, hound) was domesticated and the name of the dog may be the ancestor (linguistically speaking) of the horse (*ekwo-, cf. equus in Latin, from which we get equine, equestrian), which the I-E had by the end of the third millenium B.C., a time of great expansion and migration for them, though they probably did not have the wheel until after the dispersion of their community. Roots implying or at least suggesting the knowledge of the wheel are early, but were first used of other things [for example, *aks- 'axle' was originally 'a pivot-like junction'; *nobh-, 'nave, hub' originally meant 'navel'; *kwel- the original root of 'wheel' meant 'to go around' and was a term for the pasturing of flocks; *wegh- the root of wagon and vehicle meant 'convey'].

Metals and mining, the I-E did know. Gold, silver, copper, bronze and ore are common to the various groups; but words for iron, well-known to be a late-comer, vary in the different dialects. Words exist, too, for a variety of household activities: weaving, shaping, (of dough for bread and of mud or clay for building), crushing, cooking, sewing, weaving, spinning.

4. Environment: Some words for plants and animals and climate are especially significant: for they can help us define the geographical limits of the I-E, though their homeland is yet to be discovered with any certainty. Among the trees for which there is an I-E root is the beech: *bhago-: Latin, fagus; Greek, phēgos; Russian buziná, Serbo-Croatian, bâs; Polish, bez, Old English, bok. Since the beech is geographically limited, some scholars

have proposed that the original PIE people must have come from Europe and probably from northern Europe, but the evidence from the beech has lost most of its weight in recent years, since, for one thing, the geographical range of the beech may have changed over the millennia, and though the root appears widely in I-E languages, it is used to refer to several types of trees: the Slavic cognates designate the elder, the Greek is a type of oak. Other trees that were known to the PIE are the birch, the pine, the aspens and poplars, the willows, the maples, the alders, the elms, the ashes, the yews and the oaks.   Among the animals that were known to them are the wolf, bear, beaver, mouse, hare; and they had a generic name for wild beast, and for fish.   Specific fish for which names have survived are salmon and eel.   The birds (*awi-; cf. Latin avis, the source of English aviary) definitely known and named are the crane, eagle, thrush, starling, sparrow, finch, and woodpecker.   Nor were our distant linguistic ancestors free from insects: for there are words for wasp, hornet, fly, bedbug and louse; and of course for the bee and its honey, the source of sweetening for the ancient peoples and the base of the first certain I-E alcoholic beverage: mead.

From the lack of a common word for 'sea' the I-E are believed to have been an inland people, though they had boats and a word for rowing.   There is further a common word for 'snow,' but-- strange to say--a variety of roots for 'rain'; but common sense tells us that they must have been aware of the phenomenon.

To conclude, we can be certain that the I-E counted according to the decimal system.   Curiously, although there exist common roots for the numbers two through ten, the words for the number one vary from dialect to dialect.

	I-E	Latin	Greek	German
2	*dwo	duo	duo	zwei
3	*trei	tres, tria	treis, tria	drei
4	*kwetwer-	quattuor	tessares	fier
5	*penkwe	quinque	pente	funf
6	*sweks	sex	hex	sechs
7	*septm	septem	hepta	sieben
8	*okto	octo	oktō	acht
9	*newn	novem	ennea	neun
10	*dekm	decem	deka	zehn

The ways of expressing 11 and 12 in the various languages show that the peoples based their computational system on tens: Eleven means 'one left'; twelve means 'two left': that is, left over after ten.

undecim means one (unus) + ten (decem)
duodecim means two (duo) + ten (decem). [Latin]

hendeka means one (hen) + ten (deka)
dōdeka means two (duo) + ten (deka). [Greek]

I-E Mind and Spirit: This is not the place for a discussion of
the I-E world view. A few roots will have to suffice in lieu of a
demonstration of I-E intellectual and spiritual development. The
root *seu- [meaning self, apart, one's own] shows some degree of
self-consciousness and awareness, both of the individual and of
the social group as an entity apart from others. Is this not the
kind of awareness that is a sine qua non for all intellectualism
and art, for history, philosophy, and poetry?

There is the root *men- meaning 'to think' which has derivatives referring to various kinds of mental activity. English
words showing this root include mind (a native Teutonic word). In,
the Germanic tongues one of the meanings of the root was 'to
love' from which we get the word minion (meaning 'a favorite, a
dependent, or a subordinate'): it is interesting that love should
be a quality of mind. But when we consider that one of the Greek
derivatives of this root in mania (madness), the connection is
less strange (and the Greeks, at least the smart ones, considered
madness a gift of the gods): from this Greek connection, of
course, we have inherited an ever-expanding list of -manias, as
well as maniac, manic, mantic, and maenad (the maenads were
uninhibited worshippers of Dionysus). From Latin mens (mind) we
get mental, demented, mention. From the same root is the Latin
verb meminisse (to remember) from various prefixed forms of which
English has received memento, comment, reminiscent. Notice that
we have taken the step from thinking to remembering, obviously a
connected activity: in Greek mythology and poetry mnemosyne (memory) is the mother of the Muses, patronesses of all the arts.
Mnemonic (having to do with mnēmē, 'memory') devices, furthermore,
are to be cultivated by students because they give a decided ad-
vantage at examinations and other social activities over amnesia.

Other mental and perceptual activities are seen in the roots
*gno- 'to know' and *weid- 'to see'. From the latter English has
a number of native Germanic words including wise, wisdom, wise-
acre, wit. In Greek, different forms of the same root meant both
'to see' and 'to know': Greek derivatives of this root have given
us idea, ideo-, kaleidoscope, idol, psychedelic, history, story.
The Sanskrit sacred texts, the vedas are named from this root
(veda means both 'knowledge' and 'I have seen'). From Latin
vidēre (to see) we have borrowed video, television (a word half
Latin and half Greek), view, vision, advise, and numerous other

21

common words. The root *gno- has given us our native know and knowledge, cunning, uncouth; gnome, gnostic, agnostic, prognosis, diagnosis (from Greek); notice, noble, recognize and many others from Latin.

Nor were the Indo-Europeans devoid of religion or spirituality. Among the roots relating to other-worldly matters are *wegwh- 'to preach' which we still use in vow, votive, devout, devotions, vote (all from Latin); *gwer- 'to praise' which has given us (again through Latin) grace, gratitude, grateful, gratify, ingrate, congratulate and from Celtic, bard; AIW-, 'life force, age, etenity' survives in the English words ever, never, every, aye, nay; in the Greek derivative eon; in the Latin derivatives longevity, medieval, coeval, primeval, and in eternity, eternal, and sempiternal.

No profound conclusions can be drawn from these few brief examples, but can we not say of our ancient linguistic forbears at least that they were not brutes?

I-E: THE ITALIC BRANCH

The similarities among the modern languages, French, Italian, Spanish, Portuguese, and Rumanian make it obvious that they are related tongues. It is a well-known and never disputed fact that these languages are descended from Latin, the language of the ancient Romans: for which reason they are called the Romance languages. Latin itself is, of course, a widely studied language with a great and unique literature and a continuous tradition (that is, it has been learned by successive generations). But linguists are pleased to recognize that their reconstruction of Proto-Romance (the ancestor of the modern Romance languages) is very like the written language of Classical Latin texts, with some variations accounted for by the fact that Classical Latin is known primarily from literary texts which are somewhat different from the spoken language of the people (Vulgar Latin). The spoken language naturally had a greater effect on the formation of the modern languages than did the written language. We do have some samples of writing that are close to Vulgar Latin, especially from comedies, fiction, personal letters, lyric poetry, and handwriting on the walls (graffiti). Written Latin, on the other hand is the source of learned words: words adopted or coined by scholars.

A few examples will give an idea of the relationship between Latin and her children:

LATIN AND HER CHILDREN:
1. MATER ('mother')   Some English Derivatives:
        Italian: madre   maternal, maternity, matrix

French: mère   matron, matriculate, matrimony
Spanish: madre   matriarch, matriarchy, matri-
Portuguese: mãe   cide, matrilineal, matrilocal
Rumanian: mamă   material, matter (from Latin
materies 'tree trunk', i.e.
the tree's source of growth)

Fill in two or more additional
derivatives for each:

2. PATER ('father')   paternal
     Italian: padre
     French: père
     Spanish: padre
     Portuguese: pai

3. SOROR ('sister')   sorority
     Italian: sorella
     French: soeur
     Rumanian: soră
     The Spanish and Portuguese words for 'sister' are
     hermana and irma from the Latin word germanus 'of the
     same stock'.

4. FRATER ('brother')   fraternity
     Italian: fratello
     French: frère
     Rumanian: frate
     Spanish: hermano, Portuguese: irmão

5. FILIUS ('son')   affiliate
     (cf. FILIA, 'daughter')
     Italian: figlio
     French: fils
     Spanish: hijo
     Portuguese: filho
     Rumanian: fiu

6. NOX, base: NOCT- ('night')   nocturn
     Italian: notte
     French: nuit
     Spanish: noche
     Portuguese: noite
     Rumanian: noapte

7. CAELUM ('sky')   celestine
        Italian: cielo
        French: ciel
        Spanish: ceilo
        Portuguese: céu
        Rumanian: cer

8. DEUS ('God')   deity
        Italian: Dio
        French: Dieu
        Spanish: Dios
        Portuguese: Deus
        Rumanian: Dumnezeu

9. PRIMUS ('first')   primate
        Italian: primo
        French: premier
        Spanish: primero
        Portuguese: primeiro

10. HOMO, base: HOMIN- ('man')   hominoid
        Italian: uomo, p., uomini
        French: homme
        Spanish: hombre
        Portuguese: homem
        Rumanian: om

11. PAX, base: PAC- ('peace')   pacific
        Italian: pace
        French: paix
        Spanish: paz
        Portuguese: paz
        Rumanian: pace

12. DORMIRE ('to sleep')   dormer
        Italian: dormire
        French: dormir
        Spanish: dormir
        Portuguese: dormir
        Rumanian: dormi

13. FOCUS (in Latin 'hearth', in the Romance Languages, 'fire')
                                 focal, curfew
        Italian: fuoco
        French: feu
        Spanish: fuego
        Portuguese: fogo
        Rumanian: foc

14. NOMEN, base: NOMIN- ('name') nominal
           Italian: nome
           French: nom
           Spanish: nombre
           Portuguese: nome
           Rumanian: nume

15. PISCIS ('fish') pl. PISCES   piscary ('the right to fish',
                                              'a place to fish')
           Italian: pesce
           French: poisson
           Spanish: pescado
           Portuguese: peixe
           Rumanian: peşte

16. BIBERE ('drink')   bibulous
           Italian: bere
           French: boire
           Spanish: beber
           Portuguese: beber
           Rumanian: bea

EXERCISES

Exercise I. English and German

1. Following the rules of consonant correspondence between English and German, try to figure out the English equivalents of these German words. The vowel given in brackets is the one that appears in the English word.

Nouns and Adjectives:
    Milch
    Pflanze
    Salz
    Zoll
    Apfel
    Dorn
    Pfad
    besser
    Bad
    tief [ee]
    Durst [i]
    Wasser
    Bruder [o]
    Kupfer [o]

Verbs:
    danken
    denken [i]
    trinken
    machen
    baden
    pflücken
    brechen [ea]
    vergessen (Gm. v = Eng. f) [o]
    helfen

2. Match the German word with its English equivalent and cognate:

GERMAN		ENGLISH	
1.	Blatt	a.	clothing
2.	vierzig	b.	door
3.	zwei	c.	eat
4.	Tür	d.	forty
5.	tief	e.	two
6.	essen	f.	beard
7.	Kleidung	g.	blade
8.	Bart	h.	deep
9.	schlafen	i.	(be)hind
10.	hinten	j.	sleep
11.	Geburtstag	k.	blood
12.	Blut	l.	dream
13.	Tanz	m.	birthday
14.	Traum	n.	forbidden
15.	verboten	o.	hate
16.	hassen	p.	thick
17.	dick	q.	dance

Exercise II

Try to think of English words cognate with these German words: the definition of the German word is given as a clue (think of an English synonym that sounds more like the German word).

GERMAN WORD	DEFINITION	FILL IN ENGLISH COGNATE
1. unten	below	
2. Gürtel	belt	
3. Vogel	bird	
4. Zwart	black	
5. Kessel	boiler	
6. Knabe	boy	
7. Busen	breast	
8. Wagen	car	
9. Vorsicht	caution	
10. Fracht	cargo	
11. tragen	carry	
12. Jahrhundert	century (2 words)	
13. Stuhl	chair	
14. Burger	citizen	
15. Glocke	bell, chime	
16. Mantel	coat	
17. richtig	correct	
18. Zollhaus	customs house	
19. Worterbuch	dictionary (2 words)	

20.	Hund	dog
21.	Esel	donkey
22.	nieder	down
23.	Mehl	flour
24.	Begrabnis	funeral
25.	Kalbfleisch	veal (2 words)
26.	Blume	flower
27.	Handschuh	glove (2 words)
28.	wachsen	grow
29.	Hafen	harbor
30.	Landstrasse	highway (2 words)
31.	Sprache	language
32.	mittags	noon
33.	Schweinefleisch	pork (2 words)
34.	riechen	smell
35.	Ofen	stove
36.	Wert	value
37.	Mittwoch	Wednesday

Exercise III: Indo-European Root Canals

1. I-E NOTIONS

Using an Etymological Dictionary and a dictionary of I-E roots (the most convenient is that at the end of the American Heritage Dictionary), look up these words and these roots: find out the original meaning, try to figure out how they got to mean what they do now (if there is a remarkable change in meaning); and give other related English words.

1. pastor [root: pā-]
2. pecuniary [peku-]
3. wagon [wegh-]
4. wheel [kwel-]
5. textile [teks-]
6. dough [dheigh-]
7. mere [mori-] (mere, meaning a body of water)
8. demon [dā-]
9. mind [men-]
10. know [gno-]
11. wise [weid-]

The I-E roots are those given in the American Heritage Dictionary.

2. I-E ROOTS

Following the simplified chart of consonant correspondences, choose an English cognate from column I and an English derivative from column II to match the Greek/Latin word(s) at left.

SIMPLIFIED CHART OF I-E SOUND CORRESPONDENCES

I-E	Greek	Latin	Common Germanic	Old English	Mod. Eng. Spelling
p	p	p	f	f	f
t	t	t	th	th	th
k	k	c	h	h	h
kw	p/t/k	qu	hw	hw	wh
b	b	b	p	p	p
d	d	d	t	t	t
g	g	g	k	k	k
gw	b/d/g	v/gu	kw/k	cw/k	qu/c
bh	ph	f (b)	b	b	b
dh	th	f (d)	d	d	d
gh	ke (ch)	h	g	g	g/y
gwh	ph/th/ch	f	gw/w	w	
s	h	s	s	s	s
m	m	m	m	m	m
n	n	n	n	n	n
r	r/rh	r	r	r	r
l	l	l	l	l	l
i/y	h/z	j	j	g (y)	y
w/u		v	w	w	w

LATIN/GREEK   English Cognates   Derivative

A.

	LATIN/GREEK	I	II
1.	AD ('to') [Latin]	1. who, which	1. quiddity
2.	TO ('the') [Greek]	2. harvest	2. cornucopia
3.	PORTUS ('harbor') [L]	3. the	3. tautology
4.	CARPERE ('to pluck')[L]	4. horn	4. addition
	(cf. G. Karpos, 'fruit')		
5.	CORNU ('horn') [L]	5. wheeze	5. querulous
6.	QUID/QUID [L. interrogative]	6. at	6. carpet
7.	QUERI ('complain') [L]	7. ford	7. opportune

B.

	LATIN/GREEK	I	II
1.	BACULUM ('rod,stick') [L]	1. tusk, tooth	1. symbiosis
2.	BULLIRE ('to boil') [L]	2. kind	2. revenue
3.	DENS, DENT- ('toth') [L]	3. kneel	3. Palindrome
4.	DROMOS ('a running') [G]	4. peg	4. geranium
5.	GENOS ('race, family') [G]	5. puff, poach	5. genuflect
6.	GERANOS ('a crane') [G]	6. come	6. ebullient
7.	GENU ('knee') [L]	7. queen	7. genealogy
8.	VENIRE ('come') [L]	8. quick	8. gynecocracy
9.	BIOS ('life') [G] cf. L. vita	9. crow, crane	9. dentures
10.	GYNĒ, GYNEC- ('woman') [G]	10. tread	10. bacillus

C.

1. PHAINEIN
   ('bring to light') [G]
2. FAR ('spelt') [L]
3. FINDERE/FISSUS ('split') [L]
4. FACERE ('to do') [L]
5. THRĒNOS ('a dirge') [G]
6. FORAS/FORIS ('out-of-doors')
   (cf. G. thura, door)
7. HABĒRE ('to have/hold') [L]
8. CHASMA ('gulf') [G]
   (cf. L. haitus)
9. CHLŌROS
   ('greenish yellow') [G]

1. bite/bit
2. drone
3. give
4. gape
5. do
6. beacon
7. yellow
   [OE gealu]
8. door
9. barley

1. habitat
2. chlorophyll
3. efficiency
4. fission
5. threnody
6. farina
7. chasm
8. forest
9. phantasm

D.

1. HŌRA ('season') [G]
2. JUVENIS ('young') [L]
3. ZUGON ('yoke') [G]
   (cf. L, iugum)
4. VENTUS ('wind') [L]
   (cf. G. atmos)
5. OCHLOS ('mob') [G]
   (cf. L. vehere, 'carry')

1. yoke
2. weight
3. weather, wind
4. year
5. youth

1. syzygy
2. horoscope
3. ochlocracy
4. ventilate
5. rejuvenate

ANSWERS:

A.: 1-6,4; 2-3,3; 3-7,7; 4-2,6; 5-4,2; 6-1,1; 7-5,5.
B.: 1-4,10; 2-5,6; 3-1,9; 4-10,3; 5-2,7; 6-9,4; 7-3,5; 8-6,2;
     9-8,1; 10-7,8.
C.: 1-6,9; 2-9,6; 3-1,4; 4-5,3; 5-2,5; 6-8,8; 7-3,1; 8-4,7;
     9-7,2.
D.: 1-4,2; 2-5,5; 3-1,1; 4-3,4; 5-2,3.

3. MATCH RELATED WORDS

English natives
1. wear
2. way
3. western
4. werewolf
5. dunk
6. seven
7. yoke
8. cow
9. whom
10. hound

Derivatives from Greek/Latin
1. vespers [L]
2. heptad [G]
3. bucolic [G]
4. vest [L]
5. quorum [L]
6. cynic [G. from kuon, 'dog']
7. convey (L)
8. virile (L)
9. tint (L)
10. zeugma (G)

ANSWERS: 1-4; 2-7; 3-1; 4-8; 5-9; 6-2; 7-10; 8-3; 9-5; 10-6.

Exercise IV. Latin and Her Children

1. Look over lists of Latin words on pp. 22-24 and fill in the blanks:

   a. FILIAL duty is the obligation of the _____ to the parents.

   b. MATRIMONY is the state or condition of being a _____.

   c. PATRIMONY is the inheritance from the _____.

   d. FRATERNITIES and SORORITIES are composed of _____and _____.

   e. A NOCTURNAL predator hunts at _____.

   f. CELESTIAL beings live in the _____.

   g. A HOMINOID would resemble a _____.

   h. To PACIFY is to make _____.

   i. A DORMITORY is a place for _____.

   j. PRIMEVAL forests are from the _____ age.

   k. The PAX Romana was a time of _____.

2. Form or find:

   a. at least ten additional English derivatives of PATER and PRIMUS.

   b. at least five from these: NOX, NOCT(I)-; PAX, PAC(I)-; DORMIRE; FOCUS.

3. Fill-in with Latin words or stems:

   a. The killing of another human being is called _____cide.

   b. The "Our Father" is called in Latin the _____Noster.

   c. The greeting "peace (be) with you" in Latin is _____ vobiscum.

   d. The astrological sign of the fish is called _____.

   e. Another word for drink is im_____.

   f. A word for brotherly is _____nal.

   g. A case to establish fatherhood is called a _____nity suit.

   h. Our species is _____Sapiens.

   i. A synonym for to name is _____ate.

   j. In name only can be expressed by the word _____al.

4. Choose any one or two of these Latin words and find (if possible) the Italian, French, Spanish, Portuguese, and Rumanian forms and give several English derivatives.

   1. TOTUS (all)   2. CORPUS (body)
   3. MORS/MORT- (death) 4. LINGUA (tongue)
   5. VITA (life)   6. SCRIBERE (write)
   7. ANNUS (year)   8. VENDERE (sell)

9. MANUS (hand)
11. ARBOR (tree)
13. VETUS, VETER- (old)
15. ALTER (another)
17. OCULUS (eye)
19. VIDĒRE (see)
21. SANGUIS (blood)
23. NUX/NUC-(nut)
25. BONUS (good)
27. VENTUS (wind)

10. CRESCERE (grow)
12. FRENUM bridle:brake)
14. LIBER (free)
16. SAECULUM (age)
18. DULCUS (sweet)
20. ALTUS (high, tall)
22. VENIRE (come)
24. REX/REG- (king)
26. OVUM (egg)
28. FUMUS (smoke)

SOME DEFINITIONS

Now that you have worked with some of the concepts it is time to present some definitions. The <u>root</u> is the most basic element of the word. For many words in our language, both native and foreign, we can trace the root back to an Indo-European word element. Large vocabularies, however, grew up in the various branches after the dispersion of the original Indo-Europeans and later in the separation of the languages in the various branches. It is not possible, therefore, to discover an I-E root for every word. Nevertheless, roots are very useful in finding <u>cognates</u>: words in different languages derived from the same root. For example English KNOW is <u>cognate</u> with Latin COGNOSCERE ('to be acquainted with') and with Greek GIG<u>NŌ</u>SKEIN ('to know'), since all share the same root *GNO-.

The <u>base</u> of a word is that element from which other words are formed by adding affixes: prefixes and suffixes [AF-FIX, 'fasten to'; PRE-FIX, 'fasten before'; SUF-FIX, 'fasten under']. For example, the base of the word <u>knowledge</u> is <u>know</u>. The base of the word <u>diagnosis</u> is the Greek base <u>gnō</u>, (seen in the Greek verb <u>gig-nōskein</u>). Diagnosis breaks down to a prefix: <u>dia-</u>, meaning 'through, thoroughly, apart'; the base <u>gno</u>, 'know'; a suffix <u>-sis</u>, 'act of'. Or, take <u>acknowledgment</u> (a word that is cognate with the Greek word <u>gignōskein</u>), which is made up of:
  prefix: ac- (from Old English <u>on</u>) 'on'
  base: know 'know'
  suffix: -ledg(e), of obscure origin [alas, many things in
           language are 'of obscure origin']
  suffix: -ment, 'act or state of' [a suffix from Latin: this
           is, in fact, an early instance of the addi-
           tion of the suffix, -ment, to a native
           word].

The vocabulary of a language may be said to be made up of <u>native</u> words and words borrowed from other languages, called <u>loanwords</u>. In English, our native words are those inherited from Anglo-Saxon, the linguistic ancestor of English. These form the back-bone of our language, and are the most commonly used words. Many of our native words have close, easily recognizable cognates in the other tongues of the Germanic branch: for example, English 'good', German <u>gut</u>, Dutch <u>goed</u>, Icelandic go<u>ð</u>r. But the English language has also freely admitted words from other languages into its vocabulary. Sometimes these are words for new things picked up through contact with the foreign people. Sometimes, on the other hand, new words are borrowed from literature and learning: these are called <u>learned</u> words. The foreign languages that have added the largest numbers of words to our vocabulary are Latin (long the language of learning and culture and religion), French (through long contact with the British Isles, through diplomacy, education, and conquest), and Greek (the source of many technical words in all fields, with new entries coming in constantly in scientific terminology).

The borrowing of words from other languages has a long tradition in our culture: the Anglo-Saxon vocabulary has a number of every-day words taken from the classical tongues. For example, the word pepper is borrowed from Greek, but the Greeks themselves had long before borrowed it from an Eastern language: although the exact transmission is not known, Greek peperi is clearly related to and perhaps comes from Sanskrit pippali, 'berry'. The word street is a very early entry from Latin (from via strata, 'paved road'). Evidence that these words were borrowed at a very early date, before the Anglo-Saxons departed from Continental Europe, crossing the channel and breaking with their Teutonic linguistic cousins, is the fact that these words occur in slightly varied, but clearly cognate forms in other Germanic tongues:

1. STREET

German: Strasse
Dutch: straat
from Latin (via) strata

2. PEPPER

German: Pfeffer
Dutch: peper
Swedish: pepper
Danish: peber
Norwegian: pepper
Yiddish: fefer
from Latin piper,
from Greek peperi
perhaps from Sanskrit pippali

Besides many loan-words from Greek and Latin, English has innumerable coined words from these ancient languages, words made up from elements from one or both of them: such a word is television, from Greek tele- 'afar' and Latin vision (from visio, vision- 'sight', from visus, 'seen'). Much of the technical vocabulary in all fields is made up of words coined from Greek and Latin elements.

The long and uncomely coinage:

ANTIDISESTABLISHMENTARIANISM

(meaning, 'the doctrine of those opposed to the removal from the position of State Church') is built up from the base -establ-,

from Latin <u>stabilire</u> 'to make firm' (from Latin <u>stare</u> 'to stand':
from the I-E root STA-, 'stand') with two prefixes and an almost
unseemly number of suffixes:

PREFIXES:
    ANTI- (from Greek <u>anti</u>): 'against'
    DIS- a Latin inseparable prefix indicating reversal
SUFFIXES:
    -ISH a verbal formant influenced by French
    -MENT- 'state of' from the Latin noun-forming suffix
       <u>-mentum</u>
    -ARI- 'pertaining to' from the Latin adjective-
       forming suffix <u>-arius</u>
    -AN- 'one who' (from Latin <u>-anus</u>)
    -ISM 'doctrine of' (from Greek)

Clearly 'antidisestablishmentarianism' is a word made up (or
<u>coined</u>) from classical elements, but not representing a concept
known to the ancient Romans or Greeks.

Examples of coined words include <u>telephone</u> (tele- 'at a dis-
tance' + <u>phōnē</u> 'voice', both elements from Greek); <u>sociology</u>
(<u>socius</u>, Latin for 'companion' + <u>logia</u>, from Greek <u>logos</u> 'word,
reason'); <u>grandmother</u> (<u>grand</u> from French <u>grand</u>, from Latin <u>grandis</u>
'grand, full grown' + native English <u>mother</u>) and the somewhat il-
logical <u>grandchild</u>.

A newly coined word that has not yet gained wide acceptance
is called a <u>neologism</u> (<u>neo</u>-, 'new' + <u>logos</u>, 'word' + <u>-ism</u>,
'usage'; all Greek elements). Examples of <u>neologisms</u> include such
words as 'nixonomics', 'cocacolaization', 'Koreagate', 'telethon'.
The word <u>stagflation</u> (used to describe an anomalous economic
situation in which the economy seems to be at a standstill and yet
prices go up steadily) is a neologism coined from 'stagnation' and
'inflation'. It is also a <u>portmanteau</u> <u>word</u> (--a portmanteau is a
suitcase which opens up into two compartments--), a phrase coined
by Lewis Carroll to characterize words formed by blending the
sounds and meanings of two different words: "Well," writes Lewis
Carroll in <u>Through</u> <u>the</u> <u>Looking-Glass</u>, "'slithy' means 'lithe and
slimy' ...you see it's like a portmanteau--there are two meanings
packed up into one word."

The science which studies word origins is called ETYMOLOGY
(from <u>etumos</u> 'true' + <u>logos</u> 'word' + <u>ia</u>, noun forming suffix):
that is, etymology seeks the <u>truth</u> of words from their origins.
The word <u>etymology</u> is also used of the origin of individual words.
When we say 'what is the etymology of this word?' we mean in a
narrow sense: what are its origins, what are its component parts,
its prefix, base, and suffix, from what language does it come?

In a broader sense, however, the etymology of a word is its whole biography: not only the elements it consists of, but when and where it originated, how its form and meaning developed over the years. For some words this makes an exciting story.

EXAMPLE: VERNACULAR (a short etymology)
[meaning: as a noun: the standard native language of a country or region; the idiom of a trade or profession.
as an adjective: native to or commonly spoken by persons in a country or region.]

ORIGIN: from Latin vernaculus, an adjective meaning 'having to do with a verna,' hence, 'native, domestic': from VERNA 'a home-grown slave' (that is a slave born in the household rather than purchased); + -ar, adjective forming suffix.
USAGE: The earliest citation of the word vernacular in English is from 1601 (OED).

In Latin the words vernaculus and verna occur in a variety of uses, but the English vernacular is restricted to one reference only, that is, to language. This restriction may come from the Roman writer, Varro (of the first century B.C.) who used the phrase vernacula vocabula (native words).
Some Examples (from the OED) of VERNACULAR in English:
1788: Brown...preferred polysyllabic expressions derived from the language of ancient Rome, to his vernacular vocabulary.
1832: The congregation here being chiefly peasants and artisans, a sermon was delivered in the vernacular dialect.
1848: Low-born vernacular idioms were handed down to posterity as the poet's creation.

The dictionary that gives the most information about the life stories of words in the English language is the Oxford English Dictionary [OED] in thirteen volumes, which was compiled over the forty-five year period 1884-1928. This monumental work of lexicography is a sine qua non for the study of English vocabulary. In it, a diligent student can find out (as far as can be determined) how long a word has been in our language, how the word has changed from its original meaning, which of the meanings is in fact the original meaning, how and when the various senses of the word have developed, when a word described as obsolete had last been used. Each word is accompanied by quotations showing it in context for each use: in all, millions of quotations have been gathered by some two thousand volunteer readers to illustrate the histories of words: the first appearance and every notable point in the biography of each word.

A dictionary equally useful, for other reasons, is the American Heritage Dictionary, which, though it obviously contains fewer words than the OED, offers the student an invaluable tool in the

list of Indo-European roots in the Appendix: here are to be found
lists of cognates and derivatives. Of Etymological dictionaries
of English, Eric Partridge's ORIGINS is recommended as the one
that presents the material not only with good scholarship, but
also with good stories that make fascinating reading.

EXERCISES

Exercise I.   Natives and Naturalized Aliens

A: NATIVE ENGLISH WORDS
Using the OED and other dictionaries, find out the history of one
of these words:how did it develop; what other words are derived
from it or related to it; has its meaning, spelling, or use changed over the centuries; can you find words cognate with it in the
other Teutonic languages?

the	this	that	man	woman	daughter	son	it	and	love
will	have	be	by	for	or	he	she	if	a/an	not	in
to	then	there	tell	when	which	that	very	of	on	get

B: NATURALIZED ALIENS (in chapter one, a list of English
words derived from non-I-E tongues was given: the following words
are taken from the various branches of I-E: find out how/when/-
where the word first entered English (give first citation in OED);
what it means in English, and what it means in its original language; what language it is from and what group (branch of I-E)
that language belongs to; whether there are native English cognates, or cognates borrowed from other languages (the American
Heritage will help you with this last information).

crooked	skill	wing	smelt	rent	rich	picnic	wainscot
uproar	boor	traffic	contraband	motto	zany	umbrella
ditto	gusto	cork	sherry	cargo	rodeo	druid	shamrock
leprechaun	keen('lament')	whisky	marmalade	palaver
massage	steppe	mammoth	ukase	vodka	swastika	karma
pundit	cot	jute	tiger	mummy	magus	peri	effendi

Exercise II.   Heroes and Villains of Vocabulary

An etymology is the biography of a word, its life history.
The words in the list below are all derived from people's names:
look up one or two in the dictionary (OED and others): Find out:
1.   What does the word mean in common speech?
2.   Who was the person? How did the name of the person get
attached to the thing or act? Why was this thing or act named for
him or her?

3. Do you think the transference of the proper name to the common word was justified: did the man or woman deserve to be remembered for this one thing more than any other?

An example:

burke (vb.) 'to murder by suffocation or strangulation (originally for the purpose of selling the body for dissection in the laboratory)'

William Burke, a VILLAIN of VOCABULARY: burke, a word with a gruesome etymology, comes from the name of William Burke, hanged for murder in Edinburgh, Scotland in 1829. William Burke and his partner William Hare inhabited a rather seedy section of Edinburgh in the early nineteenth century. One evening a visitor happened to pass away in their rooming house. Rather than go to the trouble of disposing of his mortal remains in the traditional manner, the two men carted the corpse off to the University and sold it for the use of medical students. The receipt of seven pounds sterling for an otherwise useless carcase set the two on the road of crime. They began enticing men to their rooms for a drink and no longer waited for their victims to die of natural causes, but carefully smothered them so as to leave them intact for dissection in the laboratory. Fifteen or more unfortunate wayfarers were sacrificed for science and avarice in this way. Eventually the two murderers were caught and tried. The Times of London on the day of Burke's execution (2 February 1829) contained this item:

> As soon as the executioner proceeded to his duty,
> the cries of "Burke him, Burke him, give him no
> rope" were vociferated. "Burke Hare too."

To burke has been extended to mean 'to hush up, to keep quiet.' By 1840, for example, this figurative use appears in the line: The Age of Chivalry is Burked by Time. (Hood)

BIOGRAPHICAL WORDS

bloomers	abigail	babbitt	batiste	bessemer	billingsgate
bowdlerize	boycott	braille	camellia	cardigan	chauvinism
derrick	doily	dunce	thespian	frankenstein	galvanize
gardenia	gargantuan	gerrymander	graham cracker	guillotine
August	lynch	macabre	macadam	mackintosh	martinet
maudlin	mausoleum	mercerize	mesmerism	namby-pamby
nicotine	quisling	quixotic	shrapnel	silhouette	simony
spoonerism	tweed	ampere	begonia	bobby	brougham
chateaubriand	chesterfield	clerinew	daguerreotype	dahlia
derby	derringer	diesel	fahrenheit	forsythia	fuchsia
gentian	grangerize	greengage	hansom	havelock	leotard
lobelia	loganberry	magnolia	masochism	maverick	napoleon

38

ohm   pasteurize   philippic   pickle   poinsettia   pompadour
pullman   raglan   sadism   sandwich   saxophone   sequoia
sideburns   teddy bear   timothy   victoria   volt   watt   wisteria
zeppelin   zinnia   the Mae West   Levis   ferris wheel   Melba toast
bowie   knife   czar/Kaisar   mentor   pecksniffian

Exercise III. Neologisms

Neologisms come and go. They must be collected on the wing
or on the hoof as the case may be. Look and listen for them
especially in newspapers, magazines, on radio and television.
Keep a list of these with date and provenance: try not to let a
neologism or nonce-word slip away: it may be in more danger of
immediate extinction than the snail-darter.

Exercise IV. Etymologies: interesting words

The words in the list below have interesting histories:
choose three or four and find out what you can about them: where
they are from, what the elements are and what they mean. Find a
sentence using each of your words. Be prepared to tell its story.
Give other words related to it.

1. rally
2. achieve
3. anguish
4. biscuit
5. canary
6. coin
7. dame
8. dismal
9. engine
10. foreign
11. haughty
12. jest
13. Mass
14. miscreant
15. parboil
16. precocious
17. retort
18. scourge
19. solemn
20. terrier
21. delirious
22. atone

23. puny
24. romance
25. auspices
26. buckle
27. capitulate
28. copy
29. dean
30. dozen
31. era
32. gamut
33. host
34. libel
35. matriculate
36. noon
37. peculiar
38. preposterous
39. revel
40. sergeant
41. sport
42. umpire
43. alarm
44. bead

45. travesty
46. aisle
47. bachelor
48. bugle
49. chapel
50. culprit
51. denizen
52. eliminate
53. fairy
54. gin
55. insect
56. manipulate
57. mischief
58. outrage
59. porpoise
60. quintessence
61. rosemary
62. sincere
63. supercilious
64. usher
65. prevaricate
66. person

THE BEGINNINGS OF ENGLISH

English is a melting pot language. It has been shaped by political, social and intellectual forces which have taken place not only in the British Isles but, also, in Northern Europe, the Italian peninsula and the ancient Middle East. Successive waves of migration and invasion which swept over England have left indelible marks on the language. And, finally, when the English language and the people who spoke it seemed to coalesce, British imperialism in Africa, Asia, the Americas and South Pacific--a migration, so to speak, outwards--brought new ripples of linguistic influence back to the mother country.

The most significant linguistic influences were exerted on English during the first thousand years of the language's development. In that time, English grew out of a barely distinguishable group of Germanic dialects, first spoken in far northern Europe, into a magnificent amalgam of the best elements offered by Europe's rich linguistic storehouse. Upon a framework of Germanic syntax and vocabulary, the peoples of England were able to shape a new language by borrowing additional words and grammatical constructions from Latin, Greek, and other Continental European languages. The resulting vocabulary is now so diverse in origins that some scholars question whether English can be considered a Germanic language at all. But whatever its classification, English, as we know it, is one of the most remarkable inventions of Western Civilization.

To gain a reasonable understanding of the historical events which shaped our language, it is necessary to take a brief look at the larger forces which have gone into the making of European history. Some time during the later Bronze Age the ethno-political geography of the continent was carved up predominantly among three large, and within themselves, loosely related groups of peoples. In the north there were the Teutons, or Germans, a small grouping of land-starved tribes which were centered around the Baltic Sea. In the south the Greek and Italic nations prospered in a climate conducive to agriculture and civilization. While in the largest section of the continent, the vast heartland of Europe, Celtic tribes exerted a spreading influence, which at its zenith extended from Ireland to Spain and from northwestern Europe all the way to some tenuous plantings on the shores of Asia Minor.

Needless to say, our primary interest in these peoples is their language. Each of them, the Teutons, the Greeks and Italians and the Celts, spoke languages which were distinctive. Therefore, they were separated by differing linguistic traditions.

41

Within each of these groups, however, there were separate dialects and, even, languages. So that Teutonic tribes occupying differing banks of the same river were further separated by linguistic habits which affected their ways of pronouncing and arranging the words of their language--a difference of dialects. The peoples who inhabited the two major peninsulas of southern Europe, Greece and Italy, were separated by such a wide gulf in their linguistic traditions that within this group we find two recognizably different languages, Greek and Italic; of the latter Latin is the best known and most important.

Sometime about the fifth Century B.C. the peripheral groups, the Teutons to the north and the Greeks and Italians of the south, began to grow in numbers and in power, and gradually pushed towards the center of the continent. Caught in the squeeze, the Celts migrated to the British Isles, where they were eventually caught by the rapacious events of history. In the 1st Century B.C., and again in the 1st Century A.D., the Romans invaded Britain, and in the 5th Century A.D. the Germanic tribes turned in force on the island. Today Celts are found only in the isolated extremes of Europe and the British Isles.

The implications of these distant historical events may seem very remote to us at first glance. But, some 2,500 years after their initiation, the Teutonic expansion and Celtic flight still exert political and social pressure upon Western life. The causes and effects of the last three European wars, and the recent struggles in Ireland should suffice as vivid examples that large historical events rarely die easy deaths. Moreover, it should be remembered that the English language is an indirect product of those distant migrations, and the very words you now read stand as living proof that history lives.

The British islanders (mostly Celts) and the Teutons of the Continent, though at the time widely separated by geography and culture, are first mentioned in written history by a Greek merchant adventurer, Pytheas of Massilia. Around the year 300 B.C. he made a daring circumnavigation of the British Isles and other journeys to northern Europe. In the writings of Pytheas are to be found the first references to the Britanic Celts and the Teutones.

However, Britain solidly enters history in the year 55 B.C., when Julius Caesar, then a military commander in Gaul, undertook two retaliatory raids on the island in pursuit of Celtic refuges which were aiding Rome's continental enemies. Caesar's expeditions ended in all but defeat at the hands of the Britons. But, Rome's star was in the ascendency, and the lure of a new province was firmly affixed to the imperial imagination.

In the zig-zag play of history, Julius Caesar turned the force of his military and political genius onto affairs in northern Europe. He went on to plant the foundations of Roman power over the southerly most Germanic tribes. Shortly after this time, and for nearly seventy years following, while the Roman legions pushed northwards through much of what today is Germany, Roman traders and merchants ventured sporadically into the British Isles to sell manufactured goods and buy native products. "No one goes to Britain, without good reason, except the traders," commented Caesar [B.G. IV.20], perhaps in astonishment, after his brief and unfortunate brush with the islanders.

In recent years, archaeologists have helped sketch in the picture of this advance from trading contact through military and political domination. Some half a century before direct Roman contact with Britain, Celtic chieftains on that island were being buried with grave goods of Roman manufacture. These goods, mostly ceramics, had reached Britain through continental Belgic traders. But a decade before the Roman invasion of Britain actually began, small trading posts--similar to those on the North American frontier which preceded western expansion--were established by the Romans. These were tentative ventures in a barbaric and hostile land. The influence of Roman goods spread quickly throughout the island. And by the time the legions had landed in Britain, there was hardly a Briton who had not come into contact with some object of Roman culture, even if the object were something as lowly as a common kitchen pot. Therefore, it is no wonder that the Latin words mango and caupo (dealer and huckster/small-time tradesman, respectively) early entered into our language. Both words early in their careers acquired a distateful significance. Seneca says that the mangones (pl. of mango) hide any fault in their merchandise through some artificial ornament in the manner of pimps. Horace speaks of perfidus hic caupo as if dishonest were the natural word to describe a caupo. Today these words survive in altered forms, monger, as in iron-monger and war-monger, and cheap [a not overly complimentary comment on a trader's wares] and chap, which comes down to us from the older English compound word, chapman, meaning a travelling peddler. [In German too, the influence of Latin caupo can be seen in the words kaufen 'to buy' and verkaufen 'to sell'.]

Merchants: Heroes of Language

The English, as Napoleon pointed out, are a nation of shopkeepers. The Corsican emperor was actually paraphrasing and considerably shortening a statement Adam Smith made in The Wealth of Nations:

> To found a great empire for the sole purpose
> of raising up a people of customers, may at first
> sight appear a project fit only for a nation of
> shopkeepers. It is, however, a project altogether
> unfit for a nation of shopkeepers; but extremely
> fit for a nation governed by shopkeepers.

That our vocabulary reached its magnificent size in the mouths of such a people is no accident. Mercantilism and its complement, consumerism, have played an immeasurable part in the development of the English language, from the time when our ancestors were barbaric tribesmen up to our present sophisticated age of commercialism.

To face the dangers of sea and storm, of pirates and brigands and savages, to journey to far-off lands merely to sell something or buy something may at first sight seem unworthy of man's highest efforts. But the contribution to our language made by merchants is not to be underestimated. Merchants, as much as linguists, are heroes of vocabulary. New lands, new worlds are discovered for them. And as the new lands are dominated, merchants and traders and dealers and peddlers and even chapmen leave behind new things and new words, and they bring home new words for new things they have found abroad. Behind--even ahead of--Rome's legions, came merchants, ever in search of new markets. The less civilized inhabitants of Britain and Germany naturally wanted to become civilized. The most apparent aspect of the Romans' claim to greatness and higher culture was the fact that they had more things. What better way to acquire the envied civilization than through possession of the things that were its outward and visible sign? No less than ourselves, our unsophisticated forebears realized that the standard of living is based on how many things one has. And so they learned to love and need the new products. Among our earliest loan-words from Latin are the names of vessels: cup, chest, pan, pot, bin, box, sack: for the Romans, since they had more things, naturally had to have more things to put them in. Many words for textiles and clothing were borrowed at this time too [sock, belt, mat, pall, purple, silk] and words for delicacies to eat and drink: wine, butter, cheese, pepper.

Small civilian communities grew up around Roman military encampments wherever they were to be found on the imperial frontier. In Britain alone there were nearly 200,000 Romans and Romanized Celts by the middle of the first century A.D. This rapid growth in Roman population and Romanization of the natives did not spring entirely from an influx of traders and the beguiling influence of their wares. By far the largest number of Romans to enter a new territory after it had been reasonably subdued were settlers of two types who shared one purpose . . . land. Perhaps the most numerous of the settlers were cashiered legioneers, who, upon leaving the military, were given a bonus in the form of land. Of course, in newly acquired territories, such as Britain and Germany, land could be had for the taking, which is exactly what the government did. This practice of giving ex-soldiers grants of land benefited the government in two ways, not only did it satisfy its payroll and pension problems with little actual expenditure, but the veterans' presence in the territory, moreover, accelerated the pacification of the province.

The other group of Roman settlers were underemployed peasants from the Italian peninsula, who, since the second century B.C., had been leaving their homeland in search of more arable lands to farm. These peasants, in our terms, were pioneers pushing back a frontier and homesteading any land that could not be withheld from them. Neither the cashiered veterans nor the frontiersmen peasants had qualms about inter-marrying with the natives of the newly settled areas. In this manner Romanization went on apace.

However, Romanization did not go unchallenged. In A.D. 60 and 61 the bizarre and unfortunate affair of Queen Boudicca in Britain nearly brought an end to the earlier efforts of pacification on that island. Boudicca, the Celtic queen of York, had been widowed when Roman tax collectors murdered her husband who resisted exorbitant and illegal levies that the provincial officials were trying to extort from his people. Not satisfied with murder, the Romans brutally humiliated the queen. But she managed to escape, and in her wrath Boudicca raised a revolt. Long-smouldering dissatisfaction with foreign rule brought numerous Celtic tribes under her banner. And, in the course of two bloody years, the Boudiccan armies leveled the three largest Roman towns in Britain, slaughtering 70,000 Romans and Romanized Celts in a frenzy of revenge and revolt. And only by diverting a large number of troops from the Continent was Rome finally able to maintain her hold on her new island province.

A small, but poignantly human incident which occurred during the Boudiccan revolt has recently been brought to light by British archaeologists. Just before the sack of London, a Romanized Celt, aided perhaps by his family, hurriedly drank off an amphora (approximately seven gallons) of imported wine—a Roman product which probably the tippler's father had been unacquainted with. Whether this unfortunate Celt got drunk out of despair or in order to fortify his courage, he most certainly used the Latin word for the beverage, _vinum_, a word which we still use in an altered form, _wine_.

After the events of A.D. 60 and 61, the Romans realized that a vigorously fairminded policy of re-pacification was needed. Under the governorship of Agricola a crash program was instituted to build market places and Roman temples in the native centers of population. "Now," the governor's son-in-law Tacitus wrote, "he began to school the chieftains' sons in the liberal arts, with the result that those who used to wag their heads at the Latin language now were beginning to aspire to eloquence. Then even our style of clothing was an honor and the toga was seen everywhere. Step by step they fell prey to the seductions of our vices: the portico and the bath and luxurious dining. Among the inexperienced [Britons] this too was called 'Culture' [humanitas vocabatur], even though it was part of their slavery." [Agricola, 21]

Physical evidence of this period which has been recovered by archaeologists amply proves the effect of these policies. Hardly any house of this period has been discovered which was not Roman in design. The largest were equipped with every luxury that could be found in Rome itself, while none but the poorest Briton used anything but imported Samian dinnerware which was produced in Roman Gaul and styled on thoroughly Roman patterns.

The prevalence of Roman-style wearing apparel, Roman-style housing, utensils, and for that matter, Roman cuisine created an environment in which Latin influence on the native Celtic languages was inescapable. For just as today's devotee of French cooking who might live in Des Moines or Spokane is more apt to talk about a bain-marie and pommes frites collerettes than a double boiler and potato chips, so too did the Romanized Celt find it easier and more dignified to speak of those newly imported things and customs using a Latinate vocabulary for them.

Just how Latinized Britain was during Rome's hegemony of the island is a question that cannot now be answered. No doubt there was at least widespread bilingualism in the towns, especially in the south-east. Latin was the language (at least the second language) of the foreign settlers. Latin was the language of government, commerce, and culture. Latin was the language that allowed social mobility and it was at this time the only language of the written word. Latin loan-words from this period survive not only in English, but in the Celtic languages (Welsh, Cornish, Breton).

One aspect of Roman culture which never seemed to have gained acceptance in the new provinces was the semi-political, pagan religion of the State. Even though Britons, especially in the towns and cities, worshipped in typically Roman temples, they worshipped there their own native dieties. Occasionally they gave the gods of their fathers a Latin name, but never did they give them Roman personalities. Perhaps the strongest example of this atavistic conservatism concerning religious matters which our language contains is to be found in the name we know Christianity's most sacred holiday by, Easter. Eostre was a Celtic goddess whose feast day happened to coincide with the Christian holiday.

As for Christianity's influence on our language, the religion ...tered both Britain and northern Germany relatively early, though it did not become a popular religion until well after Roman power had ebbed from those parts.

Until now, insofar as the birth of the English language is concerned, we have been dealing with a situation which can best be termed pre-natal, almost genealogical. Historically our language has its roots in far-flung corners of Europe: Germany, central Italy, and its eventual place of incubation, Britain. In our historical synopsis what needs now to happen is the gathering of these diverse elements into one place so that the real process of generation may occur.

Beginning in the third century, the Roman Empire started down the inexorable road to decline. The massive military and political machine centered in a central Italian city, which for three hundred years had held in check the diverse tribal pressures of Europe, began to weaken. Economic stagnation palled the Empire; political disintegration loosened the bonds which hithertofore had made the state so cohesive; and spiritural malaise sapped citizens' morale. But, while the core of the Empire suffered, the peoples on the periphery began to realize a new vigor. The Germanic tribes moved unhaltably south and west. At the same time, resurgent Celts pushed obstinately east and south.

By the year 287 A.D. Saxon German pirates were engaged in periodic raids on the British coast. And a century later Saxons joined Celtic Scots in land-based attacks on Roman strong-holds in Britain. By the beginning of the fifth century, all of the Roman legions were withdrawn from the island to defend the city of Rome itself. But the death knell for Roman Britain was sounded a decade later when the Romano-Britons desperately beseiged by both Celtic and Germanic barbarians wrote the Emperor Honorius begging aid, his reply--called the Rescript of 410--was to wish his harried subjects well and commend them to their own devices. In light of the prevailing circumstances in the island, the Rescript of 410 told Britons, Drop Dead!

Some three hundred years after the Germanic invasion of Britain, an Anglo-Saxon monk in England, the Venerable Bede, recounted in Latin a legend about the coming of his Continental forebears to that island.

In the year of our Lord 449 . . . the Angles or

47

Saxons, sent for by the king, reached Britain in
three long ships and received lands in the eastern
part of the island on condition that they defend the
country, but in fact their intention was to conquer
it. [Historia Ecclesiastica, I. 15]

Contrary to the implied neatness of the invasion according to
Bede's contracted tale, the Germanic invasion of Britain occurred
over a long period of time and in a piecemeal fashion. So gradual
over all was the invasion that to an inhabitant of the island the
change from Romano-Celtic to barbarian German domination would
have been so incremental as to seem nearly imperceptible. Again
archaeologists show that in the mid-fifth century, when according
to Bede cataclysmic change was rending the island, Romanized Britons were still confidently building country villas in the Roman
style complete with running water and other civilized amenities.

Romanized Celtic Britain died hard. The cities lingered for
decades, most of them never really falling into disuse, where a
population basically unchanged, if but a bit more impoverished,
continued a Roman-like urban existence while the new settlers from
the continent devoted their time to agriculture in the country-
side. Gradually, in most parts of the island, through assimilation and political, economic domination, the German invaders became predominant and their language displaced the Celtic as the
standard for popular communication. However, Latin influence remained.

EXERCISES

Exercise I.   Through the Anglo-Saxon Invasion

The earliest loan-words from Latin that came into our language entered through contact with the Roman legions in Germany.
After the Anglo-Saxons arrived in England, the chief source of
Latin loan-words was the Vulgar (i.e., popular, everyday) Latin
used by the Romano-Britons. Since it is not always possible to
distinguish between words borrowed on the Continent and those borrowed during the early years of Germanic settlement, the two
groups are treated together here. As normally happens when
invaders enter a country for colonization and form a majority in
the new land, acquiring political control over it, the language of
the new-comers prevailed. Thus the language of the Anglo-Saxons
gained the upper hand though they did, of course, adopt some words
from the inhabitants they found in Britain, especially from the
Romanized Britons of the market towns and villages. Though the
Anglo-Saxons came with their language intact--for the Romans had
not colonized Germany to any great extent, nor had they become the

majority--they had quite a few loan-words from classical civilization with them already.

Go over the following list of words and then choose one or two to look up in various dictionaries, including the <u>Oxford English Dictionary</u>, to find the word's history in the English language.

Look for and note:
>The word's meaning,
>The meaning and form of the Latin original,
>The earliest spelling in English,
>The date of its earliest usage in English,
>>Any changes in meaning it has undergone during its lifetime in English--especially new meanings it has acquired--or in its transition from Latin/Greek into our language,
>>And, if possible, any words in English that are related to it, especially those derived from the same Latin or Greek root.

1. Street	12. Port ('harbor')	23. Bin	33. Pepper
2. Mile	13. Mat	24. Pan	34. Poppy
3. Camp	14. Purple	25. Kitchen	35. Ass
4. Cheap	15. Pillow	26. Kiln	36. Fever
5. Monger	16. Sack	27. Line	37. Anchor
6. Pound	17. Sock	28. Pin	38. Mortar
7. Toll	18. Candle	29. Tile	39. Pot
8. Post	19. Pipe	30. Wall	40. Fork
9. Chalk	20. Butter	31. Inch	41. Cat
10. Copper	21. Cheese	32. Pea	42. Trout
11. Belt	22. Wine		

Exercise II. Ach, mein Gott, ein <u>pot</u>! Now we can have pot roast!

The words in the previous exercise are primarily nouns, and these mostly naming concrete objects of everyday use, such things as would naturally be brought to a less civilized people by more civilized traders, who had more skills and therefore more manufactured things, as well as different plants and animals. The most natural reason for one language to adopt a word from another is that the borrower has no word of his own for such a thing.

Try to imagine the reception of the new article by our uncouth (linguistic) ancestors, and taking one of the words for a concrete object of trade write a fable telling about the first time a German (or Briton) saw this thing, how he came to find a use for it and what the reaction of his family was when he first brought it home--having traded the family cow (or some other necessity) for the newfangled gadget--and the joy he felt in communicating the new word for the new thing to his family and friends.

Words of particular interest for this exercise:

Belt	Sock	Pin	Tile
Mat	Pillow	Sack	Candle
Butter	Cheese	Wine	Bin
Pan	Pepper	Pot	Fork
Cat	Pipe	Box	

N.B.: Check out your word carefully to make sure that you have your native Teuton or Briton bringing home his article with its name in its earliest use, even if, being a visionary spirit, he invents new uses for the object.

Exercise III. Kith or Kin?

In the following groups of words some are related in sound and meaning, others are only look-alikes. Choose several groups and find which are from the same Latin root and which are unrelated.

1. A) Toll (The toll to cross the bridge is one dollar.)
    B) Toll ("Ask not for whom the bell tolls.")

2. A) Cheap (We have nothing cheap here!)
    B) Chap (He's a nice enough chap.)

3. A) Pin (as in straight-pin)
    B) Pen (as in fountain-pen)

4. A) Mint (as in US Mint at Carson City)
    B) Mint (as in peppermint and spearmint)

5. A) Street ("The sunny side of the street.")
    B) Stratum (as in "the lowest stratum of society")

6. A) Trivet (Put a trivet under the casserole!)
    B) Tripod (The camera is on a tripod.)

7. A) Kiln   (as in a potter's kiln)
    B) Culinary (as in "a culinary delight")

8. A) Inch   (as in an inch taller)
    B) Ounce   (as in "an ounce of prevention")

9. A) Line   (You have to draw the <u>line</u> somewhere.)
      B) Linen (She washed her dirty <u>linens</u> in public.)

10. A) Plum   (A <u>plum</u> is an edible fruit with a single seed.)
     B) Prune (A <u>prune</u> is a dried plum.)

11. A) Prune (as in to <u>prune</u> off the dead wood.)
     B) Prune (as in to eat a surfeit of <u>prunes</u>.)

12. A) Wine   (as in "A glass of white <u>wine</u>, please.")
     B) Vinegar (as in <u>vinegar</u> and oil)

13. A) Kipper (as in smoked <u>kippers</u>, or <u>kippered</u> herring)
     B) Copper (as in a <u>copper</u> bracelet)

14. A) Box (to <u>box</u> one's ears)
     B) Box (as in strong <u>box</u>, mail <u>box</u>, gift <u>box</u>)

15. A) Mile   ("A miss is as good as a <u>mile</u>.")
     B) Millenium ("The <u>millenium</u> is at hand.")

16. A) Fever   (She had chills and <u>fever</u>.)
     B) February (<u>February</u> is the shortest month.)

17. A) Chalk   (a chalk drawing, a piece of chalk)
     B) Calcium (Calcium is necessary for strong teeth and
                   bones.)

18. A) Must (I really <u>must</u> be going.)
     B) Must (<u>Must</u>: unfermented juice being processed for wine.)

19. A) Pound   (Sixteen ounces equal one pound.)
     B) Ponderous (This is a ponderous tome.)

20. A) Post (the wire is held up by a series of posts.)
     B) Post (as in Post Office)

21. A) Fuller (A fuller works with cloth.)
     B) Fuller (as in a fuller view of the stage.)

Exercise IV. REVIEW

Choose a word in column B that has the same Latin (or Latinized Greek) base as the word in column A.

Notice that the words in column <u>B</u>. have for the most part retained the Latin spelling of the base. Most of these words are literary, learned borrowings or coined words. The words in column <u>A</u>. are on the other hand early borrowings from the spoken

51

language. And so their spellings and pronunciations have gone
through the same shifts as native words. The words in the first
group are so thoroughly domesticated that they are now hardly
recognizable as foreign imports, except to students of etymology.

A.	B.
1. Copper	Stratigraphy
2. Chalk	Million
3. Cheese	Uncial
4. Fork	Menthol
5. Mile	Bifurcation
6. Pound	Imponderable
7. Street	Interval
8. Mint (coinage)	Cuprous
9. Mint (aromatic herb)	Monetary
10. Ounce	Calcination
11. Wall	Casein, caseous
12. Chest	Cistern

THE ANGLO-SAXONS IN ENGLAND

The Anglo-Saxons found their progress in Britain neither swift nor spectacular. For the native Celts and the Romano-Britons had discovered within themselves a new spirit of resistance and pride. Coincidental to their invigorated political systems the natives of Britain reawakened their national religion, a pagan pantheism of Celtic origins. Especially in the southeastern districts of the island a new sense of purpose put steel into British determination to withstand the Angles and the Saxons.

Around the year 500 A.D. the British won a pivotal military victory at a place called Mons Badonicus. And for the next fifty years the invaders were held at a standstill. However, growing numbers of German immigrants eventually swung the balance against the natives. The last quarter of the century found the Anglo-Saxon invaders in the ascendence. After 571 A.D., when a new and larger army of confederated English Germans routed the British, there was no doubt that the island would carry a Germanic stamp in culture, language, and politics.

During this same time most, if not all, of Europe, which previously had fallen under Mediterranean Roman influence and power, came to be dominated by one or another Germanic tribe. Rome itself was the seat of Gothic rule. English was only one, peripheral corner of the historical picture at the beginning of the Middle Ages.

While not escaping the political, cultural, and racial turmoil of the times, the oldest Roman provinces (Italy, France and Spain, for example) managed to retain their Latin based languages. But the new provinces, which had never been thoroughly Romanized, adopted or retained Germanic languages, except in Eastern Europe where Slavonic nations generally proved to be unyielding to outside pressures. However, Roman culture and religion, which now was Christianity, still remained in the eyes of the conquerors superior to their own, much in the way that European, and especially French, culture used to be thought superior by those living on the peripheries of the Western world, for example North America and the Slavic countries.

In England, as we should call the country after the Anglo-Saxons established hegemony there, Roman influence in this period was carried mostly by religion. The Germans, when they invaded the island, were heathens, worshipping a multitude of legendary gods which embodied primitive virtues. Even today we recall these deities in the names of four of our weekdays, Tuesday, Wednesday,

Thursday and Friday which are named after the old German gods, Tiw, patron of war, Woden the father of Tiw and supreme warrior, Thor a rain and cloud god, and Freyr a god of fertility. Two other weekdays are Germanic, but in their cases translations of Roman gods' names into Anglo-Saxon, Sunday and Monday.

Early Christianity, which had gained a foothold in the island during the Roman occupation, vanished from Britain with, it seems, the departure of the Roman legions. However, a branch of the Church continued to exist in Ireland, where legend held that Joseph of Arimathea was the first to preach the Gospel. It was Celtic missionaries who first undertook the conversion of the pagan Anglo-Saxons in the far north of England. Their success was rapid. And within a short time they had managed to establish a thriving series of monasteries in the kingdoms of Berenica and Northumbria.

The south was proselytized by Roman Catholic missionaries beginning with St. Augustine of Canterbury who was dispatched to England by Pope Gregory the Great with instructions to carry out a policy of gentle persuasion. The southern kingdoms of England at this time were the center of English paganism, both cultural and political. And the early missions to that part of the island suffered disappointing setbacks and hostilities unknown to the Celtic missionaries in the north. As a result of the Roman Catholic policy of gradual conversion, religious practices in the south of England took on a mixed color, assimilating some pagan aspects and vocabulary into the Christian rituals. So that today, English still uses pagan words to refer to the two holiest seasons of the Christian calendar, Easter (see the preceding chapter) and Yule which comes from giuli, the name of an end of the year pagan feast the date of which coincided with Christmas (cf. yule log, Yuletide).

In time the two strains of Christianity came into conflict over theological and political matters. The ostensible clash was fought over the dating of Easter, which was a problem that sorely vexed Christians. Through the superiority of its scientific calculations and theological evidence the Roman Catholic Church based in the south was able to persuade the majority of the English Christians represented by their Bishops of its position on the question at the Synod of Whitby. The resulting decline of Celtic thought on English Christianity, insured the continuing influence of Latin, the language of the Roman Church, in England. Also, another consequence of the triumph of the Catholic Church over the Celtic Church insured the use of the Roman alphabet, which we now use. The earliest writing system used to transcribe the native language of England was one called Runes, which, though ultimately derived from the Roman alphabet, had developed into a series of characters radically different from those which we are used to. The Celtic Christians being little influenced by European culture wrote mostly in Runes. The Catholics on the other hand held close ties to Europe and wrote mostly in the Roman alphabet. The final adoption of our present writing system facilitated the entry into our language of Latin words and ideas.

The quelling of religious opposition and the ascendency of the Roman alphabet, opened England to the full force of Continental culture. Roman monastic houses were vigorously established throughout the island, and monk-scholars travelled back and forth from England to European centers of learning. Two centuries after arriving in England, the English still retained memories of their continental origins. Within the climate of religious expansion at home, English monks felt it their fraternal responsibility to take Christianity to their Germanic homeland. And for some half century, English missionaries pursued the conversion of the continental Germans with something bordering on fanaticism.

The high point of this phase of Anglo-Saxon culture came in the late seventh and the early eighth centuries with the appearance of two north English monks, Bede and Alcuin, in the kingdom of Northumbria. Although, Alcuin made his career at the court of Charlemagne and is thus considered more European than English, Bede spent his life at the monastery of Jarrow, writing Biblical and theological commentaries, studies which, in those times, were held to be the highest form of scholarship. For his work in theology he earned the name, Venerable Bede. Another Englishman, St. Boniface said of Bede that he was "the candle of the Church." Today, however, we consider the monk of Jarrow's most important work to be his History of the Church in England, which traces the history of the island up to his own times.

Both Bede and Alcuin, along with all of their educated contemporaries, wrote in Latin; a fact which is not surprising when it is considered that the Anglo-Saxon word laedina (a corruption of Latina) not only meant the Latin language, but also meant any literate language and, even grammar itself. Since Latin was the universal medium of instruction and of learned writing at this time, the most educated people of the day fell naturally into bilingualism. They spoke of trivial matters in their native tongue, and of intellectual matters in Latin. Bede, in the History of the Church in England, tells us that in England there were four distinct groups of people and five languages spoken among them, the fifth and universal language, he states, was Latin. However, throughout his History, Bede makes reference to vernacular literature written in England, usually verse, by authors such as Caedmon and Cynewulf.

The age of Bede and that phase of Anglo-Saxon culture was soon brought to an end by a renewal of migratory movement. This time the far northern Germanic tribes of Scandanavia were on the move, pushing south and west. During the respite from external threat, the English had built up a monastic establishment located on the coast and on coastal islets because there they could be most easily protected from secular intrusions and land-based brigandage. But the monasteries and the towns were unprotected from the sea by either walls or standing militia. The rich, undefended prizes of England were a magnet for these blond barbarians who had been set roaming by the barrenness of their native fjords. The Norse hordes began first to pick at England with small, sporadic sallying raids, which year after year grew in intensity and ferocity. Within three years, 793, 794 and 795, the three richest and most prestigious seats of monastic learning in England were sacked by the sea raiders. Lindisfarne, Jarrow, and Iona were each in turn obliterated. Within less than a century the Danish Vikings shifted from a pattern of seasonal raids to one of sustained attack. The Scandanavians began to look upon England as a place to conquer and to settle.

For over a century, the island lacked both the stability of government and the tranquillity of learning without which no country can progress. But the period of the Norse invasions was not entirely unrelieved. For the Vikings, whose name has come to be associated with savagery and piracy, brought to the English language the word law and along with it a new concept of the law to the island.

In the last decade of the ninth century a remarkable man ascended to the throne of the kingdom of Wessex in southern England. Hard pressed by the Danish menace, he manoeuvred his scanty forces cunningly, knowing when to retreat, when to compromise with the foreign enemy, and when to attack, in the end, he earned the title which has since followed him through history, Alfred the Great, by beating back the Danes.

Alfred the Great, in his fortieth year, after military and political victory was his, began to study Latin; for the preceding times--fraught as they were with alarms--were not conducive to study. And, in his last years, Alfred devoted his time to the revival of learning in England, as he wrote in his preface to a translation of Orosius' universal history.

Unlike his predecessors of the eighth and early ninth centuries, Alfred wrote the bulk of his works in Anglo-Saxon, concentrating mostly on translations of essential Latin works in order to facilitate the business of education in his country. Because the foregoing hundred years had all but obliterated formal

education in the island, Alfred felt he had to appeal to his subjects in a language they already knew, rather than in an alien
tongue. And only by stepping over the niceties of classical education was he able to start a sizeable body of Englishmen back on
the road to education. His royal patronage lent authority to his
educational reforms and imparted prestige to the particular dialect of Anglo-Saxon in which he wrote. Therefore, the Anglo-Saxon
of Alfred became the foundation of the standard English language
which we use today.

The Alfredian renaissance did not revive learning in England
immediately, it only started it on its way. For nearly a century
later, Aelfric, a monk, schoolmaster and author, tells us that the
old priest who first undertook to teach him Latin himself under-
stood "little Latin". But at this time, the beginning of the ele-
venth century, England was caught up in a Pan-European reform of
monasticism and learning. Monasteries, then as earlier, were the
principal seats of learning, occupying a place in the intellectual
life of their times something akin to universities today. English
Bishops, notably Oswald, Dunstan, and Aethelwold, brought a new
spirit of educational excellence to the island. Aelfric himself
took what we would call his college training from Aethelwold at
the Cathedral school of Winchester, where the Bishop took pleasure
in personally teaching the students. As Aelfric later recounted,
Aethelwold "exhorted them with pleasant words to do better
things."

As the first age of Anglo-Saxon culture in the eighth century
was predominated by the Venerable Bede, and the ninth century can
be called the age of Alfred the Great, so the tenth century is
known as the age of Aelfric. He wrote many works, both in Anglo-
Saxon and in Latin, putting his peculiarly English stamp on Christian orthodoxy and European philosophy. But he is most remembered
still for several small textbooks. One, a Latin grammar written
in Anglo-Saxon, which Aelfric tells his readers can be used to
teach either Latin or Anglo-Saxon (the latter language, one ima-
gines, if Latin happened to be the student's mother tongue).
Another textbook of Aelfric's is an elementary Latin language
reader called the Colloquy. This book is made up of a series of
short, witty dialogues between the schoolmaster and various ordinary folks, fishermen, farmers, bakers, and so forth, concerning
their day to day lives. Because of this book's intrinsic value
and good humor, the Colloquy is still used today to teach Latin!

As a natural consequence growing out of the nature of King
Alfred the Great's educational reforms in which Latin works were
taught in translations, the vernacular became, alongside of Latin
the language of scholars in England. So that that country became
the first in Europe where the intelligentsia was truly bilingual.

Today it might seem slightly amiss to have two languages, one ordinary and one learned, coexisting in the same country, but during the European Middle Ages no one saw the oddness in such an arrangement. But the English, Alfred and Aelfric, perhaps unwittingly, conspired to make the ordinary language of the people a respectable vehicle of intellectual communication. However, owing to the way language was taught in the schools of that day, wherein English was never completely divorced from Latin in the classroom, changes were wrought upon the vernacular, giving it, through osmosis, free access to a rich and varied vocabulary from the Latin dictionary. In short order, Latin words learned in school seeped into the students' everyday English conversation, and soon the Latin vocabulary seemed as natural to the English speakers as were the words of Germanic origin.

EXERCISES

Exercise I. Words from the Conversion

The full-scale conversion of the Anglo-Saxons to Christianity (beginning in 597) and the accompanying spread of scholarship brought many more new words to our language. Many of these words naturally refer to ecclesiastical matters: from this group, the list below is taken. Since Christianity existed among the Roman-Britons who inhabited the towns before the A-S arrived, some religious terms survived from this earlier period. There are furthermore a few words adopted from ecclesiastical Greek, perhaps first by the Goths, which spread to other Germanic tribes before they became Christians themselves.

Go over this list of words and choose one or two to look up. Find out:

1. When and where (if possible) it first entered our language.
2. What was its first spelling in our language?
3. What was the original word in Latin or Greek?
4. What is the meaning of the original word?
5. Has the word changed in meaning?
6. Are there other words from the same Latin or Greek word used in English?
7. Has the word had a continuous history from its earliest entrance or was it reborrowed from Latin or French?
8. Does the word come from a specific work?

1. angel	2. church	3. nun
4. alms	5. Mass	6. pope
7. cope	8. altar	9. cleric

10. deacon	11. passion	12. priest
13. monk	14. relic	15. creed
16. noon	17. paradise	18. abbot
19. apostate	20. cross	21. sabbath (Hebr.)
22. preach	23. devil	24. minister
25. bishop	26. disciple	27. offer
28. alb	29. acolyte	30. apostle
31. dean	32. martyr	33. saint

Exercise II. Words from Literature

The Venerable Bede, writing in the early eighth century in Latin, says: "At present peoples of Britain study and confess one and the same knowledge...in five tongues--equal to the number of books of divine law--English, British, Scots, Pictish, and Latin, which through study of the Scriptures has become common to all." [Historia Ecclesiastica, I, 1]

The influence of literature on language should not be under-estimated: the Latin translation of Scripture brought many coined words into respectable Latin. Likewise, the reading of religious and other literary texts in Latin gave many new words to English. In this way Bede himself influenced the English language, though he wrote in Latin: in the Old English translation of Bede's Historia Ecclesiastica a good number of learned words, usually following Bede's Latin occur: for example antemn (antiphon, anthem), letania (litany), archidiacon (archdeacon); canon, capitol (for 'chapter'), cometa (comet), eretic (heretic), subdiacon (sub-deacon) as well as most of the words listed in exercise 1.

Many of these early literary loan-words did not survive. Some have ceased to be used altogether in English, but many others were replaced or reborrowed either directly from Latin or Greek or through French. It is natural that words borrowed from literature should first enter our own language in its written form: sometimes such words pass into the spoken language and become fixed there. But probably the majority of these words remain among 'learned' words and never reach the lips of the average speaker.

In the following list, are some early loan-words from Latin. These have all dropped out of our language and have been replaced by other words: 1. Give the modern word for the OE word or 2. if no word from the same source has replaced it, give a modern English word derived from the same source.

For example:
1. plaetse, plaece [from Greek plateia hodos 'broad street' from platus 'broad' (cf. platy-) through Latin platea] was

replaced by PLACE from the Latin version of the same Greek word, this time influenced by Old French, with the meaning 'an open place in a town.' We have furthermore borrowed the word again in the forms PLAZA (from Spanish) and PIAZZA (from Italian) because PLACE has become so generalized that it no longer means 'a public square' or 'an open area in a city or town', but any area. We therefore reborrowed the word from other Romance languages in its original sense (though even plaza is becoming more generalized so that it is now used for parking lots, even covered ones, and for roofed shopping centers).

2. fenester (window) on the other hand has dropped out of every-day English and was not reborrowed; but we do have some derivatives of the Latin word fenestra in the words FENESTRATED ('having windows or window-like openings'), FENESTRATION (an architectural term meaning 'the design and placement of windows in a building'; and a surgical term, 'the cutting of an opening from the external auditory canal to the labyrinth of the internal ear to restore hearing'), DEFENESTRATION (an urbane way of indicating the act of 'throwing something or someone out of a window'), and finally in scientific terminology, we have the Latinism FENESTRA (used to mean 'a window-like opening' or 'a transparent marking on an insect's wing').

Early English form   (Meaning)   Latin   Fill-in replacing
                                                word or derivatives

1. plaetse, plaece (open place in a town) from PLATEA
   Give word that replaced plaetse and some additional derivatives: _____

2. fenester (window) from FENESTRA
   Give some derivatives: _____

3. Milite (soldiers) from MILITES
   Give derivatives: _____

4. fers (a line of poetry) from VERSUS
   Give derivatives of versus: _____
   Fers was replaced by: _____

5. ymen (a song of praise) fr. HYMNUS Replaced by _____

6. carte (paper, deed) from CHARTES
   Replaced by: _____
   Derivatives:_____

7. punct (dot) from PUNCTUS
   Replaced by: _____
   Derivatives: _____

8. titol (superscription) from TITULUS
   Replaced by: _____

9. calend (month) Latin CALENDAE (the first of the month)
   Derivative: _____

10. studdian (to see, take care of) from STUDERE
    Replaced by: _____
    Derivatives: _____

11. castel (village, small town) from CASTELLUM
    Replaced by: _____

12. clauster (enclosure, a place devoted to religious seclusion)
    from Lat. CLAUSTRUM; Replaced by: _____

13. columne (pillar) from COLUMNA; Replaced by: _____

14. antefn (sung response) from antiphona
    Replaced by: _____

15. cantere (singer) from CANTOR: Replaced by: _____

Exercise III. Literature and Vocabulary: GLOSSES [optional]

Of the English scholars and authors of the late 10th century, the greatest was the abbot Aelfric of Eynsham, whose work reflects better than that of any other, the spirit and quality of the age. It was an age of mixed cultural and intellectual traditions: the Germanic, the Classical, and the Christian. Perhaps the most charming of his works--which include Homilies, Lives of Saints, interpretations of Biblical and Christian works, a Glossary, a Grammar and numerous Epistles--is a small work called Colloquy, a dialogue in Latin between a teacher and his pupils on everyday life in and around a monastic school. Since Latin was the language of learning, students were discouraged from using the vernacular, but they needed elementary work to learn to speak in Latin of the common things around them: to meet this pedagogical need, the Colloquy was written. It gained an added importance from the fact that it was glossed by an anonymous monk shortly after it was written: that is, an Old English translation was written above the Latin text, probably for the use of teachers whose Latin was a little hesitant. This is the only extended piece of sustained dialogue in Old English. The little work, consisting of question and answer between the master and a series of workers, a ploughman, a shepherd, a fisherman, a merchant, a cook, a baker, a hunter, and a smith, parts to be taken by the students in the class, gives us a witty glance at life in the 10th century.

Aelfric's <u>Colloquy</u> in the Old English version contains about three dozen words derived from Latin (or Greek) including a number of fish named by the fisherman and quite a few objects of trade mentioned by the merchant. For these exercises we will single out only two of the Anglo-Saxon glosses for special consideration: Ceaster ('city') and Kempa ('soldier').

A. CEASTER

The master asks the fisherman where he sells his catch and the reply is : A-S: on <u>ceastre</u> Lat. <u>in</u> <u>civitate</u> ('in the city') "And who buys them," asks the master. The fisherman answers: A-S <u>ceasterwara</u> Lat. <u>cives</u> ('citizens, town-dwellers') CEASTER is one of our earliest loan-words from Latin. It comes from the Latin word CASTRA meaning 'camp'. Since the Romano-Britons built their towns around military camps, the word <u>ceaster</u> became the common word for city/fortified town. It survives today in place names such as <u>Chester</u> and those ending in -<u>chester</u>, -<u>caster</u>, -<u>cester</u>.

1. Give the names of several cities and towns in England and the U.S. ending in -chester, -caster, -cester.

We no longer speak of the Chester (or ceaster) but have replaced this word with <u>city</u>, derived through French from Latin <u>civitas</u> (stem <u>civitat</u>-), the word which is glossed by <u>ceaster</u> in the A-S translation. Nor do we use the word ceasterwara for city- or town-dwellers which glosses the Latin word <u>cives</u> (from which <u>civitas</u> is derived), 'citizens' [English 'citizen' is also derived from <u>civitas</u>, through French, so that the earliest meaning of <u>citizen</u> is 'city-dweller'].

2. Can you think of some other words derived from CIV- (the base of <u>cives</u>)?

B. KEMPA

Another word of interest in the text is the word <u>kempa</u>, glossing the Latin word <u>miles</u> 'soldier'. <u>Kempa</u> very probably comes from the Latin <u>campus</u>, 'field'. <u>Kempa</u> has fallen out of use in English, having been replaced by <u>soldier</u> which also ultimately comes from Latin [Middle English <u>souldeur</u> from Old French <u>soudier</u>, <u>soldier</u> from <u>soulde</u>, 'pay' from Latin <u>solidus</u>, an ancient Roman coin; so that a 'soldier' was originally a mercenary, one hired for pay]. The meaning of soldier has become generalized so that we have had to borrow yet another word from Latin through French

62

for the soldier who hires himself out to foreign armies, Mercenary from Latin <u>merces</u> 'pay, wages'. From the same stem comes
<u>merchant</u>. The god <u>Mercury</u>, who was among other things the
protector of merchants and thieves, is possibly from the same
stem.

Questions:

Give three other English derivatives from
1. <u>merces</u> or from merx, <u>merc-</u> 'goods, wares'
2. <u>campus</u>
3. <u>solidus</u>

Exercise IV. Words From Latin Culture

The most important English prose of the 9th century is the
writing of King Alfred himself. Much of his work is translation
of Latin texts, for example, a version of <u>Historia</u> <u>adversus</u>
<u>Paganos</u> of Paulus Orosius (a compendium of world history from the
beginnings to Alaric's sack of Rome, written in the 5th century
and seeking to show that Christianity was not the cause of the
fall of Rome). This work, because of its subject matter, introduces a number of words that are connected with Roman history into
the English language.

Words describing Roman cultural and political institutions
have come into our language at various periods. In this list (A)
of words referring to Roman culture, the form used by Alfred is
given in brackets. List B contains words that came in later.
Choose two words from either list and find out all you can about
the institution or person [use the Oxford Classical Dictionary or
an encyclopedia; you may have to look under a more general subject
area.] Using the OED, find out when the word came into English
and what reborrowings (if any) it underwent. Give an example of
the word in a sentence, any other words derived from it in English
and explain any changes of meaning that it has undergone.

A. 1. Caesar [casere] Modern: czar, tsar, Kaiser
    2. centurian [centur]
    3. consul [consul]
    4. cohort [coorte]
    5. legion [legie]
    6. palace [palendse]
    7. triumph [triumphan]
    8. talent [talente]
    9. dictator [tictator]
   10. tunic [tunece]
   11. noon [non] from <u>nona</u> <u>hora</u> 'ninth hour'

63

B. 12. forum
15. salary
18. farce
21. tribune
24. fanatic
27. applause
30. paterfamilias
33. Fascist
36. succint

13. senate
16. pagan
19. sacrosanct
22. rostrum
25. sacrament
28. June
31. candidate
34. censor
37. July

14. auspice
17. manumission
20. August
23. augury
26. emancipate
29. profane
32. pontificate
35. municipal

Exercise V.   REVIEW

Match words from same stem

A		B	
1.	forum	1.	diabolical
2.	bishop	2.	castle
3.	creed	3.	reliquary
4.	alb	4.	credulous
5.	cross	5.	palatine
6.	saint	6.	diaconate
7.	deacon	7.	predicate
8.	place	8.	missal
9.	offer	9.	forensic
10.	Mass	10.	oleomargarine
11.	relic	11.	episcopal
12.	wine	12.	plaza
13.	oil	13.	albino
14.	Chester	14.	sanctify
15.	merchant	15.	oblation
16.	city	16.	vintage
17.	Palace	17.	commercial
18.	augury	18.	civilian
19.	devil	19.	inaugurate
20.	capitol	20.	chapter
21.	preach	21.	crucifixion

Give the meanings of the base-words.

SCANDINAVIAN WORDS in English: Explanations & Exercises

A large number of Scandinavian words were adopted during the Old English and Middle English periods as a result of the Viking invasions (of the 8th, 9th, and 10th centuries) and especially of the peaceful settlement of the Scandinavians and their association with Englishmen in the 11th and 12th centuries.   The earliest of the Scandinavian words have to do with the sea and the law primarily, though later loan-words are more general, including some of the most ordinary words and implying no introduction of new things or new ideas.

64

The Scandinavian dialects used by the invaders resembled the English dialects of the time, especially in vocabulary, since all were Germanic. Bilingualism or at least mutual intelligibility was quite common. It is for this reason that the Scandinanvian influence was so great and yet so imperceptible, since the words that were borrowed did not really feel like foreign words. The fact that many words in the two groups of dialects are cognates and some even identical, makes it difficult to know for certain whether a word is a loan-word or not. Sometimes the meaning of an English word has been changed under Scandinavian influence, since the meaning of common words were sometimes different in the two groups. Another indication of borrowing may be the spelling of the word: the most noticeable variation being the sk- sound for which old English had sh-: so that the word skirt (of Scandinavian origin) is a double for the English shirt. Sky, skill, skulk, skull, skin, score, scrape, scrap, scare and some words borrowed later (since the 16th century), scud, scrag, scuffle, scrub, skit, skittles, skewer, ski are of Scandinavian origin.

SOME SCANDINAVIAN WORDS to work with: Choose any one of the words in this list and find out: what was its Scandinavian ancestor; what is its original meaning; when did it enter English, did it have cognates in English already, has its meaning changed?

LEGAL AND QUASI-LEGAL TERMS

1.	law	2.	wapentake
3.	loan	4.	wrong
5.	crook	6.	fellow
7.	husband	8.	crooked
9.	husting	10.	bond

NAUTICAL TERMS: 1. haven   2. boatswain

COMMONPLACE WORDS from Scandinavian

1.	call	2.	take	3.	let	4.	knife
5.	loft	6.	wing	7.	band	8.	score
9.	they, their, them (developed under Scandinavian influence)						
10.	egg	11.	gape	12.	get	13.	skin
14.	skill	15.	leg	16.	bait	17.	sale
18.	die	19.	cast	20.	give (replaced OE yive)		
21.	root	22.	bull	23.	anger	24.	booth
25.	rag	26.	hit	27.	want	28.	snare
29.	boon	30.	awe	31.	thrall	32.	meek

SECTION ONE: Chapter Six

THE NORMANS IN ENGLAND

Though 1066 A.D. is commonly taken as the year in which Norman French influence began to be felt in England, the ground for this influence was laid many decades earlier. As the English were not natives of the British Isles, but Baltic Teutons, neither were the Normans natives of France. Their very name tells us that they were Northmen or Scandinavians, who had invaded France around the year 900 A.D. and stayed to become French. Like the English, who accepted the religion of southern Europe, Christianity, the Normans converted after they settled in their new home. But, unlike their neighbors across the English Channel, the Normans did not retain their Teutonic language, but readily adopted the Romance, Vulgar Latin of France. And, one other point of similarity between the Normans and the English is that once they both settled in their new homes, they resisted further incursions by the still southward pushing Scandinavian Teutons.

Close commercial and intellectual ties linked Normandy and England for some time. And their common struggle against raiding Vikings had drawn them into an on again off again alliance. However, the Normans were not only pursuing a defensive policy, protecting what was theirs as were the English, but they were also, after the Scandinavian pattern, expansionistic. For the Normans needed elbow room, and so their younger sons went roaming, planting Norman rule as far afield as Southern Italy, Sicily, and the Holy Land. So that they could carry out this practice of keeping their French lands unhindered by Vikings and at the same time expand their federated empire, the Normans occasionally came to tacit agreements with the raiding Scandinavians not to oppose them. And occasionally the English suffered because of the loss of their ally.

Even after Emma, the sister of the Duke of Normandy, married King Aethelred of England, the alliance between those two countries was not guaranteed. And so when the Danes made a bold thrust into the heartland of England in 1013, the Normans did nothing more than offer refuge to the fleeing English royal family for the sake of their kinswoman, the Queen. This Danish invasion succeeded to a degree none of the earlier Scandinavian raids had done, and a Viking was placed on the throne of England. Canute became king both of Denmark and of England. His English policy, however, was one of reconciliation to the traditional families. He championed the cause of English Christianity, and brought a measure of stability to the island.

Once again the Normans managed to insinuate themselves into English history even after the island had been lost to the Scandinavian invader. For by this time Aethelred had died and his Norman widow was available for another marriage. One more time she married the king of England, Canute the Dane. By her first marriage to the Anglo-Saxon king she was the mother of an heir to the throne, and by Canute she became the mother of another heir to the throne, Hardacanute.

The zig-zag course of English history nowhere becomes so remarkably confused and romantic as it does at this juncture. In the twice married, twice Queen of England, we see the intersecting cross currents which have affected the British Isles throughout history. The island is held prisoner by its geographical location, caught on the north-south migratory routes of the Teutonic tribes and placed on the outer path of the south-north road of Mediterranean cultural expansion. These varying influences, northern and southern, meet and merge in England. And, it is in the person of Emma, that the various strains seem to be most vividly embodied. As a Norman, she was by nationality a Scandinavian. But by culture she was Mediterranean. She spoke a language which was derived from the type of Latin spoken by the Roman legionaires and farmers who settled in Gaul in the wake of Caesar's conquest. She was devoted to a religion which carried the stamp of its non-European origins. But as a Norman, Emma was a vigorous adherent to practical expansionism common to those people.

The marriage between Emma and the Anglo-Saxon Aethelred, seemed to the English to give them a permanent claim on Normandy's support. But in this they were wrong, as we have seen. The Danish King of England, Canute, it seems, married Emma with the idea that somehow she, being the widow of the former native king of the island, would impart to him and the heirs of their marriage a certain degree of Anglo-Saxon legitimacy in the eyes of his English subjects. However wisely Canute had calculated the benefits of this marriage, his Queen had other motives.

While Emma was back in England, bearing and raising a Scandinavian heir to the English throne, her first son by Aethelred remained with his Norman kinsmen in France. As the years slipped by, it seemed that the English had become acclimatized to Danish rule, and that the new rulers were gradually becoming acclimatized to the island. The impression that the Danish rulers were being accepted by the English seemed to be strengthened in 1035 when Canute died. In rapid succession two of his sons came to the throne of England, and each was in turn protected by English noblemen from threats launched by Aethelred's children who had taken the opportunity to regain their lost heritage. Emma's

Danish son, Hardacanute was eventually enthroned in England. And by 1040, he felt secure enough to invite his half brother Edward, to return to England. No doubt, Emma their mother was instrumental in this reconciliation. But within two years, Edward succeeded to the throne of England. This relieved the English since he represented, as the son of Aethelred, the continuity of Anglo-Saxon political rule in England.

However Edward's thirty years' exile in France left its mark on him. He brought a Normanized attitude towards government and culture back to England with him, and he showed preference to his Norman French aquaintances in making appointments to political and ecclesiastical posts. Edward, in fact, was so Norman in his preferments that he even went so far as to name as his heir to the English throne, as was the Anglo-Saxon custom, his cousin William, Duke of Normandy. But the Anglo-Saxon nobility did not take kindly to their king's French leanings, since they had expected his restoration would mean a complete restoration of their power as well, and a civil war followed. The struggle failed to unseat Edward, but the nobles did, in the end, force the king to submit to their will for the rest of his reign. During the last fourteen years of his life, Edward acquired a reputation for piety, centering around his activities in building churches and monasteries, which were politically neutral activities which could not incite Anglo-Saxon mistrust, and he came to be known as Edward the Confessor.

When he died in January 1066, Edward left no natural heir to the crown and the Anglo-Saxon nobles were not anxious to see his chosen successor, the Duke of Normandy, ascend to the throne. One after the other two Englishmen quickly took the throne. But the events were unsettled. There was the matter William's claim on England which was worrisome and represented an ever present threat to the Anglo-Saxons. And then there was in the same year a renewed Viking invasion. While King Harold II was in the north of England trying to stave off the Norsemen, William the Norman earned his nickname, the Conqueror, by landing a force in the undefended south of England. Then, when the harried English king hurried to fight him, William conquered him at the Battle of Hastings on the 14th of October. On Christmas day of 1066, less than a year after his cousin Edward's death, William the Conqueror was formally crowned king of England at Westminster Abbey.

When the Normans conquered England, they were met with a culture far more advanced than their own. Literacy and education was relatively common in England in comparison to Normandy. This showed in the fact that the English kept numerous records of public and private doings, whereas written records of any kind were virtually unknown to the Norman French. Also, the English were the first in Europe to find their own daily language worthy of writing, whereas other peoples wrote only in Latin.

However, the pen, in an open fight, is not mightier than the sword, and the literate English were conquered by the mostly illiterate Normans, both politically and for the time linguistically. Perhaps because William the Conqueror, shortly after his coronation, tried to learn English and failed, the Normans decided to retain their own language instead of adopting the language which they found on the island. But even in the face of the overwhelming military superiority of the French conquerors, who took complete control of the island, the Anglo-Saxon Chronicles were still being written in English a hundred years after the Conquest. Nonetheless, the upper classes of English society at any rate came to speak French.

Within a scant generation of the Battle of Hastings, nearly all of the leading personages of England were either French by birth or French speakers by preference. However, the adoption of the language of the Norman French invaders did not necessarily mean that the English also adopted their conquerors' anti-intellectual attitude towards literacy and culture. For in the year 1140 a remarkable event occurred in the midlands of England; an event which is as notable in the history of ideas and culture as the Invasion had been in the annals of politics. In that year it is reported that the Lady Constance Fitz Gilbert of Lincolnshire had not only gone to the expense of paying one Mark in silver to have a vernacular poem on the life of King Henry I copied out for herself, but that she also often read the poem in her room to herself. On the face of it, this may not seem too extraordinary, but this is the first recorded instance we know of in post Roman Europe that popular literature written in the everyday language was purchased and read by an invidivual for pleasure. Within a quarter of a century of this momentous date there was in England a thriving trade in manuscripts of vernacular poetry which was fueled mostly by well-born ladies who sought light reading material.

At this time the Vernacular language which the Anglo-Norman aristocracy spoke and read was the French of the Conqueror. An English writer, some two hundred years later, commenting on those times, tells us that well-born children then were taught to "leve here oune longage [leave their own language]" for French from the time they were "yrokked in here cradel [rocked in their cradle]". However, what was true of the aristocracy, who feared the politically dominant Normans and feared more that they might seem ignorant if they could not speak French, was not true of the majority of Englishmen who continued to speak their native language throughout this period.

70

During this period of some two hundred and fifty years Anglo-Saxon was not only spoken by the masses of common men but it was also written. Around 1205, Layamon of Worcestershire wrote a verse chronicle of English history of nearly 30,000 lines using fewer than fifty words borrowed from French. However, Anglo-Saxon could not resist for long the influence of the conquerors' language. And gradually not only bilingual Englishmen, but also the lower classes who spoke only their native tongue began to assimilate a growing number of French words into their everyday speech. Certainly, during this period, the vocabulary of Anglo-Saxon changed and its grammar was affected, but English still managed to maintain a distinct identity. And many Englishmen began to view their native language with nationalistic pride.

In 1295 the Anglo-Norman king of England found himself at war with the king of France. He was not able to muster much enthusiasm for this particular war among his English subjects until he made the claim that his French adversary had threatened to utterly wipe out the English language in the event of his victory. This appeal to linguistic nationalism swung the vote.

At the beginning of the fourteenth century, French was still a compulsory subject in the grammar schools of England. But the tide rapidly changed within less than two generations. A schoolmaster named John Cornwell, it seems, was the first to experiment with a curriculum based on English rather than French. And his reforms were carried further by one of his students, Richard Pencritch. Before long French was nearly unheard in the class rooms of English grammar schools. By 1362 a statute was decreed changing the official language of the law courts from French to English, because the former was "much unknown in the realm".

EXERCISES

Exercise I: Daily Life

A. "The Raw and the Cooked"

In an oft-quoted scene from <u>Ivanhoe</u>, the jester assures the swineherd that his herd of pigs will be converted into Normans before morning.

> The swine turned Normans to my comfort!"
> quoth Gurth "expound that to me, Wamba, for my
> brain is too dull and my mind too vexed to read
> riddles.

71

Why, how call you those grunting brutes running about on four legs?" demanded Wamba
   "Swine, fool--swine," said the herd;
"every fool knows that."
   "And swine is good Saxon," said the jester;
"but how call you the sow when she is flayed, and
drawn, and quar- tered, and hung up by the heels
like a traitor?"
   "Pork," answered the swineherd. "I am glad
every fool knows that, too," said Wamba, "and pork,
I think, is good Norman French; and so when the
brute lives and is in charge of a Saxon slave, she
goes by her Saxon name, but becomes a Norman and is
called pork when she is carried to the castlehall to
feast among the nobles. . ."

And so Wamba goes through several other animals that on the hoof
are Saxon, but Norman on the table, concluding, "he is Saxon when
he requires tendance, and takes a Norman name when he becomes a
matter of enjoyment."

For example:

ALIVE	COOKED
oxen, kine	beef
calf	veal
deer	venison
sheep	mutton

   The social significance of the Norman Conquest is clearly
seen in the language not only of domestic animals on the hoof and
on the platter, but in all aspects of life, from the kitchen to
the court, from the bedroom to the battlefield. By the fifteenth
century no form of business or pleasure could be talked about
without the use of French words.

Foods and Cooking Terms 11th to 15th centuries:

lentil	beef	mutton	veal	pork	bacon
venison	oyster	gravy	almond	mace	clove
sugar	ginger	onion	potage	gelatin	sauce
vinegar	oil	fig	spice	crepes	flour
grease	batter	suet	capon	mallard	date
saffron	raisin	paste	fruit	supper	dinner
bottle	banquet	table	feast	diet	plate
grape	blanche	boil	parboil	mince	fry

And of course many more culinary terms have entered our language
from French more recently: for example: casserole, croquette,
meringue, ramekin, rissole, tureen, ragout, praline, liqueur,

72

cuisine, aspic, hors d'oeurve, cafe, gourmet, restaurant, menu, souffle, puree, fondant, mousse.

TWO RECIPES: Find words from FRENCH

(1) A 15th century English recipe for Crepes (quoted from M.I. Serjeantson, p., 150)
      Take white of eyren, Milke, and fyne floure, and bete hit togidre, and drawe hit thorgh a streynour, so that hit be rennyng, and noght to stiff; and caste there-to sugur and salt, And then take a chaffur full of fresh grece boyling; and then put thi honde in the batur and lete the bater ren thorgh thi fingers into the chaffur; And when it is ren togidre in the chaffre, and is ynowe, take a Skymour, and take hit oute of the chaffur, and putte oute al the grece. And lete ren; And putte hit in a faire dissh, and cast sugur thereon ynow, and serve it forth.

(2) A 20th century recipe for Pancakes (from Better Homes & Gardens New Cookbook, p. 79). This modern recipe is surprisingly similar except that spoons of various sizes are now recommended instead of fingers and hands to the hygienic houseperson.
1 1/4 cups sifted all-purpose flour
3 teaspoons baking powder
1 teaspoon sugar
1/2 teaspoon salt
1 beaten egg
1 cup milk
2 tablespoons salad oil or melted shortening or bacon fat.

      Sift together flour, baking powder, sugar, and salt. Combine egg, milk, and salad oil; add to dry ingredients, stirring just till flour is moistened. (Batter will be lumpy.) Bake on a hot griddle.

Notice too that in the second recipe, English spelling has become standardized.

Underline the words borrowed from French in the two recipes.

PROJECT: Take a typical lunch or dinner menu and find out how many of the names of the dishes and their ingredients are from French.

B. GAUDEAMUS IGITUR
     Besides the pleasures of the table, many of our daily de-lights are of French origin. These words, for example, entered

the English language within three centuries of the Norman Conquest.

joy	delight	ease	folly	park	letter
parlour	music	tavern	revel	lodge	journey
sojourn	juggler	minstrel	dance	diamonds	rubies
chair	lamp	ornament	vestment	habit	attire
color	tryst				

PROJECT: Write a story using these words (or most of them) and then substitute a native English synonym or a phrase with about the same meaning for each of the imported words. Which of the words in the list are for things we can do very well without and which name things that you would consider necessary for a civilized and comfortable life?

C. SINE QUA NON

Many words for things, actions, feelings which we could not conceivably do without also came into our speech with the Normans. Life would be difficult if we should suddenly decide to amputate the French element from our vocabulary. Try to think of native synonyms for the following words: it may be difficult since the words from the classical tongues through French are in many instances the common ones.

air	rock	desert	beast	cave	gravel
river	flower	change	cry	delay	pass
fail	pay	sign	strive	record(vb)	catch
depart	disturb	place	age	manner	fame
perfection	discipline	silence	noise	cellar	city
country	figure	sponge	towel	cage	lesson
chapter	story	cause	merit	plenty	envy
glutton	feeble	jealous	circumstance		

D. FAMILY TREE

Only our closest kin are named in Anglo-Saxon terms: <u>mother</u>, <u>father</u>, <u>son</u>, <u>daughter</u>, <u>brother</u>, <u>sister</u> (and even <u>sister</u> has been affected by Scandinavian: the modern 'sister' is not directly descended from A-S <u>sweoster</u> but from Old Norse <u>syster</u>). But <u>aunt</u>, <u>uncle</u>, <u>niece</u>, <u>nephew</u>, <u>cousin</u> are from French and ultimately from Latin. Even the <u>grand-</u> of grand-parents and grand-children is from French: in the 13th century, <u>grandsire</u> and <u>grandame</u> (taken directly from French) were used, but were replaced in the 15th century by <u>grandfather</u> and <u>grandmother</u>, words half-English and half-French. The element <u>grand-</u> ('great, full-grown, grand') was later rather illogically extended to the words <u>grandchild</u>, <u>granddaughter</u>, <u>grandson</u>, formations that are unknown to the French language which uses <u>petits-enfants</u> (pl.), <u>petite-fille</u>, petit-fils, which one must admit make more sense. Our in-laws, mother-in-law, father-in-law and so forth are made up of English elements (with the Scandinavian 'law') but are direct translations of Old French compounds. The words sire and dame, now dam, once terms of respect for one's parents have suffered a degradation which has reduced them to terms almost exclusively used to refer to animals: Secretariat is said to have sire and dam, but not so the Secretary of State. Dame has become in American English a slang designation for one whom there ain't nothin' like. But sir (which is of the same origin as sire, the Latin senior 'elder') and, in England, dame have retained their respectful usage.

PROJECT: Work over one of your imported kin: find out how he or she got into our language, what were the Latin and French words from which she or he was derived. Or make up a family tree, giving the etymologies of each relative. Find out where family, spouse, wife and husband come from.

E. STRATA OF SOCIETY

Many of our terms describing status in society, from the lowest to the highest came into English with the Norman Conquest as a result of the rapid and complete Normanizing of the ruling classes: William and his Normans held not only the throne and the administration of the realm, but had even dispossessed the important English land-owners and had replaced the native bishops and abbots with Frenchmen. The language of life and business for nearly all persons with ambitions became French.

Among the French words describing status in society that entered after the conquest are:

| master | servant | butler |

Many of the degrees of the English titled class:

| duke | marquis | viscount | baron |

Count was not adopted because the native (or nearly native) earl came to have approximately the same meaning as French count; but countess was borrowed to apply to the earl's lady, in keeping with the French custom of giving the wife of a titled man a title as well. Knight (OE cniht) was also retained.

The words applying to royal power and court life are also largely French. The top of the royal family, the KING and QUEEN retained their native titles, but their children, the PRINCE and PRINCESS are of French origin. Some other words applying to royalty from French are:

| castle | crown | majesty | reign |
| sceptre | throne | sovereign | realm |

```
        state       power      emperor     empress
        royal       court      [all from Latin or Greek]
Take one of these words and trace it back to its beginning.
```

F. WAR is l'enfer
    ARMY and NAVY and our military ranks
    are from French:

```
    officer     corporal    sergeant    lieutenant
    captain     major       colonel     general
    soldier     private     ensign      commander
    admiral (cf. emir: from Arabic)
```

PROJECT: Choose one of these and find its derivation: what is the literal meaning (e.g. lieutenant is from Fr. lieu tenant, from Latin locum tenentem, 'place holding'); how is this meaning applied to the actual duty of the officer? What other English words are from the same stem?

Many other military terms of various types were also adopted at this time: choose one of the following and find out its history:

```
war         peace       battle      enemy         tower
assail      assault      challenge   tournament    arms
armor       archer      conquer     victory       siege
standard    ensign      banner      pennon
(N.B. flag is a native word.)
```

G. PEOPLE, PROFESSIONS, WAYS OF LIFE

The French influence is to be found in all aspects of daily life and business. All of these people are called by French names:

```
chancellor  minister    attorney    legate       messenger  nurse
squire      mason       mariner     porter       physician   clerk
host        hostage     bachelor    virgin       harlot      felon
marshall    page        rebel       parson       person      friar
```

In the world of business we have these borrowings:

```
market       rent        treasure    rich         poor      to seal
robber       poverty     adversity   prosperity   ransom    debt
relief       pay         heir        heritage     grant     purse
merchandise  coffer      bargain     extortion    profit    purchase
guile
```

ASSIGNMENT: Trace the history of one word in each list; try to think of a native English word or phrase for the same thing.

H. LAW & ORDER

prison	justice	privilege	degree	judge	jury
term	gibbet	charter	counsel	court	felony
advocate	assize	common	evidence	franchise	govern
homage	jurisdiction	crime	pardon	warrant	accuse
defendant	penalty	plaintiff	plead	property	session
suit	summon	tenure	senator	senate	constable
peer	parliament	noble	mayor	official	

PROJECT: In the News of Record section of your local paper, find words relating to the legal system that came into English with the Conqueror.

I. FAITH & MORALS

A very large number of words relating to religion are from French, among them:

service	abbot	religion	cardinal	sacrament	chaplain
miracle	mercy	prophet	baptist	pilgrim	procession
saint	chapel	grace	nativity	passion	evangelist
cell	sermon	disciple	archangel	patriarch	orison
clerk	grief	chalice	chasten	simony	confess
paten	pity	covetous	charity	envious	trespass
bible	savior	trinity	penitence	advent	hermit
prelate	primate	angel	purgatory	nunnery	crucifix
image	tempt	abbey	assumption	collect	abstinence
purity	blame	preach	blaspheme	praise	parishioner
temptation					

PROJECT: Go through the list and look up the meanings and origins of any words that you do not know and any ones that interest you. Most are ultimately from Latin, though several are from Greek. In some instances the French influence is at second hand since the word had already been borrowed (e.g. abbot replaced the earlier abbod and angel replaced the earlier engel).

Exercise II. Doubles

A. A result of the Norman Conquest has been the doubling of English vocabulary. Often the French word did not replace the native word but lived side by side with it. In formal and legal and religious usage we have many expressions which show this tendency to keep the native word and adopt the French word and use them together in a formulaic phrase, as in:

last WILL and TESTAMENT
to ASSEMBLE and MEET TOGETHER
to PARDON and FORGIVE

77

to AID and ABET

(both aid and abet are actually from French, but abet was borrowed from the Scandinavians.)

by ACT and DEED
to ACKNOWLEDGE and CONFESS
SAFE and SOUND
we have ERRED and STRAYED
not DISSEMBLE nor CLOAK
PRAY and   BESEECH
as many as are HERE PRESENT
all who PROFESS and CALL themselves
from all the PERILS and DANGERS of this night
POOR and NEEDY
SAVE and DELIVER us
CONFIRM and STRENGTHEN
FLOURISH and ABOUND
DEARTH and FAMINE
SCARCITY and DEARTH

Assignment: Taking one such pair: tell which is the French/Latin word and which the native, and the origins and meanings of both. Give some other words from the same root of both the native and the alien. What (if anything) is the difference in meaning; what is the difference in usage? Use each in a sentence without the other. Which is the more common word (which would you be more likely to use, which have you heard or seen more often)?

B. We have many other doubles in English, though in everyday speech they would not be used together:

I	II	III (give some derivatives of Latin stem of word in II)
foe	enemy	
friendly	amicable	
begin	commence	
shut	close	
wish	desire	
buy	purchase	
sell	vend	
tale	story (Gk.)	
dread	terror	
work	labor	
try	attempt, endeavor	
meal	flour	
forerunner	precursor	
writer	scribe	
wedding	nuptials	
teachable	docile	

twofold	double
truly	verily
feeling	sentiment
lawful	legal
bloom	flower
blessing	benediction

Once again go over the list: decide which word in each pair is the more common, which you are more familiar with (if either). In Column III, give one or more English derivative from the Latin root of each word in column II.

C. Match the word in Col. I with a native English synonym from Col. II.

I	II
1. felicity	1. feeder
2. provide	2. teaching
3. fraternity	3. freedom
4. illegality	4. manifold
5. script	5. lively
6. pastor	6. burdensome
7. verity	7. brotherhood
8. doctrine	8. heavenly
9. cordial	9. childish
10. multiple	10. writing
11. incredible	11. deathly
12. carnal	12. foretell
13. vital	13. behead
14. royal	14. hearty
15. regal	15. truthfulness
16. celestial	16. happiness
17. liberty	17. fiery
18. mortal	18. unbelievable
19. onerous	19. kingly (use twice)
20. puerile	20. foresee
21. predict	21. lawlessness
22. igneous	22. oversee
23. decapitate	23. fleshy
24. supervise	

Exercise III

D. MORE DOUBLES

Sometimes the native word remains the common or only word for the thing or action, but adjectives used to describe it are from French or Latin.

Examples:

 Life: lively or VITAL (Lat. vita, 'life')
 Death: deadly or MORTAL (Lat. mors, mort-, 'death')
 Birth: NATAL (Lat. natus, 'born')
 Moon: LUNAR (Lat. luna, 'moon')
 Sun: SOLAR (Lat. sol, 'sun')
 Tail: CAUDAL (Lat. cauda, 'tail')

 Fill in the adjective in -al, based on the Latin noun (-ar is used if l occurs in one of the two preceding syllables):

ENGLISH PART	ADJECTIVE	LATIN BASE
Ex: eye	OCULAR	oculus
Ex: ear	AURAL	auris
mouth		os, or-
nose		nasus
tongue		lingua
head		caput, capit-
body		corpus, corpor-
flesh		caro, carn-
hand		manus, manu-
foot		pes, ped-
finger, toe		digitus
tooth		dens, dent-
lip		labium
mind		mens, ment-

 Sometimes the noun and adjective are both from Latin, but they appear different because the noun was borrowed through French and the adjective directly from Latin: for example:

voice	vocal	from:	vox, voc-
ray	radial		radius
judge	judicial		judex, judic-
beast	bestial		bestia
doubt	dubious		dubitare
feast	festal		festum
nurse	nutritious		nutrire

 The further complication of dialectal differences in French (especially between Norman French and Parisian) results in another small series of doubles, twice-borrowed words. Find the Latin original of each word and the differences in meaning between the two words in each pair:

	Norman		Parisian
hard c		ch	
	catch		chase
	capital		chapter

80

| | cancel | | chancel |
| | cattle | | chattel |

w   gu

         wage   gage
         warden   guardian

g   i

         gaud   joy

Exercise IV

The words in this list have been borrowed twice or even more often than that: once from French and then directly from Latin or once from popular French and again from literary French. Such pairs usually differ in meaning if only slightly.

Choose two pairs (or groups): look up the origin of both words in each group and explain the differences in meaning between the words in each group and use each word in a sentence:

1. abbreviate/abridge
2. aggravate / aggrieve
3. amicable / amiable
4. carnal / charnal
5. compute / count
6. fact / feat
7. defect / defeat
8. estimate / esteem
9. fragile / frail
10. ratio / ration / reason
11. pauper / poor
12. prosecute / pursue
13. respect / respite
14. pungent / poignant
15. quiet / coy
16. cohort / court
17. corona / crown
18. faction / fashion
19. gentile / genteel / gentle
20. invidious / envious
21. legal / leal / loyal
22. major / mayor
23. pallid / pale
24. piety / pity
25. senior / sire / sir
26. vocal / vowel
27. species / spice
28. tradition / treason
29. dignity / dainty
30. conception / conceit

81

31. hospital / hostel / hotel
32. potion / poison
33. penitence / penance
34. particle / parcel
35. redemption / ransom

SECTION ONE: AFTERWORD

MODERN ENGLISH

With the fifteenth century begins a remarkable development in the English language. It is the time of the beginning of the Great Vowel Shift, when all our long vowels begin to be pronounced with the tongue higher in the mouth, a change which differentiates the sound of Modern English from that of Middle English. In the Middle English period, the vowel sounds were very close to the standard European vowels. As a result of the vowel shift, we now pronounce, for example a long a as most pronounce a long e and a long e as most pronounce i. That the change in pronunciation was not accompanied by a change in spelling is a major cause of the present confusion in English spelling, in which the same letter represents different sounds and the same sound may be spelled by different letters: in short a cacographical spelling system. Also in the late fifteenth century came the introduction of printing. The printed book exercises a tyranny over the written language that the manuscript could never achieve. Literacy in England became more widespread and books proliferated. Little by little spelling became standardized, but not rationalized.

In the previous chapters we have introduced the foreign influence on English: although some of the borrowed words at all periods came from literature, most entered in the natural way, from the spoken tongues of the people with whom the English came in contact. But during the English Renaissance (the sixteenth and first half of the seventeenth centuries) the growth of English vocabulary is enormous. Words are taken in right and left from Latin and Greek called--by those who opposed the wholesale borrowing from the classical tongues--inkhorn (or inkpot) words. There was, in fact, on the part of many writers and scholars a conscious effort to enlarge the vocabulary of English and to make of their native tongue a means of communication to rival Latin. The spread of education had produced a literate but semi-Latinless public for whom translations and epitomes of Latin literature were made. Anyone familiar with the process of translation will recognize that it is natural to translate a word with a word like itself. Often the native equivalent does not occur at once, or there is no native equivalent, and rather than go through a long periphrasis, the translator simply Englishes the Latin word. The exuberance of certain writers at times went too far, so that their words must have sounded to more moderate readers and writers like the bureaucratic and administrative jargon--with its proliferation of minimizings and maximizings--that rings so harshly in the ears of literary men and women today. Many words (words like eximious, impetrate, adminiculation) missed the mark and were dropped before they ever caught on; but others have become so popular that we cannot imagine living without them: words like maturity, education, affability, and scores of others. And if ever we begin to think of Latin as a dead language, it is a good exercise to try to write a paragraph without any words from Latin or to take a page from a newspaper or magazine and cross out the words from Latin.

The size of vocabulary is one of the most conspicuous aspects of English. It has given English the capability of expressing extremely subtle shades of meaning and has made our language one of the most remarkable inventions of mankind. The growth of our vocabulary goes on apace. Technical terms are invented daily, mostly from Greek and Latin, as human beings continue to use their first prerogative, naming things. And although some sensitive souls lament the loss of ability in our language to invent new native compounds, it might be well to rejoice in the philoxenous nature of English which has accepted foreign words so readily and not cast a snobbish eye upon them. These immigrant words have given us more tools with which to forge compounds of various heritage.

The following sections treat, in the main, learned words of the type that began to flood our language during the Renaissance and though some may smell of the inkpot, most will be seen if not heard and can be used without fear.

VADE MECUM

So many Latin words have entered the English language, both into our every-day word-stock and into our scientific and technical vocabularies, that a speaker of English totally ignorant of Latin can only flounder about helplessly among the masses of words met at all levels of cerebral activity. Even the briefest encounter with Latin can help immeasurably in understanding and organizing this vocabulary and its possibilities for expanding consciousness.

To begin: a little grammar is necessary for organizing Latin vocabulary. English and Latin--though they have some aspects in common, representing their shared heritage from Indo-European--are quite different in grammatical organization. Sometimes this difference is obfuscated by the fact that our grammatical vocabulary is derived from Latin (and, in fact, ultimately from Greek: for the Romans were much taken with Greek Scholarship; although the Latin words referring to grammar are not derived from Greek, they are for the most part simply literal translations of Greek words: an important if often overlooked chapter in the history of ideas). Whether or not this was a happy occurrence, the reader is invited to see for himself or herself, after consulting the list below, selected from the Abbot Aelfric's coined Anglo-Saxon equivalents of the Latinate grammatical terminology.

Modern English Term	Aelfric's Coinage
noun	name
verb	word
pronoun	namen speliend
interjection	betwuxaworpennys
participle	dael nimend
syllable	staefgefeg
vowels	clypiendlice
semivowels	healfclypiendlice
subjunctive	undertheodendlic

Traditionally in speaking of Grammar, we start with what are called 'parts of speech' [a translation of the Latin phrase partes orationis, itself a translation of the Greek expression ta merē ta tēs phōnēs]. These parts are:

ENGLISH	LATIN
noun	nomen (=name)

verb	verbum [=word]
adjective	adjectivum [thing thrown/put beside]
adverb	adverbium [beside the word (or verb)]
pronoun	pronomen [instead of noun]
preposition	praepositio [a putting before]
conjunction	conjunctio [a joining together]
interjection	interjectio [a throwing between]

These 'parts of speech' in the two languages correspond to a degree at least. In a simple sentence we would probably use a noun to translate a noun or a verb to translate a verb, and so forth. But naturally, differences in structure and usage and idiom between the two languages make the process of translation a much more difficult process than a mere one for one correspondence.

How in an English sentence do we determine what part of speech a given word is? It is not always easy to do. But in general, we go by function in the sentence of a word in relation to other words. We ask "what part or role does this word play in the sentence?" In Latin, on the other hand, not only function, but form (how the word looks) tells us what part of speech a word is.

This is a major difference between English and Latin grammars, and one that has plagued generations of students who were taught English as if it were more like Latin than it is.

Latin, as is clear from these remarks, has some things that English does not have to any great extent to enable a reader or listener to determine the part of speech by the shape of the word. Latin has <u>inflections</u>. Latin is, in fact, what we call an inflected language. What this means is that it changes the form of the word to show its relation to other words in the sentence. How does English show these relations? Not, in general, by changing the form, but by the placement of words, although we do have a few inflections (primarily in our verbs and pronouns). Usually we can tell what a sentence means by its adherence to accepted word order. Not so in Latin. In Latin, the order of words is much more flexible, because the form of the word tells what its relation is to the other words.

EXAMPLE:

In English we might say, to take a simple, historical example:

Brutus killed Caesar.

From the order of the words we know who did it and who got it. But if we changed these words around, we would get either the anti-historical statement:[1]

    Caesar killed Brutus

or a jumble of words. There are, as common sense and the rules for permutations show us, six possibilities for arranging the three words. The first two make grammatical sense, but only one is right historically. The next two could make sense, but are poetic affectations which could be made clear by the tone of voice:

      Brutus Caesar killed.
      Caesar, Brutus killed.

The last two are more outrageous still:
      killed Brutus Caesar.
      killed Caesar Brutus.

The words can be listed in any of these ways, but only the first one "Brutus killed Caesar" says what we want it to say in

---

1.   On the Ides of March, 44 B.C., a group of dissident republicans (in the ancient sense: advocates of the restoration and revitalization of the Roman Republic) attacked and killed the dictator Julius Caesar in the Senate chamber. They were acting in the ancient tradition of tyrannicide (a Greco-Roman word tyrannos + cide, from caedere 'to kill') by which, among others, the Athenians Harmodious and Aristogeiton won undying glory (even though they killed the wrong man). The founder of the Roman Republic, furthermore, Lucius Junius Brutus, by ridding the state of its last king, Tarquin the Proud, both achieved greatness and became the eponymous hero of the month of June (that is, it was named after him). Among the conspirators against Caesar who numbered about sixty was one Marcus Junius Brutus, a descendant of the original republican. And this latter day hater of one man rule was a close friend to Ceaser. For such disloyalty, he is placed by Dante in the lowest rung of Hell with only Judas Iscariot below him. But Shakespeare through the mouth of Marc Antony went so far as to say of him, after his demise in the play: "This was the noblest Roman of them all." This incident has added much to our language, through Shakespeare's retelling in Julius Caesar: for example, 'et tu Brute', 'beware the Ides of March', 'it was Greek to me', 'friends, Romans, countrymen', 'the fault, dear Brutus, is not in our stars, but in ourselves', 'yon Cassius has a lean and hungry look', 'ambition should be made of sterner stuff', phrases that are heard often. The incident also gives us our example, a simple declarative sentence the meaning of which is clear and the accuracy of which may be put to historical test.

unaffected style. It is the only order acceptable for prose.

In Latin, to make the same statement, we also have three words:

Brutus: Brutus
interfecit: (he) killed
Caesarem: Caesar

The word Brutus in Latin says something more than the name of the man. Because the ending in -us is a nominative ending, it says that Brutus is the subject of the sentence, the one who did it, the actor in the plot: the one who performed the action of the active verb interfecit. The other noun in the sentence, Caesarem can be only the object of the sentence, the victim in the plot, the one who received the action of the active verb. The ending -em tells us this. And what is most important is that we can arrange these words in any of the six orders possible for three words without changing the relationship between doer and receiver, between (in this instance) killer and victim, between subject and object: a relationship of more than routine importance in the grammatical drama of this sentence.

In Latin, the most normal arrangment would be:

Brutus Caesarem interfecit.
subject-object-verb

But any of the others would be possible and would in no way offend the ears of a Roman. The emphasis would be changed somewhat if we put the victim first in the sentence and the killer last or if we interposed the action (i.e. the verb) between the killer and his victim: BUT THE GRAMMATICAL RELATIONSHIP WOULD REMAIN UNCHANGED.

Because: Brutus is nominative and therefore the subject of the verb. And Caesarem is accusative and therefore the object of the verb.

Nominative and accusative are the names of cases. CASE (from Latin casus, "a falling", translated from Greek ptōsis, "a falling") tells the relation of nouns or pronouns to one another in the context (or environment) of a sentence. The cases of Latin nouns, pronouns, and adjectives are:

NOMINATIVE: (from nomen, nomin-, NAME), the subject of the sentence.

GENITIVE: (from genus, BIRTH, ORIGIN), the case of origin, that is, of direct dependence of one noun on another; one of the most

common uses of the genitive is to show possession: e.g. <u>Caesar's</u>
death/the death <u>of Caesar</u>: Caesar<u>is</u>

DATIVE: (from <u>datum</u>, past participle of <u>do</u>, <u>dare</u>, GIVE), the case
of giving, used for the indirect object, and other relationships
implied by English <u>to</u> or <u>for</u>: he gave <u>Caesar</u> a wound/a wound <u>to</u>
<u>Caesar</u>: Caesar<u>i</u>.

ACCUSATIVE: (from <u>accusare</u>, from <u>causa</u>: CAUSE), the case of the
thing caused by the action of the verb, used for the direct object, the one that receives directly the action of a transitive
verb: he killed <u>Caesar</u>. Caesar<u>em</u>. The accusative is also used
for other relationships and with certain prepositions, as the ob-
jective case is used in English.

ABLATIVE: (from <u>ab</u>, AWAY + <u>latum</u>, the past participle of <u>fero</u>,
<u>ferre</u>, CARRY), the case of SEPARATION (for which we use <u>from</u>); al-
so used for INSTRUMENT (for which we use <u>with</u>, <u>by</u>) and LOCATION
(<u>in</u>, <u>at</u>, <u>on</u>). It was done <u>by Caesar</u> (ablative of agent: <u>a</u>
<u>Caesare</u>. He killed him <u>with a sword</u> (ablative of means or instru-
ment: <u>GLADIO</u>).

VOCATIVE: (from <u>vocatum</u>, past participle of <u>voco</u>, <u>vocare</u>, CALL)
the case of calling or addressing someone directly: et tu <u>Brute</u>
("even you, Brutus"). Take that, Caesar: <u>Caesar</u>, vocative (same
form as nominative in the third declension, see below).

It is clear from the foregoing that English is perfectly capable of expressing the same relationships as Latin, but that where
Latin changes the endings of the nouns, English either puts the
words in a certain word order [subject, verb (indirect object) direct object] or uses prepositional phrases. The branch of grammar
which deals with the way words are put together to form phrases
and sentences is called SYNTAX (a Greek derivative from <u>sun</u>-
"with, together" and <u>tassein</u> "to arrange"). The <u>syntax</u> of Latin
is basically inflectional (relationships are shown by different
endings); that of English is <u>positional</u> (relationships are shown
by the place of the words in the context). An inflected language
like Latin is also called (in the jargon of linguistics) <u>synthetic</u>
(from Greek, <u>sun</u>- + <u>tithenai</u> 'to put'); an essentially uninflected
language like English (and Turkish and Chinese) is called <u>analytic</u>
(from Greek, <u>ana</u>- 'up, throughout' + <u>luein</u>, 'to break, <u>loosen</u>')
because it tends to use two or more words instead of a single inflected form: for example we break up into two (or more) words
expressions like 'to him', 'with a dagger', for which Latin would
use a single inflected word.

On the other hand, English still uses inflected forms for its personal pronouns (I, my, me; he, his, him; she, her, her; they, their, them; we, our, us) and for the relative and interrogative pronouns (who, whose, whom); but these still must go into their proper places.

Further Characteristics of Nouns:

Besides case, nouns have _number_, which tells _how many_ are involved: one (singular) or more than one (plural). Latin has a variety of endings to show number, a separate ending for each case in singular and again in the plural (making twelve forms for each noun, except that the vocative is usually the same as the nominative); English shows plural regularly by adding -s, or -es to the singular; in a few words by vowel gradation (that is by changing the stem vowel as in woman, women; man, men; mouse, mice; louse, lice; goose, geese) and in even fewer words in other ways (child, children; fish, fish; ox, oxen).

In Latin, nouns, all nouns, have _gender_, whether or not we attach to them any kind of natural characteristics which would make gender-identification easy. In general, nouns referring to natural females are _feminine_; those referring to males are _masculine_; but other nouns referring to things to which our minds attach no gender are masculine or feminine or neuter. This perversity is called grammatical gender. According to grammatical gender a _sword_ in Latin (gladius) is masculine; its _sheath_ in Latin (vagina) is feminine; the _wound_ (vulnus) it makes is neuter; a _book_ (liber) is masculine; the quality of _manliness_ (virtus) is feminine; the _sea_ (mare) is neuter. In English we do not put up with such arbitrary regulations: only male people or animals are masculine: for them we substitute _he, his, him_; only females are feminine and take _she, her, hers_. Everything else is called _it_: except for some vehicles and machines and disasters (heavy winds, for example, until the advent of hurricane Bob) to which we imaginatively fix feminine personalities and pronouns (as, "she's a beaut" or "thar she blows"). That is, we use gender only when we think or mean to say that someone or something is masculine or feminine. Notice that in the plural our pronouns make no distinction in gender.

Finally, nouns in Latin are said to belong to _declensions_: English once had them too, but has shaken them off along with its case endings and grammatical genders. A declension is simply a pattern of inflection according to which a group of nouns changes its endings for case and number. The classification of nouns according to declension is a useful tool without deeper significance. Latin has five declensions (usually called by the ordinal numerals first to fifth). Each noun belongs to one declension and does not change to another. The cases have the same use no matter what declension the noun belongs to.

Examples of the declensions (for reference only) are given in the chart on page 106.

There are some variations, but these are the basic patterns and are sufficient for the purposes of this book.

Adjectives, which will be treated next, follow the patterns for the first three declensions, except that in the third declension there are some variations (most notably, -i in the ablative instead of -e; -ia in the neuter plural, and -ium in the gen, pl.).

How to recognize nouns: When a Latin noun is given in a vocabulary list or in a dictionary, the nominative, genitive and gender (m., f., n.) are given. The genitive is given for two reasons: (1) to show the stem, which is not always clear from the nominative and (2) to show which pattern or declension the noun follows: this is clear from the combination of nominative and genitive.

For example:

amicus, amici, m. "friend" obviously belongs to the second declension which is the only declension which shows nom. -us, gen. -i.

rex, regis, m. "king" belongs to the third declension, which is the only one that shows -is in the genitive singular. The base is reg- which is not clear from the nominative.

Rule: the base of a noun is found by removing the case ending from the genitive singular. It is from the base that English derivatives are usually formed. For example, from rex, regis, regal, regicide, regalia.

In the vocabularies in this book, abbreviated forms will be used, for example, amicus, -i, m. 'friend; ancilla, -ae, f. 'serving maid' unless the stem changes between nom. and gen. as in rex, regis, m., dux, ducis, m. 'leader', nox, noctis, f. 'night', corpus, corporis, n. 'body'. The important things to learn are the nom., the base and the meaning.

Other examples:

genus, generis, 'race, origin, kind' belongs to the third

91

declension. The -us ending, which is also a second declension ending, does not make this clear. But the genitive not only shows the stem but indicates the declension. In English we use the word genus, but other derivatives come from the stem [e.g. general, generic, generous, degenerate].

poeta, -ae, m. 'poet'
agricola, -ae, m. 'farmer'

These two nouns along with a few others belong to the first declension and yet are masculine, although most first declension nouns are feminine, like via, ancilla, puella, alumna etc. For students of Latin it is necessary to realize that membership in a declension does not necessarily imply gender.

The accusative singular of the various declensions should be noted if not learned, since this is the form that most often carried over from Latin into the Romance languages and thence into English, so that dictionaries usually give the accusative form when explaining the etymology of a word from Latin, if it has first passed through one of the Romance languages.

PLURALS: learn these!

For words that have come into English directly from Latin with no change in ending, it is sometimes necessary to know the nominative plural as well as the nominative singular. Although some words taken from Latin form their plurals in the English manner by adding -s, others retain their Latin plural.

Examples:

    I alumna: plural alumnae
    II alumnus: plural alumni
    datum: plural data
    masculines in -us have plural in -i
    neuters in -um have plural in -a
    III appendix: plural appendices (or appendixes, Eng.)
        the base of appendix is appendic-
    genus: plural genera
    masculines and feminines have plurals in -es
    neuters have plurals in -a
    V species: plural species
    nouns of the fifth declension show no change for the plural

EXERCISES

Exercise I. Plurals

Form the plurals of: (numbers indicate declensions)

1. datum (II)
2. memorandum (II)
3. corpus, corporis (III,n.)
4. focus (II)
5. addendum (II)
6. formula (I)
7. curriculum (II)
8. stadium (II)
9. index, indicis (III, m.)
10. medium (II)
11. dictum (II)
12. antenna (I)
13. axis, base: ax- (III)
14. basis, base: bas- (III)
15. gladiolus (II)
16. locus (II)
17. Magus (II)
18. nucleus (II)
19. ovum (II)
20. nebula (I)
21. series (V)
22. opus, operis (III, n)
23. propositus (Law: 'one from whom a line of descent is traced; the person immediately affected by the action') (II)
24. salmonella (New Latin from Daniel E. Salmon) (I)
25. talus (II) 'ankle'
26. sternum (II) 'breast'
27. primordium (II)
28.   cloaca (I) ('sewer': Zoology, 'tract into which intestinal, genital, and urinary tracts open in fish, birds, reptiles, and some primitive mammals)
29. carpus (II) 'wrist'
30. rostrum (II)
31. erratum (II)

ADJECTIVES: Adjectives in Latin have the same characteristics as nouns; they belong to declensions and have case, number, and gender. The major difference between them and nouns is that the gender is not inherent to them. Adjectives add qualities, characteristics, attributes to nouns and they change gender to agree with their nouns. Adjectives must agree with their nouns in gender, number, and case, but they do not have to agree in declension.

The most common groups of adjectives are the -us, -a, -um type and the -is, -e type. The former belongs to the first and second declensions with -us (II) used for the masculine, -a (I) for the feminine, and -um (II) for the neuter. Their cases follow those of the declension to which they belong [e.g. genitive: -i (m.) -ae (f.) -i (n.)]. The second type belongs to the third declension: -is for masculine and feminine, and -e for neuter. There are a number of other types but these are sufficient for our purposes.

Adjectives can be recognized in the vocabulary by their three genders or two genders. The few one-termination adjectives will be explained as they come up. The base, if not clear in the masculine can be found in the feminine or neuter.

Adjectives are compared: that is, they have comparative and superlative degrees, comparable to English -er, -est (more, most). In Latin the regular formation is base + ior (m,f), -ius (n.) for the comparative; -issimus, -a, -um for the superlative. The comparatives and superlatives that have most commonly become English words, however, are the irregularly formed ones: these have to be learned as separate vocabulary entries.

For example:

magnus, magna, magnum 'great, large

Comparative: major, majus 'greater'
Superlative: maximus, -a, -um 'greatest'
Think of some words from each of these.

Exercise II. Adjectives: Agreement

Choose the correct form of the adjective to agree with the noun in the expression. Various hints are provided. Give meanings of expressions marked with an asterisk [*].

1. res _____ (fem.) adjudicatus adjudicata adjudicatum
('a case already decided')

* 2. Pater _____ (m.) noster nostra nostrum

* 3. _____ opus (n.) magnus magna magnum

* 4. _____ ego (m.) alter altera alterum

94

*   5. _____ fide (f., ablative)   bono   bonā   bonam

*   6. _____ bonum (n. N.B. adjectives can be used as nouns)
communis   commune

    7. ceteris _____ (abl. pl.)   pares   paribus   pari   ['other
    things being equal']

*   8. Deo _____ (abl.)   volens   volente

    9. fraus _____(f.)   pius   pia   pium   ('a pious deception')

    10. in _____ res (f., accus., pl)   medius   medias   medios,
    media   ('into the midst of things')

    11. in _____ persona (f. abl.) propriae   propriā   proprio
    ('in one's own person')

*   12. _____ verba (n. pl.)   ipsissimum   ipsissima

*   13. _____ facto (n. abl.)   ipso   ipsum   ipsa

*   14. loco _____ (m. abl.) citatus   citato   citatis

*   15. _____ Charta (f.)   magnus   magna   magnum

*   16. _____ cum laude (f. abl.)   summo   summā   summis

*   17. _____ homo (m. nom.) novus   nova   novum   (one who
gains distinction on his own rather than through the influence
of his family)

*   18. _____ facie (f., abl.)   primus   primo   primā

*   19. _____ avis (f.)   rarum   rara   rarus

*   20. _____ generis (n. gen.)   suum   suo   sui

*   21. terra _____ (f)   firmus   firmas   firma

ADVERBS: An adverb even in Latin is not declined. It is used to
qualify a verb, an adjective or another adverb.

A few Latin adverbs have come directly into English; some have
come in as adverbs but others as nouns.

alibi   Latin meaning: 'elsewhere'

95

alias	'otherwise'
interim	'meanwhile'
item	'likewise'
tandem	'at length'
verbatim	'word for word'
gratis	'for free'
extra	'beyond'
passim	'everywhere, throughout'

Exercise III

Give the English meaning of each of these Latin adverbs, tell what part of speech it is and use it in a sentence. Look up any you do not know.

PRONOUNS

In Latin as in English, pronouns fall into several categories: personal (I, ego; we: nos; you, tu, vos, etc.); reflexive (-self: herself, himself, themselves, itself, etc.: sui); relative (who, which, that: qui, quae, quod); interrogative (who? what?: quis, quid); intensive (-self: ipse); demonstrative (this, that: hic, haec, hoc; is, ea, id; ille, illa, illud); indefinite (someone, anyone; aliquis and a number of others in Latin). The pronouns in Latin are declined according to case, number, gender, as are the nouns for which they stand. They are often irregular and are learned with great difficulty. But fortunately more than enough has already been said about them since they do not go into the making of many English words.

Some English words from Latin Pronouns:

Ego, super-ego, id: the Freudian terms for parts of the psyche
suicide: self-slaughter
quiddity: 'what-ness': that which a thing is, that which differentiates it from all others; also used to mean 'a quibble, a hair-splitting distinction'
quidnunc: 'what now?' (someone who is always saying 'quidnunc?'), a busybody or gossip

Tell what type of pronoun each of these is derived from.

There are also a number of common phrases that use Latin pronouns, for example:
1. ad hoc [literally 'to/for this']
2. ipse dixit 'he himself said [it]'
3. quid pro quo [literally 'what for what?']

4. status quo ['state at which']
5. alter ego ['another I']
6. ipso facto ['by the very fact/fact itself']
7. per se (v. also ampersand) ['through itself']
8. sui generis ['of its own kind']
9. sine quā non ['without which not']
10. pax vobiscum ['peace (be) with you']
11. cui bono ['for whose good']
12. inter nos ['among us/ourselves']
13. post hoc ergo propter hoc ['after this, therefore on account of this']
14. Q.E.D. [quod erat demonstrandum: 'which was to be demonstrated']
15. Te Deum (laudamus) ['(we praise) You, God']
16. terminus ad quem ['the end to which']
17. i.e. [id est: 'that is']
18. q.v. [quod vide: 'which see']
19. me judice ['with me as the judge', 'in my opinion']
20. vade mecum ['go with me' one's constant companion]

Exercise III. Pronouns

1. Identify each pronoun by type (personal, relative, demonstrative, etc.).
2. Use each expression in a sentence.

PREPOSITIONS: Latin prepositions are used with the accusative and ablative cases and in general further define the meaning of the case with which they are used. Their influence on English is primarily as prefixes added to verbs and to adjectives. Prepositions will be treated in detail in the lessons to follow.

Some examples of Latin prepositions:

Latin with case	Meaning of preposition	Meaning as prefix
a, ab ablative	from, away from	off, away
Examples of derivatives: avert, abduct		
e, ex ablative	out of, from	out, completely
Examples of derivatives: eject, exact		
per accusative	through	through, throughly
Examples of derivatives: perfect, perennial		

Although the Latin prepositions are most important to our study as prefixes, their force as prepositions can be seen in these common Latin expressions:

1. ab initio 'from the beginning'

2. ad infinitum 'to the endless'
3. ad litteram 'to the letter'
4. ad rem 'to the matter'
5. cum laude 'with praise'
6. de facto 'from the thing done'
7. e pluribus unum 'one out of more'
8. ex tempore 'from the time'
9. in absentia 'in absence'
10. in extremis 'in the last'
11. inter nos 'among/between us'
12. per annum 'through the year'
13. per se 'through itself'
14. pro tempore 'for the time'
15. sine qua non 'without which not'
16. de profundis 'from the depths'
17. in toto 'on the whole'
18. sub judice 'under the judge'
19. sub rosa 'under the rose'
20. a priori 'from the former'

EXERCISE IV.

Learn the expressions.
The definitions given are literal: explain the meaning and use of each.
Use each in a sentence.

Of the other parts of speech, only verbs need detain us long: interjections and conjunctions--except in a few expressions--have little effect on English vocabulary.

Learn these expressions and give their meanings:

1. ecce Homo. (ecce, interjection meaning 'behold')
2. et tu Brute.
3. et al. = et alii, et aliae, et alia
4. etc. = et cetera
5. O tempora! O mores!

VERBS:

The VERB is the word of the sentence as its name implies in Latin [verbum = 'word'] and often was saved for the end of the Latin sentence. The verb is the one word that is most necessary to produce a grammatical sentence. A verb alone can make a complete and grammatical sentence (as, 'Go!' 'Stop!' 'Help!'). A baby may point at a feline quadruped and announce 'cat!'; but although we understand perfectly what is meant, we do not accept this as a grammatical sentence, though it may be pronounced with as much urgency as the verb forms quoted above.

A final definition of VERB has yet to be devised: generally we say that a verb is that part of speech which expresses action, existence, or occurrence. This is a definition according to function and meaning. A formal definition of the English verb (which is almost but not quite accurate) can also be concocted: a verb is that which undergoes certain changes in form: -s for the third person singular (work: he/she works, sing; sings) -ing for the present participle (working, singing); -ed or other change for a past tense (worked; sang); -ed or other change for a past participle (have worked, have sung). At most, the regular verb has five different forms. The verb 'to be' has a few more, but some verbs have only two or one (that is only one change or none at all); and yet we call these 'verbs' having no other name for them: these are such verbs as may/might; can/could; will/would; shall/should and must. They are auxiliary verbs, often called modal auxiliaries because they express the mood or attitude of the speaker or writer toward the reality of the action of the verb (modal and mood from Latin modus, 'manner').

In Latin, VERB is easier to define. In form the Latin verb differs from the English in a very important aspect: the Latin verb is highly inflected. It has a multiplicity of forms that give more information than the few English inflections. First, the form contains its own subject: that is, endings vary according to person and number: in English we have to use two words to say 'I see,' 'you see,' 'he/she/it sees' etc.: a pronoun (or a noun) and the verb; but in Latin the forms video, vides, videt are sufficient and the pronoun is omitted unless for contrast or special emphasis. Of course if the Latin wants to make the subject clearer than the vague 'third person singular person or thing sees' a subject can be added to the form: Caesar videt: "Caesar sees." In English the verb form see is not sufficient because it can be anything (except third person singular) from first person singular (I see) to third person plural (they see) to an infinitive (able to see; must see) to an imperative (See!): but in Latin, a new form of the verb is needed for each of these utterances (respectively: video (first person), vident (third pl.), vidēre (infinitive), vide (imperative singular), videte (imperative plural).

The forms with personal endings are called finite forms [from Latin finis 'end, boundary, limit'] because they are defined or limited to one grammatical person and number. Opposed to finite forms are infinitives, so called because they are not limited either by person or number. Infinitives can be used as nouns, as in 'to err is human' (errare est humanum) and they can be used for any person or either number (possum videre: I am able to see, I can see; possunt videre: they are able to see, they can see) without change in form.

Other characteristics of Latin verbs (besides person and number) are tense, voice, and mood. Tense tells the TIME of the action, occurrence, or existence: Latin has six tenses all of which are represented by different forms of the verb: present, imperfect, future, perfect, pluperfect, future perfect. English has many more tenses, but--except for present and past--these are indicated by compound (also called periphrastic) tenses, using participles or infinitives with various auxiliary verbs.

EXAMPLES:

LATIN   ENGLISH

PRESENT:
duco   'I lead' (simple present)
                               'I am leading' [present progressive:
                               formed by the verb 'to be' + present
                               participle (-ing form)] 'I do lead'

[other forms of the present active: ducis (you...); ducit (he/
she/it...) ducimus, ducitis, ducunt (we, you, pl., they).]

IMPERFECT:
ducebam   'I was leading' (past progressive)
                               'I used to lead'
                               'I kept on leading'

[other forms of imperfect: active: ducebas, ducebat; ducebamus,
ducebatis, ducebant]

FUTURE:
ducam   'I will/shall lead'
                               (also: 'I am going to lead')

[other forms of the future: duces, ducet; ducemus, ducetis,
ducent]

PERFECT:
duxi   'I led' (simple past)
                               'I have led' (present perfect)

100

[other forms of the perfect: duxisti, duxit; duximus, duxistis, duxerunt]

PLUPERFECT:
duxeram   'I had led' (past perfect)

[other forms of the pluperfect: duxeras, duxerat; duxeramus, duxeratis, duxerant]

FUTURE PERFECT:
duxero   'I shall/will have led' (future perfect)

[other forms of the future perfect: duxeris, duxerit; duxerimus, duxeritis, duxerint]

Although this does not cover all the possibilities of the English system of compound tenses, it should give an idea of the enormous flexibility of English for producing a multiplicity of verbal times with a very limited supply of different forms. Notice how few forms of the verb 'lead' are needed in English. In Latin however the thirty-six forms of DUCO that are given above barely scratches the surface. We have yet to glance at the passive voice, the subjunctive and imperative moods, the infinitives, and participles. But all the parts of the English verb have already been laid out: all we have to do to form the other voice and other moods is change the auxiliaries.

Voice tells us the relationship of the subject to the action of the verb. The examples given above are all active: the subject performs the action, does the leading (in our example). But in the passive [from Latin passus, past participle of patior, pati, 'suffer, experience'] the subject is acted upon, he experiences or (in grammatical jargon) suffers the action: he is led (in our example). The distinction is important, even vital: to hark back to our earlier example: turned into the passive it reads, "Caesar was killed by Brutus." But Caesar, though he has become the grammatical subject of the passive verb, still is the one to get it. For each of the tenses given above, Latin has a separate form of the verb (except that in the perfect system, compound tenses are used: a participle with forms of the Latin verb esse, 'to be'). English forms all the tenses of the passive with forms of the verb be and the past participle.

LATIN   ENGLISH

PRESENT PASSIVE:
ducor   'I am led, I am being led'

101

[other forms of the present passive: duceris, ducitur; ducimur, ducimini, ducuntur]

IMPERFECT PASSIVE:
ducebar   'I was being led/I used to be led'

[other forms of the imperfect passive: ducebaris, ducebatur; ducebamur, ducebamini, ducebantur]

FUTURE PASSIVE:
ducar   'I will/shall be led'

[other forms of the future passive: duceris, ducetur; ducemur, ducemini, ducentur]

PERFECT PASSIVE:
ductus (ducta) sum   'I was led/I have been led'

[other forms of the perfect passive: ductus/-a es, ductus-a-um est; ducti/-ae sumus, ducti/-ae estis, ducti/-ae/-a sunt]

PLUPERFECT PASSIVE:
ductus/-a eram   'I had been led'

[other forms of the pluperfect passive: ductus/-a eras, ductus/-a/-um erat; ducti/-ae eramus, ducti/-ae eratis, ducti/-ae/-a erant]

FUTURE PERFECT PASSIVE:
ductus/-a ero   'I will/shall have been led'

[other forms of the future perfect passive: ductus/-a eris, ductus/-a/-um erit; ducti/-ae erimus, ducti/-ae eritis, ducti/-ae/-a erunt]

    <u>Mood</u> tells the attitude of the speaker or writer toward the action: is it a fact or is it a supposition, a hope, a possibility, or is it a command? The three moods in Latin are <u>indicative</u> [from Latin <u>indicare</u>: 'point out'] which is used for stating facts, for talking about reality, for asking questions about facts; the <u>subjunctive</u> [from Latin <u>sub</u> 'under' + <u>jungere</u> 'join'] used for a variety of less than factual attitudes such as purpose or intention, result or consequence, some conditions, possibilities, hopes and fears; and the <u>imperative</u> [from Latin <u>imperare</u> 'to command'] which gives an order. Latin, predictably, has different forms for the different moods, but English equally predictably, uses the same forms, but with a variety of auxiliaries for the

subjunctive; and for the imperative just the simplest form of the verb alone, without a subject: Go!, Stop!, Eat, drink, and be merry! The auxiliaries of mood (called modals) express all the varieties of attitude which the different Latin forms express. The English verb system is simple and yet varied and flexible; the Latin verb system is complex, but it too allows for flexibility and subtlety in the language.

Finally we come to participles and infinitives. A participle is a verbal adjective; an infinitive is a verbal noun. Latin participles are especially important for our study of English vocabulary, because so many of them--especially from forms of present participles--have entered our language. As a verbal adjective, a participle [from Latin particeps from pars; partis 'part' + capere 'take', therefore 'a part-taker or sharer, a translation of Greek metoche, 'sharer'] shares the characteristics of adjectives and verbs: as an adjective it is used to qualify nouns (in Latin participles are declined so they can agree with their nouns); and as a verb it is derived from the verb stem, has tense and voice, and can take an object. Most of the Latin participles that have come into English have entered as adjectives or nouns so that their double aspect is no longer felt.

Principal Parts: how to recognize a verb in the vocabulary lists.

Latin verbs are listed with their principal parts (of which a complete and regular verb has four) which give all the forms necessary to conjugate the verb in full (provided that one knows the appropriate endings). The principal parts are:

1. the first person singular, present active indicative (amo, 'I love'; video, 'I see'; duco, 'I lead')
2. the present active infinitive (amare, 'to love'; vidēre, 'to see'; ducere, 'to lead')
3. the first person singular, perfect active indicative (amavi, 'I loved'; vidi, 'I saw'; duxi, 'I led')
4. the perfect passive participle (amatum, 'having been loved'; visum, 'having been seen'; ductum, 'having been led')
For English word formation, the important principal parts to learn are numbers 2 and 4. The others will be given only for reference.

Verbs are divided into conjugations, which--like the declensions of nouns--indicate the pattern which the forms follow. There are four conjugations of regular verbs in Latin, recognizable by the stem vowel in the present infinitive.

I First conjugation: or -A- conjugation (The present infinitive

103

ends in -are)
>   amo <u>amare</u> amavi <u>amatum</u>, 'love' (Nearly all first conjuga-
>   tion verbs follow this pattern: -are, -avi, -atum). First
>   conjugation verbs, unless they differ from this pattern will
>   be marked <u>I</u> and the reader may supply the principal parts ac-
>   cording to the regular pattern.

II Second Conjugation: or -Ē- (long -e-))the present infinitive
ends in -ēre.)
>   video, <u>vidēre</u> vidi <u>visum</u> 'see'
>   teneo <u>tenere</u> tenui <u>tentum</u> 'hold'

III Third Conjugation: or -E- (short -e-) (present infinitive
ends in -ere)
>   duco <u>ducere</u> duxi <u>ductum</u> 'lead'
>   mitto <u>mittere</u> misi <u>missum</u> 'send'

A second type of third conjugation verb shows -io in the first
form and this -i- is usually retained in words that come into
English from the present stem.
>   <u>capio</u> <u>capere</u> cepi <u>captum</u> 'take'
For such verbs, it is worthwhile to learn the first principal part
along with the second and fourth.

IV Fourth Conjugation: or -I- (present infinitive ends in -ire)
>   audio <u>audire</u> audivi <u>auditum</u> 'hear
>   venio <u>venire</u> veni <u>ventum</u> 'come'

Deponent verbs:
>   Verbs that have no active forms, but occur only in the pas-
>   sive are called deponents. They may belong to any of the conjuga-
>   tions:
>   I.   -ari, -atum: conor, <u>conari</u>, <u>conatum</u> 'try'
>   II. -eri: fateor, <u>fatēri</u>, <u>fassum</u> 'acknowledge'
>   III. -i: nascor, <u>nasci</u>, <u>natum</u> 'be born'
>   patior, <u>pati</u>, <u>passum</u> 'suffer'
>   IV. -iri: experior, <u>experiri</u>, <u>expertum</u> 'experience'

Exercise V. Verbs

1. Translate the principal parts of the verbs given above. [For
example: AMO = 'I love'; AMARE = 'to love'; AMAVI = 'I loved';
AMATUM = 'having been loved']

2. Many Latin verbs have been very productive of English words:
for example, a partial listing of derivatives of DUCO includes:

adduce   educe   induce   produce   seduce   reduce   conduce

induct   abduct   duct   aqueduct   viaduct   ductile   conduct
induction   abduction   seduction   reduction   inductive
conducive   traduce   introduce   introduction

Taking these words, try to think up 10 English derivatives:
a) MITTO: Stems mit(t)- and miss-
b) PORTO 'carry': stems port-, portat-
c) VENIO: stems: veni- and vent-
d) VIDEO: stems: vide- and vis-

3. LATIN PARTS OF SPEECH

The words in the list below are unusual: they all entered English with their Latin inflectional endings intact: that is they show things like case, number; tense, voice, mood, person. Choose two and find out:

a. What is the literal meaning of the Latin word?
b. What part of speech is it in Latin? (The dictionary should give this information.)
c. What ending does it have?
d. What is the meaning of the English word?
e. What part of speech is it in English?
f. Find some uses of your word in English sentences (use the Oxford English Dictionary): try substituting the literal meaning of the word in these sentences: does it work, or does it cause stylistic havoc?
g. Note any peculiarities of your word. When and how did it come into English? Does it come from a specific work or expression?
h. Is it a common word? Did you know it before?

1. via	2. placebo	3. quorum	4. imprimatur
5. introit	6. nostrum	7. specie	8. ignoramus
9. propaganda	10. exit; exeunt	11. rebus	12. fiat
13. recto	14. caveat	15. posse	16. numero
17. vim	18. innuendo	19. recipe	20. omnibus
21. credo	22. verso	23. deficit	24. habitat
25. proviso	26. affidavit	27. interest	28. tenet
29. veto	30. habeas corpus	31. floruit	32. memento
33. limbo	34. requiem	35. caret	36. mandamus
37. variorum			

	1st fem.	2nd masc.	2nd neut.	3rd f.,m.	3rd n	4th f.,m.	4th neut.	5th
Nominative	via	modus	donum	rex	genus	manus	cornu	res
Genitive	viae	modi	doni	regis	generis	manūs	cornūs	rei
Dative	viae	modo	dono	regi	generi	manu(i)	cornu	rei
Accusative	viam	modum	donum	regem	genus	manum	cornu	rem
Ablative	viā	modo	dono	rege	genere	manu	cornu	re

PLURAL

	1st fem.	2nd masc.	2nd neut.	3rd f.,m.	3rd n	4th f.,m.	4th neut.	5th
Nominative	viae	modi	dona	reges	genera	manūs	cornua	res
Genitive	viarum	modorum	donorum	regum	generum	manuum	cornuum	rerum
Dative	viis	modis	donis	regibus	generibus	manibus	cornibus	rebus
Accusative	vias	modos	dona	reges	genera	manus	cornua	res
Ablative	viis	modis	donis	regibus	generibus	manibus	cornibus	rebus

VIA, VIAE, f 'road, way'

MODUS, MODI, m. 'manner'

DONUM, DONI, n. 'gift'

REX, REGIS, m. 'king'

GENUS, GENERIS, n. 'race, birth'

MANUS, MANUS, f. 'hand'

CORNU, CORNUS, n. 'horn'

RES, REI, f. 'thing, matter, affair'

N.B. Long marks are indicated only where they are needed to distinguish one case from another.

106

ENGLISH WORDS FROM LATIN NOUNS AND ADJECTIVES: DIRECT AND NEARLY DIRECT ENTRIES

Many words, especially, nouns, have come directly into English from Latin nouns and adjectives, or in spite of certain historical changes, have ended up in English looking exactly like their Latin originals.

Examples of direct entries: NOUNS

actor, actoris, m. 'a doer' ACTOR

delirium, -ii, n. 'a going off track' [in Latin, a word from agriculture: lira is a furrow; delirare, a verb derived from lira means 'to go out of the furrow' and thence 'to be off one's track'] DELIRIUM

omen, ominis, n. 'a sign of the future' [note that the base is omin- so that derivatives will show -i- in the stem, as ominous, abominate] OMEN

Some words have changed from their Latin counterparts, but come around to the same spellings as they have in Latin. In the exercises these will be treated as direct entries.

Examples:

labor, laboris, m.: accusative, laborem: O.F. labor/labour (Modern French labeur): English labor/labour [Note that the American spelling of words in -or is identical to the Latin, while the British -our takes the Old French spelling]. The accusative case is very commonly the form from which the Romance languages derive nouns: this can be more clearly seen in the Italian form: labore. LABOR

Orator, oratoris, m.: accusative oratorem: Old French orateur; Anglo-French oratour, relatinized to ORATOR

Direct entries: ADJECTIVES

bonus, bona, bonum 'good': the masculine form bonus provides an English noun meaning 'a good thing, an extra dividend or payment' [The English word bonus is a made-up word, invented by students or office boys as a joke: no doubt, if scholars had coined it for serious purpose the neuter form, bonum would have been used, since bonus properly means 'a good man'] BONUS

albus, alba, album 'white': here, the neuter form of the adjective comes in as an English noun. Album was used in Latin too as a noun meaning a white or blank tablet of entries for lists of dates or names of officials: it was first used in English as a Latin word. Johnson's definition: "a book in which foreigners have long been accustomed to insert the autographs of celebrated people." ALBUM

similis, simile 'like': <u>simile</u>, a likeness or comparison, was also used as a noun in Latin: the use of neuter adjectives as abstract nouns is very common in Latin, evidence of the Roman preference for the concrete and avoidance of abstraction. <u>Bona</u> (neuter plural) means 'good things, goods'; <u>mala</u> 'bad things, evils', concepts more meaningful to the Roman mind than 'goodness' and 'badness', abstracts removed from particular events or facts. <u>Simile</u>, literally 'a thing like' is now used in a technical sense in English, in the field of literary criticism, "a figure of speech in which an explicit comparison is made between two essentially unlike things, by the use of 'like, as'." SIMILE

Examples of similes:
1. O my Luve's like a red, red rose
   That's newly sprung in June:
   O my Luve's like the melodie
   That's sweetly played in tune.   Robert Burns
2. Love is like the measles; we all have to go through it.
   Jerome K. Jerome

Among the direct entries from Latin are both common and unusual words. The words in the following lists are words that are found in both English and Latin dictionaries.

Exercise I.

Check off the words that are familiar to you and jot down an English synonym or a brief definition.

Look up in an English dictionary any unfamiliar words, noting if the word has undergone any change in meaning during its passage from Latin to English. [Such information is given in the etymological part of the dictionary entry.]

Look up words marked with an asterisk (*) even if you know their meanings to find their origins. Some of the words listed here are compounds, showing prefixes and suffixes which will be treated later when we take up compounding rules.

| LATIN & ENGLISH WORD | MEANING | COMMENTS (*) |

1. vapor
2. honor
3. color
4. odor
5. * murmur
6. * minister
7. rumor
8. acumen
9. furor
10. * abecedarium
11. * aegis
12. * animal
13. animus
14. ardor
15. * senator
16. appendix
17. arbiter
18. locus
19. lector
20. libido
21. magisterium
22. monitor
23. mores (pl. in Latin, listed under <u>mos</u>, moris)
24. onus
25. opus: find plural
26. * doctor
27. opprobrium
28. dolor (find out what a dolorimeter is)
29. * error
30. exemplar
31. facetiae
32. * fasces
33. * formula
34. * fungus
35. genus
36. * horror
37. * index
38. * cancer
39. cantor
40. * cervix
41. *circus
42. clamor
43. compendium
44. corpus
45. * crux
46. vector
47. * tutor
48. virago

49. terminus
50. dementia

Exercise II. Words that have changed meanings

A. Tell whether the word has become more generalized or more specialized (that is, respectively, does the modern English word apply to more or less than the Latin word?). [use dictionary]

1. area
2. campus
3. camera
4. arena
5. corona
6. focus
7. fulcrum
8. humus
9. imago
10. integer
11. nausea
12. rabies
13. radius
14. ratio
15. Africa
16. Asia
17. farina
18. liquor
19. virus

B. Metaphors: these words have changed their applications, as delirium in Latin originally applied to agriculture, but now is used of one's mental state: what were these applied to in Latin and what now? [use dictionary]

1. cirrus
2. pastor
3. candor
4. columbarium
5. incunabula
6. nucleus
7. persona
8. prevaricator
9. rostrum
10. larva
11. calculus
12. codex
13. genius
14. placenta

110

Exercise III.   Noun or Adjective

Tell what part of speech each is in Latin and what part in English; give meaning in Latin and in English.   Use glossary.

1. major
2. medium
3. odium
4. miser
5. quota
6. sanctus
7. species
8. minor
9. vacuum
10. exterior
12. peculator
13. quantum
14. pauper

Exercise IV.

Using bases, find five (5) or more English words from each of these Latin nouns or adjectives: use a dictionary; if you get stumped, use an etymological dictionary.

E.g. albus -a-um 'white': album, alb, albino, albinism, albumen, albuminoid, albuminous, albedo, albescent, albite, daub, auburn

1. animus, -i, m. [stem; anim-] 'spirit'
2. finis, finis, m. 'end, limit' [stem: fin-]
3. similis, -e 'like'
4. rex, regis, m. 'king'
5. opus, operis, n. 'work'
6. locus, loci, m. 'place'
7. genus, generis, n. 'race, kind'
8. species, speciei, f. 'sight, appearance'
9. annus, -i, m. 'year'
10. domus, -ūs, f. 'home'
11. terra, -ae, f. 'land, earth'
Learn these Latin words and their meanings.

Exercise V.   Ancient Culture

In the following list of words, check those that are used to describe aspects of modern society.   Look up the others and find out what they meant to the Romans:

1. lictor	2. latifundium	3. toga (cf. 'togs')
4. paterfamilias	5. lar (lares)	6. plebs
7. forum	8. censor	9. dictator
10. atrium	11. consul	12. praetorium
13. procurator	14. curia	15. lustrum

Exercise VI. Direct entries from Latin in English literary sentences

Define underlined words.

1. And after 'Amor vincit omnia' [conquers all]. Chaucer

2. Beyond the Atlantic things civil and things spiritual move in their separate spheres, without any need for an arbiter between them. Gladstone

3. The condition of true naming on the poet's part, is his resigning himself to the divine aura which breathes through forms. Emerson

4. Like a dismall Clangor heard from farre. Shakespeare

5. With this exordium . . . Nickleby took a newspaper from his pocket. Dickens

6. Those deserts whose fervors scarce allowed a bird to live. Shelley

7. The hiatus in Phutatorius's breeches was sufficiently wide to receive the chesnut. Sterne

8. Apollonius . . . by some probable conjectures, found her out to be a serpent, a Lamia. Burton

9. The progenitors of Birds and the progenitors of Man at a very remote period were probably one. Drummond

10. Hovel piled upon hovel--squalor immortalized in undecaying tone. Hawthorne

11. They included all learning in the seven liberal arts; of which grammar, rhetoric, and dialectics, formed what they called

the trivium. Rankin

12. And crowne your heads with heavenly coronall,
    Such as the Angels weare before Gods tribunall. [tribunal]
Spenser

QUISQUILIA

Some interesting direct entries and their relations.

1. AUGUR, in Latin, 'a diviner, soothsayer, seer, one who predict-
ed the future by interpreting the flights and notes of birds, the
lightning and any unusual occurrences'; in English, as a noun, 'a
seer or prophet'; as a verb, 'to predict from signs or omens; or
'to be a sign or omen' (as 'this augurs well'). Augur comes from
Latin AUGERE, 'to increase': the stems of the Latin verb are
AUG(E)- and AUCT-, which produce these English words: augment,
augmentation, augmentative, author (from Lat. auctor), authority,
authorize, auction, augend, augury, inaugurate, inaugural;
Augustus ('majestic, venerable, magnificent', a title taken by the
emperor Octavius), august, the month August (named after the
emperor Augustus), auxiliary (from auxilium, 'aid').

The I-E root of these words is AUG-, meaning 'to increase'.
The native English cognate to Latin augere is the Old English word
eacan from which we get the verb eke ('to strain to fill out, to
make a living with great effort') and the noun nickname (originally 'an ekename' from O.E. eaca 'in addition'). In an extended
form (WEGS-, OE weaxan) the same root gives us wax, meaning
'grow', used especially of the moon which waxes and wanes, and of
public speakers who occasionally wax eloquent.

The Greek auxein from the same root has given us several scientific derivatives: auxin (a plant hormone that affects growth);
auxesis (an increase in the size of a cell without cell division);
the suffix -auxe (enlargement, as in hepatauxe, 'enlargement of
the liver').

2. FETUS, in Latin: 'a bringing forth, bearing, hatching; young,
offspring, brood': from fetus-a-um, (adjective from the participle of obsolete *feo 'to bear'), 'pregnant, breeding, fruitful,
productive; newly delivered.' In English, "the unborn young of a
viviparous vertebrate; in humans, the unborn young from the end of
the eighth week to the moment of birth as distinquished from the
earlier embryo." (American Heritage Dictionary)
From fetus, we get also fetal, feticide, effete (literally 'worn
out by child-bearing'), superfetate. The I-E root from which
fetus is derived is DHEI- meaning 'to suck'. Other Latin words
from this root are (1) FEMINA 'woman' [that is, she who suckles']

113

from which are derived the English words _female_, _feminine_, _effemi-nate_; (2) _fecundus_, 'fruitful' which gives us _fecund_, _fecundity_; (3) _felix_ 'fruitful, happy, lucky' which gives us the name _Felix_; _felicity_, _infelicity_, _felicitate_.

The Greek word _thelus_ meaning 'female' is from the same I-E root and gives us _theelin_, a female hormone.

END GAME: Choose the Classical Words:

state   constitution   cheer   felicity   cook   culinary   nurse
nutrition   charm   incantation   add   subtract   poor   pauper joy
gaudy   damn   condemn   boil   fail   face   infallible integrity
faith   course   clear   doubt   cursive   clarity indubitably   false
veracity   fierce   feast   school   pray   imprecate   pain   penalty
ebullient   festive   semiferal chance   cadence   force   fortitude

Check the words in this list which you believe to be derived from Latin or Greek. Look up any that you do not check for your edification and surprise.

NOUNS AND ADJECTIVES ENTERING FROM LATIN WITH SLIGHT CHANGES

Many Latin Words come into English showing very slight change, so that the words are recognizable in Latin to an English speaker, especially to one who has learned what the common changes are.

1. The Latin ending is often dropped, so that the base of the Latin word becomes the English word.

Examples:

Nouns:

ars, artis 'skill' becomes English ART
[for ars, see the common expression, ars gratia artis the motto of MGM and ars longa, vita brevis; and ars gratia pecuniae (the motto of the producers in Silent Movie)]

verbum, -i, n. 'word': VERB

Adjectives:

absurdus-a-um 'unmusical, senseless': ABSURD
grandis, -e 'large, tall, old': GRAND

2. English often adds a silent -e to the base; words ending in -o usually drop the -o and add a silent -e.

Nouns:

magnitudo (magnitudinis, f) 'greatness, size' MAGNITUDE
nodus, -i, m. 'knot': NODE

Adjectives:

arcanus-a-um 'secret': ARCANE
gravis, -e 'heavy, serious' GRAVE

3. A final -ia, -ius, -ium often becomes -y; final -tas becomes -ty.
-tia, -tius, -tium and -cia, -cium become -ce, -cy. -gium becomes -ge.

Nouns:

penuria, -ae, f. 'poverty': PENURY
pietas, pietatis, f. 'devotion to duty': PIETY
alimonium, ii, n. 'nourishment': ALIMONY
collegium, -ii, n. 'association in office, guild': COLLEGE
gratia, -ae, f. 'thanks, favor': GRACE
contumacia, -ae, f. 'obstinacy': CONTUMACY

silentium, -ii, n. 'stillness': SILENCE
provincia, -ae, f. 'province': PROVINCE

Adjectives:
amatorius, -a, -um 'of love': AMATORY
litterarius-a-um 'of letters/reading and writing': LITERARY

4. The -us ending often becomes -ous

Adjectives:
noxius, -a,-um 'harmful' NOXIOUS
pius-a-um 'devoted to duty' (v. "sum pius Aeneas"): PIOUS
anxius-a-um 'troubled': ANXIOUS

5. The Catch-22 Rule: other, unpredictable changes some-times take place: this is especially true of words that have en-tered English after serving time in the French language.

Some examples:
English JOY is from Latin <u>gaudia</u> (pl. of gaudium, 'delight, enjoy-ment'); the Latin stem shows up in the word <u>gaudy</u>
AUTHOR is from Latin <u>auctor</u> which is from the same stem as auction (from <u>auctus,</u> past participle of <u>augere</u> 'to increase')
REASON is from Latin <u>ratio</u>, accusative <u>rationem</u> ('reason, propor-tion') from which we have also received <u>ration</u>, <u>rational</u>, <u>ratio.</u>
LARCENY is from Latin <u>latrocinium</u>, 'robbery, piracy'
COUPLE is from Latin <u>copula</u>, 'bond, rope'

EXERCISES

Exercise I.

Following the rules in this and the previous lesson:
a.   give the English word derived from each of these Latin words.
b.   tell what rule it follows (how the English word is formed).
c.   state whether it is a noun or adjective.
d.   give its meaning if that has changed markedly from the Latin meaning [such words are marked with an asterisk (*)].

Examples:
nullus (no, none): NULL drops ending (rule #1) adjective, now means 'not valid'
facilis (easy) FACILE adds silent -e (rule #2) adjective
tumor (swelling) TUMOR no change noun
custodia (care) CUSTODY -ia becomes -y (rule #3) noun

116

NOTE: Latin ae becomes English e.
1. *auctio, auctionis (act of increasing)
2. dubius-a-um (doubtful)
3. extremus (outermost, last)
4. calumnia (false accusation)
5. *egregius (outstanding, out of the flock)
6. aedificium (building)
7. aptus (fitted to)
8. fiduciarius (to be held in trust)
9. luridus (yellow)
10. justitia (rightness, fairness)
11. amplitudo (size, distinction, fulness)
12. antiquus (old, ancient)
13. fanum (temple)
14. docilis (easily taught)
15. aequitas (condition of being even)
16. agilis (easily moved)
17. familia (household)
18. mimus (actor in farce)
19. contumelia (abuse, insult)
20. digitus (finger)
21. *immunis (exempt from taxes)
22. *seminarium (a place for seeds, nursery)
23. *sermo, sermonis (talk, conversation)
24. *stipendium (tax, tribute, penalty, income)
25. *cliens, clientis (dependent)
26. *suavis, (sweet)
27. benignus (kind)
28. *rota (wheel)
29. silentium (stillness)
30. *paganus (rural)
31. *obesus (wasted away, eaten away: fat)
32. *profanus (before, and therefore, outside the temple)
33. obscenus (filthy, ominous)
34. *integer (whole, untouched)

Exercise II.

Change the Latin word to its English form in the following quotations:

1. _____ should be made of sterner stuff. Shakespeare
   ambitio, ambitionis 'a going around: canvassing for votes'

2. Thus _____ does make cowards of us all.   Shakespeare
   conscientia 'joint knowledge'

117

3. _____ indications of the better marriages she might have made shown athwart the awful gloom of her composure. Dickens
   <u>luridus</u> 'pale yellow, ghastly'

4. The short _____ way in mathematiques will not do in metaphysiques. Berkeley
   <u>jejunus</u> 'without food, fasting'

5. To forgive is the most _____ pitch human nature can arrive at. Steele
   <u>arduus</u> 'high, steep, difficult'

6. Teachinge thinges which they ought not, because of filthy _____. Tindale
   <u>lucrum</u> 'gain, profit'

7. The oppressors wrong, the poore mans _____.
Shakespeare
   <u>contumelia</u> 'abuse, insult, reproach'

Exercise III

   Additional exercises for words showing slight change from Latin: change each to its English spelling; mark noun or adjective; know meanings; learn unfamiliar words.

NOTE: Latin <u>ae</u> becomes English <u>e</u>.

   1. abortio, abortionis 'miscarriage'
   2. advocatus 'one called to (another's aid)'
   3. caerimonia 'sacredness, sacred work'
   4. gratia 'favor, charm, service'
   5. divinus 'of deity, godly'
   6. exemptus 'taken away'
   7. inanis 'empty, void'
   8. indecorus 'unseemly, unbecoming'
   9. arcus 'bow'
   10. experientia 'experiment, practice'
   11. devius 'out of the way'
   12. cella 'storeroom'
   13. adventus 'a coming to'
   14. fortuitus 'casual, accidental'
   15. dignitas 'worthiness'
   16. conscius 'knowing with'
   17. gloria 'fame'
   18. diffidentia 'mistrust'
   19. luteus 'yellow'
   21. juvenilis 'youthful'

22. modus 'manner'
23. mimus 'farcical actor'
24. merus 'pure, undiluted'
25. mutus 'speechless'
26. beneficium 'kindness'
27. frons, frontis 'forehead'
28. artificium 'trade, handicraft, skill'
29. forma 'shape, beauty'
30. accentus 'signal, tone'
31. clementia 'mildness'
32. acerbus 'harsh to the taste, sharp, sour'
33. firmus 'strong, stable'
34. editio, editionis 'a publishing'
35. praemium 'a reward'
36. audientia 'a hearing'
37. decens, decentis (adj.) 'seemly, becoming'
38. alienus 'belonging to another'
39. aemulatio, aemulationis 'rivalry'
40. arrogantia 'haughtiness'
41. furtivus 'of a thief'
42. frigidus 'cold'
43. junctura 'a joining'
44. germanus 'genuine, born of the same parents'
45. fatum 'the thing said'
46. futurus 'about to be'
47. abstrusus 'pushed away, concealed'
48. dirus 'fearful'
49. justus 'fair, lawful'
50. causa 'reason, purpose, case'
51. pius 'devoted to duty'
52. vividus 'lively'
53. norma 'carpenter's square'
54. rudis 'unwrought, rough'
55. nasturtium 'cress'
56. polus 'end of an axis'
57. squalidus 'stiff with dirt'
58. aurora 'dawn'
59. pronus 'leaning forward'
60. farrago 'fodder for cattle, mash'
61. primus 'first'
62. pyra 'funeral pile'
63. specimen 'that by which a thing is seen, mark, token, proof'
64. sordidus 'dirty'
65. index 'a pointer'
66. quartanus 'belonging to the fourth'
67. curator 'one who cares for'
68. prudentia 'a foreseeing'
69. vastus 'empty, desolate'
70. pallor 'paleness'

71. scaena 'stage'
72. osseus 'bony'
73. hiatus 'opening, gap'
74. ornatus 'fitted out'
75. rarus 'porous, thin'
76. cicada 'tree-cricket'
77. sensus 'feeling, perception'
78. potentia 'power, ability'
79. ruina 'downfall'
80. quadrivium 'four ways'
81. viscera (pl.) 'internal organs'
82. copia 'abundance, resources'
83. sonorus 'noisy'
84. octavus 'eighth'
85. patens, patentis 'lying open'
86. tribus 'a division of the people'
87. obsoletus 'worn out'
88. vertigo 'a turning around'
89. pictura 'a painting'
90. uxorius 'fond of one's wife; hen-pecked'
91. ulcus, ulceris 'sore'
92. marsuppium 'pouch'
93. praecursor 'forerunner'
94. usus 'employment, exercise'
95. opportunus 'fit, suitable'
96. fiscus 'money basket'
97. patronus 'protector'
98. noxius 'harmful'
99. popularis 'of the people'
100. caduceus 'a herald's staff'

Exercise III. Unpredictable Changes

In the English words listed below, the Latin base has been obscured: try to find an English derivative from each of the Latin originals that more clearly shows the Latin base (if no word occurs to you, use the dictionary):

Example: ABLE from Latin habilis, -e (manageable, handy): HABILE, REHABILITATE

English	from Latin	derivative showing base
HEIR	heres, heredis 'heir'	
CLEAR	clarus 'bright, clear, famous'	
DEBT	debitum 'something owed'	
GOVERNOR	gubernator 'pilot'	
EMPIRE	imperium 'supreme power'	

JUDGE	judex, judicis 'judge'
LAGOON	lacuna 'hole, pit'
GRAIN	granum 'grain'
HUMBLE	humilis 'lowly'
MISTER, MASTER	magister, magistri, 'teacher'
MERCHANT	mercator 'tradesman'
POOR	pauper 'poor'
PEACE	pax, pacis 'peace'
PENCIL	penicillus 'little brush'
POUND	pondus, ponderis 'weight'
PEOPLE	populus 'people'
SAINT	sanctus 'holy'
TOWER	turris 'tower'
ROYAL	rex, regis 'king'
BRIEF	brevis 'short'
VOW	votum 'vow'
BEEF	bos, bovis 'cow, ox'
ISLE	insula 'island'
COURT	cohors, cohortis
UNCLE	avunculus 'uncle', lit. 'company of soldiers'
MEMOIR	memoria 'memory'
PAIR	paria (pl.) 'equals'
DEIGN	dignus 'worthy'
COUNT	computare 'reckon'
FLAIL	flagellum 'whip'
AVENGE	vindicare 'lay claim to'
VAIN	vanus 'empty'
ROUND	rotundus 'round, wheel-shaped'
POISON	potio, potionis 'a drink'
FOUNT	fons, fontis 'spring, source'
SOUND	sonus 'noise'
NUMBER	numerus 'number'
POWDER	pulvis, pulveris 'dust'
TERM	terminus 'limit, end'
TAVERN	taberna 'shed, shop,
CAGE, JAIL, GAOL	cavea 'hollow'
JOURNAL	diurnalis 'daily'
CHEF, CHIEF	caput, capitis 'head'
CORPS	corpus, corporis 'body'
ETUDE	studium 'zeal'
MENU	minutum 'a little thing, detail'
NAIVE	nativus 'natural, inborn'
SAVANT	sapiens, sapientis 'wise'
SEANCE	sedere 'sit'
ANTIC	antiquus 'old, ancient'
ENSIGN	insignis 'distinguished'

WORDS TO LEARN: study this vocabulary list. Fill in two English derivatives for each. [This will help you remember the Latin words.]

Adjectives:
amplus-a-um   large, spacious
antiquus-a-um   old, ancient
bonus-a-um   good
     bene (adv.) well
brevis, -e   short
clarus-a-um   bright, clear, famous
dignus-a-um   worthy
divus-a-um   of a god; as a noun, a god
facilis-e   easy
difficilis-e   difficult
humilis-e   lowly
par (gen. paris)   equal
primus-a-um   first
sanctus-a-um   holy

Nouns:
caput, capitis, n.   head
causa, -ae, f.   cause, reason, case
corpus, corporis, n., body
fatum, -i, n. the thing said, fate
gratia, -ae, f. favor, grace
ius, iuris, n.   right, law
modus, -i, m.   manner, means, limit
pax, pacis, f.   peace
populus, -im m.   the people
rota, -ae, f.   wheel
studium, -ii, n.   eagerness, zeal, study
terminus, -i, m.   end, boundary, limit
via, -ae, f.   way, road

QUISQUILIA

BACK-TO-BACK: some surprising relations

Latin dorsum means 'back' and is used in English as an anatomical term for the back or any backlike part or organ.   The adjective derived from this noun is dorsal, meaning 'having to do with the back' or in plants, 'with the outer surface or underside of an organ.'   The dorsal fin, for example, is the main fin on the back (or dorsal surface) of fish and certain marine mammals.   A number of scientific or semi-scientific terms come directly from dorsum used as a prefix (dorso-, dorsi, dors-):   for example:

     dorsad   'toward the back'
     dorsibranchiate   'having gills on the back'
     dorsicumbant   'lying on the back'

dorsiduct   'carry towards the back'
dorsifixed   'fastened by the back'
dorsigrade   'walking on the backs of the toes'
dorsimedian, dorsimesal 'in the middle line of the back'
dorsispinal   'of the spinous processes of the vertebrae'
dorsiferous   'bearing fructification on the back of the frond'
dorsigerous   'carrying the young upon the back'
dorsiparous   'hatching the young on the back'
dorsocaudal   'relating to back and tail'
dorsolateral 'relating to back and side'
dorsosternal 'relating to back and breastbone'
dorsoventral 'extending from a dorsal to a ventral surface'

The words in this list are all predictable: their elements are clearly recognizable because they are put together from Latin and Greek word elements, keeping the whole of the base. Some other words, however, derived from dorsum are not so easily recognizable:

endorse 'to countersign' [i.e. 'to sign on the back']
do-si-do   a square dance movement in which the partners circle each other back to back. From French dos-a-dos 'back to back'. A dos-a-dos is also a seat or carriage for seating two people back to back. (Dorsum becomes dos in French.)
a doss house is in English slang the equivalent of a flophouse, a cheap sleeping house, where presumably one lies down on one's back.
dosser is a large pack basket or an ornamental hanging for the back of a chair or throne (the latter is also called a dossal).
dorse an obsolete verb 'to throw someone on his back'
a dossier is a file of papers and documents on a particular person or subject, so named because of the label placed on the back of it.
extrados 'the upper curve of an arch' (literally, outside the back)
intrados 'the inner curve of an arch' (inside the back)
reredos 'the structure forming the back of an altar' or 'the back of an open hearth or fireplace' [from ad retro dorsum (to) behind the back]

Exercise IV.   ENDGAME

Find the Malapropisms:

Mrs. Malaprop, a delightful creation of Richard Brinsley Sheridan, and now a household word (as in "Mother is a veritable Mrs. Malaprop."), in scene after scene of The Rivals allows her

123

love of language to get the better of her, as she tries to prevent her niece and ward, Lydia Languish, from throwing herself away on a mere Ensign. Find malapropisms in the quotations below: what is Mrs. M. saying and what does she mean to say?

1. But the point we would request of you is, that you promise to forget this fellow--to illiterate him, I say, quite from your memory.

2. Now don't attempt to extirpate yourself from the matter; you know I have proof controvertible of it.

3. Observe me, Sir Anthony, I would by no means wish a daughter of mine to be a progeny of learning; I don't think so much learning becomes a young woman; for instance, I would never let her meddle with Greek, or Hebrew, or algebra, or simony, or fluxions, or paradoxes, or such inflammatory branches of learning--neither would it be necessary for her to handle any of your mathematical, astronomical, diabolical instruments. --But, Sir Anthony, I would send her, at nine years old, to a boarding-school, in order to learn a little ingenuity and artifice. Then, sir, she should have a supercilious knowledge in accounts; --and as she grew up, I would have her instructed in geometry, that she might know something of the contagious countries; --but above all, Sir Anthony, she should be mistress of orthodoxy, that she might not mis-spell and mis-pronounce so shamefully as girls usually do; and likewise that she might reprehend the true meaning of what she is saying. This, Sir Anthony, is what I would have a woman know; and there is not a superstitious article in it.

4. He is the very pine-apple of politness!

5. Long ago I laid positive conjunctions on her, never to think of the fellow again; --I have since laid Sir Anthony's preposition before her; but I am sorry to say, she seems resolved to decline every particle that I enjoin her.

6. Oh! it gives me the hydrostatics to such a degree. I thought she had persisted from corresponding with him; but behold, this very day, I have interceded another letter from the fellow; I believe I have it in my pocket.

7. There, sir, an attack on my parts of speech! was ever such a brute! Sure, if I reprehend any thing in this world it is the use of my oracular tongue, and a nice derangement of epitaphs!

8. No caparisons, miss, if you please. Caparisons don't become a young woman. No! Captain Absolute is indeed a fine gentleman... then he's so well bred; so full of alacrity, and adulation! --and

has so much to say for himself: --in such good language, too! His physiognomy so grammatical! Then his presence so noble! I protest, when I saw him, I thought of what Hamlet says in the play:--"Hesperian curls--the front of Job himself!--An eye, like March, to threaten at command!--A station, like Harry Mercury, new--" Something about kissing--on a hill--however, the similitude struck me directly.

SECTION TWO: Chapter Four

ADJECTIVE-FORMING SUFFIXES

In Latin, as in English, there are a variety of endings added
to nouns to make them into adjectives.

English suffixes used to turn nouns into adjectives include:
-y (-ey for words ending in -y), -ish, -ly which mean '-of, belonging to, of the nature or character of (the thing or person
named by the noun to which the ending is attached)'; -ish also
implies 'tending to'.

Examples:

NOUN	ADJECTIVE
might	mighty
sky	skyey
girl	girlish
book	bookish
world	worldly
king	kingly

Following these, form English adjectives from:
mood, thirst, health, meal, noise, home, nose, clay;
boy, ape, clown, fool, self, hell, ghoul, brute;
beast, love, scholar, time, man, woman, day, night, year.

All of these are very productive suffixes, used constantly to form
new words and nonce-words (formations made on the spur of the moment, for the nonce or the occasion, not meant to become a lasting
part of the vocabulary). The suffixes -y, -ish, -ly are, we may
say, used for instant adjectives: take one noun, or even a
phrase, add -y, -ish, or -ly and you have an adjective:

Is the dressing too garlicky?
Don't be so stand-offish!

-y and -ish are often used for describing colors: maroonish;
orangy-red. -y is also frequently used for flavors and textures:
oniony, peppery, peanutty, creamy, runny. -ish is often used for
styles and pretensions: Queen Annish; Jet Settish, modish. -ish
is also common for forming adjectives for national names: English, Welsh, Irish, Jewish, Polish, Scottish, Flemish, etc.

EXERCISE: Make up or find five additional adjectives in each of
these suffixes -y, -ish, -ly and use each in a sentence.

Corresponding to English -y, -ly, -ish are several Latin

suffixes meaning: 'of or pertaining to, belonging to, of/having the nature or character of'. These suffixes are added to the base of the noun.

Latin suffixes:
-alis becomes English -al [i.e. the base alone comes into English] e.g. caput, capitis 'head': capitalis 'of the head': CAPITAL
corpus, corporis 'body': corporalis 'of the body': CORPORAL

-aris becomes English -ar [base alone comes into English]
-aris is used instead of -alis if -l- occurs in one of the last two syllables of the base to which the suffix is added.
E.G. populus 'the people': popularis 'of the people': POPULAR
joculus 'a little joke': jocularis 'having the character of a little joke': JOCULAR
*Sometimes -aris becomes -ary in English
E.g. capillary is from capillaris (adj. of capillus, 'hair') military is from militaris (adj. of miles, militis, 'soldier')

-arius usually becomes English -ary [-ius becomes -y]
E.g. tempus, temporis 'time': temporarius 'belonging to the time': TEMPORARY
*Sometimes -arius becomes -arious [-us becomes -ous]
E.g. grex, gregis 'flock, herd': gregarius 'belonging to the herd': GREGARIOUS
Other irregular changes sometimes (but rarely) take place:
mountaineer is from montanarius
primier is from primarius (from which we also get primary in the regular way). French influence is responsible for both -eer and -ier.

*-arius can also be used to form nouns in-ary (and -arium): the masculine (in -arius) forms nouns meaning 'one who, one concerned with.' The neuter -arium forms nouns meaning 'a place' for' in either -ary or -arium.
E.g. 'one opposing': ADVERSARY from adversus, 'against'
'a place for plants': HERBARIUM from herba 'plant'
'the place of the skull': CALVARY from calva 'skull'

-ilis becomes English -ile [base + silent -e]
sometimes English -il [base alone]
This suffix, added to noun bases is identical in meaning to -alis, -aris, but less common; another -ilis suffix is added to verb bases and means 'capable of, able to'; it will be treated in a later lesson.

E.g. civis (base: civ-), 'citizen': <u>civilis</u> 'characteristic of citizens, relating to citizens, relating to the body politic': CIVIL

vir, <u>viri</u>, 'man': <u>virilis</u> 'manly': VIRILE

<u>-anus</u> becomes in English <u>-ane</u> (base + silent <u>-e</u>)
OR <u>-an</u> (base alone)
E.g. urbs, <u>urbis</u> 'city': <u>urbanus</u> 'pertaining to the city': URBAN
mundus 'world': <u>mundanus</u> 'worldly': MUNDANE
Other changes, of which the most common is that -anus becomes <u>-ain</u>, result from French influence:
E.g. <u>montanus</u>: MOUNTAIN
      <u>certanus</u>: CERTAIN
      <u>capitanus</u>: CAPTAIN
MEAN is from <u>medianus</u> (which also gives MEDIAN, according to the rule).

<u>-inus</u> becomes in English <u>-ine</u> (base + silent <u>-e</u>)
canis 'dog': <u>caninus</u> 'having to do with dogs': CANINE

<u>-icus</u>, <u>-ticus</u> become <u>-ic</u>, <u>-tic</u> in English (base alone)
E.g. civis 'citizen': <u>civicus</u> 'relating to the citizens': CIVIC
aqua 'water': <u>aquaticus</u> 'having to do with water': AQUATIC

WORDS TO LEARN: Study these words before doing exercises. For review, after you have done the exercises, fill in one or two English derivatives beside each.

aqua, -ae, f. water
caro, <u>carnis</u>, f. flesh
civis, <u>civis</u>, m. citizen
fanum, -i, n. temple
latus, <u>lateris</u>, n. side
lex, <u>legis</u>, f. law
luna, lunae, f. moon
manus, <u>manūs</u>, f. hand
mare, <u>maris</u>, n. sea
miles, <u>militis</u>, m. soldier
mors, <u>mortis</u>, f. death
mos, <u>moris</u>, m. manner, mood, custom; pl. character
murus, -i, m. wall
navis, <u>navis</u>, f. ship
necesse (indeclinable) unavoidable
nomen, <u>nominis</u>, n. name
oculus, -i, m. eye
ordo, <u>ordinis</u>, m. rank, row
radix, <u>radicis</u>, f. root

ratio, <u>ration</u>is, f. reckoning, account, reason
rex, <u>reg</u>is, m. king
rus, <u>rur</u>is, n. (bases: rus-, rur-) the country
saeculum, -i, n. age, the times
salus, <u>salut</u>is, f. health
sol, <u>sol</u>is, m. the sun
tempus, <u>tempor</u>is, n. time
urbs, <u>urb</u>is, f. city
verbum, -i, n. word
vox, <u>voc</u>is, f. voice

In doing the early exercises to follow, do not hesitate to refer
back to the vocabulary list: you will learn the words by using
them.

EXERCISES

EXERCISE I. Latin Adjectives

a. give Latin base word with meaning (unless it is given).
b. change Latin adjective into an English adjective
c. give meaning of English adjective

Examples:
a. familiaris: Latin base word: FAMILIA, 'household, family'
    English adjective: FAMILIAR
    Meaning: 'having to do with the household, common, well-
        known'
b. finalis: FINIS, 'end'; FINAL: 'of/at the end' (also, FINIAL,
    'an end piece')

1. rationalis
2. vulgaris (vulgus, -i, n. 'the masses, the crowd')
3. gradualis (gradus, -us, m., 'step')
4. carnalis
5. gregarius (grex, <u>greg</u>is, m. 'flock, herd')
6. primarius
7. militaris
8. salutaris
9. divinus
10. urbanus
11. lupinus (lupus, 'wolf')
12. rusticus
13. civicus
14. civilis
15. classicus (classis, 'fleet, class')
16. dualis (duo, 'two')
17. cardinalis (cardo, <u>cardin</u>is, m. 'hinge')

130

18. necessarius
19. equinus (equus, -i, m. 'horse')
20. lunaris
21. mortalis
22. lateralis
23. paganus (pagus, 'village, country district')
24. muralis
25. auxiliaris (auxilium 'aid, reinforcements')
26. saecularis
27. humanus (from homo, hominis, m. 'human being')
28. singularis (from singuli 'one at a time')
29. manualis
30. mercenarius (merces, mercedis, 'pay, wages')
31. lunaticus
32. fanaticus
33. causalis
34. capitalis
35. corporalis
36. popularis
37. modalis
38. ancillaris (ancilla, 'maid-servant')
39. regalis
40. puerilis (puer 'boy')
41. generalis
42. annualis
43. specialis
44. fatalis

Exercise II

Form English adjectives from the following Latin nouns and give their meanings.

Example: mos, moris (custom): MORAL 'pertaining to custom'

1. tempus, temporis
2. femina (woman)
3. canis (dog)
4. aqua
5. mare
6. vox, vocis
7. judicium (judgment)
8. joculus (a little joke)
9. lympha (water)
10. mundus (world)
11. ordo, ordinis
12. sensus (base: sensu-, 'feeling')
13. navis

14. oculus
15. lex, legis
16. sol
17. nomen, nominis
18. radix, radicis

Exercise III

From the Latin word, form an English noun with the given meaning: ending in -ary, or -arium.

Example: aqua: 'a place for water' AQUARIUM

1. herba: 'a place for plants'
2. adversus: 'one opposing'
3. terra: 'a place for earth'
4. lapis, lapidis: 'one having to do with stones'
5. volpuptas (base: voluptu-): 'one devoted to pleasure'
6. calva: 'the place of the skull'
7. liber, libri: 'a place for books'
8. emissus: 'one sent out'
9. apis: 'a place for bees'
10. avis: 'a place for birds'
11. aestus: 'a place subject to tides'
12. antiquus: 'one interested in old (things)'
13. veterinus: 'one interested in beasts'
14. dies: 'an allowance for the day'
15. granum: 'a place for grain'
16. semen, seminis: 'a place for seed'
17. sal: 'an allowance for salt'
18. nota: 'a writer of notes'
19. mortuus: 'a place for dead bodies'
20. os, ossis (use ossu- as base): 'place for bones'
20-21. vicis (a change): from vicarius 'taking another's place' form a noun and an adjective:

Exercise IV

Define each of the following and use it in a sentence:

1. secular
2. ordinal
3. salutary
4. gregarious
5. auxiliary
6. mundane
7. classic
8. libertine

9. mercenary
10. subsidiary

Some Latin sayings using the lesson vocabulary:

o tempora o mores!
per saecula saeculorum
tempus fugit
Roma, urbs aeterna
sic transit gloria mundi
puer nobis natus est
cave canem
dux femina facti
vox populi, vox Dei
homo sum, humani nihil a me alienum puto.

Lesson 4, part 2: MORE ADJECTIVE-FORMING SUFFIXES

Two other Latin suffixes corresponding to English -y, -ish, -ly are:

-eus which usually becomes -eous [-us becomes -ous], but sometimes
-eus drops the ending (-us) and adds an additional -al: -eal
-eus is frequently found in combination with -ac- or -an-:
-aceus becomes -aceous; -aneus becomes -aneous

E.g. ignis 'fire: igneus 'fiery': IGNEOUS
corpus, corporis 'body': corporeus 'of body': CORPOREAL
miscellus 'mixed': miscellaneus: MISCELLANEOUS
creta 'chalk': cretaceus 'chalky': CRETACEOUS
sanguis, sanguinis 'blood': sanguineus 'bloody': SANGUINE
    (base alone)

-ernus, -urnus, -nus usually add -al to the base in English
forms:
-ernal, -urnal, -nal
E.g. fraternus (frater, 'brother') 'brotherly': FRATERNAL
nocturnus (nox, noctis 'night') 'at night': NOCTURNAL
vernalis (ver 'spring') 'of spring': VERNAL

A few English derivatives do not add the -al:
    for example:
    taciturn
    nocturn
    modern

In dividing a word like paternal (from paternus)
    pater = base 'father'
    -n- from Latin suffix -nus 'of, having to do with'

133

-al additional Latin suffix 'of, having to do with'

Native English adjectives are also formed by the addition of -ful and -some to noun or adjective bases. The original meaning of -ful was 'full of', but this sense has been weakened to 'having'.

Some English adjectives using -ful are:
mournful
woeful
beautiful
graceful
prideful

The meaning of -some is 'being or tending to be', as in:
burdensome
loathsome
wholesome
handsome
cumbersome

The suffix is used for new formations like cuddlesome; but many older words in -some are becoming endangered species: one hardly hears such lovesome words as winsome, longsome, fulsome, gladsome, darksome these days.

Exercise

Find or invent three English words using -ful as a suffix, and three using -some; and compose a sentence using each.

Corresponding to our native English suffixes -ful and -some are two Latin suffixes meaning 'full of, having; being, tending to be, disposed to, abounding in'

-osus becomes English -ous or -ose
[note that -ous also corresponds to the -us adjective ending: often, the only way you can tell is by looking up the Latin word.]
E.g. gratiosus (from gratis): GRACIOUS (N.B. -ti- becomes -ci-)
otiosus (otium, 'leisure'): OTIOSE

-lentus (-olentus; -ulentus) becomes English -lent (-olent, ulent)
corpulentus (from corpus): CORPULENT 'developed in body'
violentus (vis 'force'): VIOLENT 'disposed to force'

134

WORDS TO STUDY: go over this list; after you have done the exercises fill in one or two English derivatives for each word.

copia -ae, f. abundance
dies, diei, m. day
funus, funeris, n. funeral, death
ignis, ignis, m. fire
jocus, -i, m. joke
mater, matris, f. mother
nervus, -i, m. tendon, sinew
nox, noctis, f. night
numerus, -i, m. number
odium, -ii, n. hatred
onus, oneris, n. burden
os, ossis, n. bone
pater, patris, m. father
pes, pedis, m. foot
pestis, pestis, f. plague
radius, -ii, m. ray, rod
sanguis, sanginis, m. blood
somnus, -i, m. sleep
vinum, -i, n. wine
virus, -i, m. slime, poison
vitium, -ii, n. fault, flaw, offence

Exercise I

a. Give Latin base word with meaning.
b. Change the Latin adjectives to their English equivalents (check any unfamiliar ones in the dictionary).
c. Give literal meanings. (Those marked with an asterisk have meanings that differ markedly from the literal meanings.) If necessary, review previous vocabulary list.

1. * morosus
2. somnolentus
3. maternus
4. onerosus
5. verbosus
6. spontaneus (sponte, adv. 'of one's own accord')
7. externus ('outside')
8. osseus
9. vitiosus
10. *ambitiosus (ambitio 'a going around')
11. ramosus (ramus, 'branch')
12. diurnus

135

13. copiosus
14. flatu-lentus (Mod. Latin from flatus-us, m. 'a blowing')
15. funereus
16. callosus (callum 'hard skin')
17. prodigiosus (prodigium, 'a portent')
18. truculentus (trux, trucis, adj. 'wild, rough')
19. * nervosus
20. infernus ('beneath')
21. paternus
22. jocosus
23. nemorosus (nemus, nemoris, 'grove')
24. vinolentus
25. studiosus

Exercise II

Form Latin adjectives meaning 'full of, etc.', using A.
-osus; B. -lentus from these Latin nouns. Give meaning and English form. Example: ingenium 'native talent': INGENIOSUS
'having innate ability': INGENIOUS
vis (vi-) 'force': VIOLENTUS 'given to force': VIOLENT

A. [-osus]
1. fama ('fame')
2. sumptus (sumptu- 'expense')
3. victoria ('victory')
4. odium
5. injuria ('injury')
6. insidiae ('ambush, trap')
7. perfidia ('faithlessness')
8. lachryma (Med. Lat. spelling of classical lacrima, 'tear')
9. numerus
10. contumelia ('insult, invective')

B. [-lentus]
1. ops, opis, f. (-u-) ('means, resources, wealth')
2. fraus, fraudis (-u-)
3. virus
4. pestis (pesti-)
5. turba (-u-) ('uproar')

Exercise III: for review

Take these words apart: divide into base-word, suffix(es),
giving meaning of each part. Use each word in a sentence.
Example: sylvan (or silvan): base silva 'woods, forest' + anus
'of, having to do with'; Pan was a silvan god.

1. urbane	2. radial
3. libertine (libertus 'freedman')	4. pedal
5. venal (venum 'sale')	6. callous
7. otiose	8. radical
9. truculent	10. morose
11. insidious	12. prodigious
13. prodigal (prodigus 'wasteful')	14. corpulent
15. verbose	16. breviary
17. terminal	18. funereal
19. lunatic	20. marine

Exercise IV. Matching (for review)

A. Match words from Latin with their native English equivalents.
In column C form another English word from the Latin base.

A		B	C
1. bloody	1.	annual	
2. wordy	2.	verbose	
3. kingly	3.	somnolent	
4. nightly	4.	regal	
5. yearly	5.	odious	
6. childish	6.	igneous	
7. sleepy	7.	nasal	
8. burdensome	8.	sanguine	
9. hateful	9.	virile	
10. fiery	10.	puerile	
11. nosey	11.	onerous	
12. manly	12.	nocturnal	

B. Match meanings. In column C give a word using the same suffix
as the word in column B.

A		B	C
1. timely	1.	mundane	
2. homey	2.	copious	
3. beastly	3.	aqueous	
4. worldly	4.	vicious	
5. watery	5.	temporary	
6. boney	6.	maternal	
7. fulsome	7.	lachrymose	
8. faulty	8.	domestic	
9. motherly	9.	osseous	
10. tearful	10.	opulent	
11. wealthy	11.	corporeal	
12. bodily	12.	bestial	

QUISQUILIA

Bobbed Words
Some words have lost large parts of themselves in their transition into English.

MOB comes from <u>mobile</u> <u>vulgus</u>, 'the moving or fickle crowd'.

BUS is almost meaningless: in Latin it is only a case ending (in this instance, the dative plural, signifying the relationship to or <u>for</u>). BUS has been shortened from OMNIBUS, meaning 'for all'.

ANA, too, is only an ending in Latin, but has come to be an English word meaning 'a collection' or 'an anthology'. It developed from the custom of calling a collection of verses or sayings of a particular author by the author's name with -ana added to it (from the adjective ending -anus 'belonging to': so that -ana, the neuter plural means 'things belonging to') as in Vergiliana, Shakespeariana. (Likewise in words like Americana, and other collectibles.) Southey, in 1834 wrote that Boswell's Life of Johnson 'for its intrinsic worth, is the Ana of all Anas.'

FAN 'a devotee or avid admirer' (of a team, sport, art, or person) is short for fanatic, from Latin <u>fanaticus</u>, literally, 'of the temple [fanum]', that is, 'inspired or maddened by a god'.

BIB is from Latin <u>bibere</u> 'to drink'

FENCE is short for <u>defense</u> from Latin <u>defendere</u> 'defend, protect'

SCOUR comes from Middle Dutch <u>scuren</u> which in turn stems from Old French <u>escurer</u> which is from Late Latin <u>excurare</u> 'to clean out': <u>ex-</u> 'out' + <u>curare</u> 'to take care of' from <u>cura</u> 'care'.

SCOUT similarly has lost its first syllable, having come through Old French from Latin <u>auscultare</u> 'to listen'

SPORT is shortened from <u>disportare</u> 'to carry (oneself) away (from work)' and so 'to amuse oneself' How then can it be <u>sport</u>, you may well ask, if it is professional?

ENDGAME:

In the last lesson, Mrs. Malaprop amused us. For a modern version of this remarkable lady, listen to Archie Bunker's delicious misuse of language and keep a list of Bunkerisms.

NOUN-FORMING SUFFIXES

In English we have a number of suffixes to convert adjectives into nouns that express the state or quality of being what is named by the adjective: such nouns are called abstract nouns. For example, -ness is a very productive English suffix for forming abstract nouns: it is the English suffix most commonly attached to adjectives (and to past participles) to form nouns expressing the state or condition of being.

    hard: hardness
    dark: darkness
    red: redness

-ness has been used continually to form new words and it can be added to any adjective, whatever its origin: so that we can add -ness to adjectives derived from Latin as well as to natives of English (e.g. graciousness, dubiousness). It is even possible to add -ness to phrases, pronouns, and adverbs: witness these fine formations: togetherness, uptightness, clean-shirtedness, kind heartedness, get-atableness, up-to-dateness, other-worldliness, in-itselfness, self-centeredness, and the exquisite dislike-to-getting-up-in-the-morningness of George Eliot. And consider the flexibility of English in this phrase, where -ness is used as a noun in its own right:

    'cheerfulness, kindliness, cleverness and contentedness, and all the other good nesses.' (Lowell, 1888)

As useful as -ness is to the creative speaker of English, we are not to be caught short; there are several other native abstract-noun forming suffixes, including: -ship (corresponding to German -schaft); -dom (cf. German -tum); -hood (cognate with German -heit).

-ship, like -ness, is added to adjectives and past participles; it is also added to nouns to express the state or condition of being or to denote the office, position, dignity or rank (and most of the new formations are of the latter type).

    hard: hardship
    friend: friendship
    partner: partnership
    king: kingship
    son: sonship
    steward: stewardship
    associate professor: associate professorship

-dom is a noun-forming suffix which has grown out of an independent noun meaning 'putting, setting, position, statute'; it is now a living suffix used to form nouns expressing 'condition, state, dignity, domain, realm' and is attached to nouns as well as adjectives:

kingdom	martyrdom
freedom	thralldom
wisdom	boredom
Christendom	

And, more than -ship, though less than -ness, -dom is used for nonce-formations (instant abstractions in this case): peachdom and pineappledom, B.A.dom, officialdom, do-you-own-thingdom.

-hood, like -dom, started as a separate noun, meaning 'person, personality, condition, sex, quality, rank' but was so freely combined with other words that it ceased to be used as a noun in its own right and is used now only as a suffix added to nouns and sometimes to adjectives to denote condition or state:

childhood	priesthood
girlhood	dog-hood
womanhood	state-hood
maidenhood	duck-hood

The number of such formations, like those in -ness cannot be determined, because these suffixes are very lively and in constant use.

Exercise

1. Find or make up five words each using -ness and -hood; and three each using -dom and -ship. Use each in a sentence.

2. Using a German dictionary find one word each in -nis (cognate of -ness), -shaft, -tum, -heit. Divide each word into base and suffix and define each part.

Example:
    Wissenschaft ('wisdom, learning, science') wise + ship
    Erkenntnis ('knowledge') knowing + ness
    Gesundheit ('health, wholesomeness') sound + hood
    Konigtum ('realm') king + dom

LATIN NOUN FORMING SUFFIXES

Corresponding to -hood, -ship, -dom, -ness are a number of

Latin suffixes which come into English with the meanings state of being, condition of being, quality of being such and such (as expressed by the base-word).

<u>Part A</u>   Suffixes added to adjective bases (and sometimes to nouns)

-tas forms nouns expressing quality and becomes English -TY. Usually -i- precedes the suffix, though -ety is used if the base word ends in -i-, as in adjectives in -ius. In a few words, there is no connecting vowel.

E.g.   loquax, gen. <u>loquacis</u> ('talky'):   <u>loquacitas</u> 'talkiness': LOQUACITY

sobrius, 'sober': <u>sobrietas</u> 'soberness': SOBRIETY

difficilis 'difficult, hard': <u>difficultas</u> 'hardship': DIFFICULTY

Sometimes -tas is added to noun bases;

socius 'comrade': <u>societas</u> 'comradeship': SOCIETY

-ia becomes English -Y

E.g. memor 'mindful': <u>memoria</u> 'mindfulness': MEMORY

Sometimes added to noun bases:

victor 'conqueror': <u>victoria</u> 'conquerorhood': VICTORY

-itia becomes English -ICE

E.g. notus 'known': <u>notitia</u>: NOTICE

-tudo (base in -<u>tudin</u>-, which is used in forming adjectives from the abstract nouns) becomes English -TUDE (-i- is used as the connecting vowel before this suffix)

E.g. altus 'high': <u>altitudo</u> 'highness': ALTITUDE

multus 'much': <u>multitudo</u>: MULTITUDE

The base of Latin multitudo is multitudin-: from which we can form an English adjective by adding -ous. MULTITUDINOUS [v. Macbeth: No, this my hand will rather the multitudinous seas incarnadine, making the green one red.]

-monia, -monium becomes English -MONY

E.g. sanctus 'sacred, holy': <u>sanctimonium</u> 'holiness': SANCTIMONY

acer, base acr(-i-) 'sharp, bitter': <u>acrimonia</u> 'bitterness' ACRIMONY

WORDS TO LEARN   Fill in derivatives:

acer, <u>acris</u>, <u>acre</u> sharp, bitter
altus-a-um high, steep
animus-i, m. mind, soul
anima-ae, f. breath, soul, mind
beatus-a-um happy, blessed

celeber, celebris, -e   crowded, honored
fortis, -e   strong, brave
gratus-a-um   pleasing, welcome, thankful
gravis, -e   heavy, serious
heres, heredis, m.   heir
humanus-a-um   of man [from homo, hominis, m.   'human being']
latus-a-um   wide
levis, -e   light
liber, libera, liberum   free
longus-a-um   long
magnus-a-um   big, great, large
    major, majus (comparative of magnus) greater
    maximus-a-um (superlative of magnus) greatest
malus-a-um   bad
    pejor, pejus (comparative of malus) worse
    pessimus-a-um (superlative of malus) worst
miser, misera, miserum   unhappy, wretched
pauci-ae-a (adj. pl.)   few
pius-a-um   devoted to duty
posterus-a-um   next, following
proprius-a-um   one's own, peculiar
pulcher, pulchra, pulchrum   beautiful, handsome
qualis-e   of what sort, what kind of
quantus-a-um   how great, how much
satis   enough (not declined)
socius-i, m.   companion, comrade
testis, testis, m.   witness
unus-a-um   one
varius-a-um   diverse
vicus, -i, m.   quarter (section of a city), village

EXERCISES

Exercise I

    a. give Latin base word with meaning
    b. define the compound word
    c. give English spelling

Example: facilitas a.   facilis 'easy'; b.   'easiness'
c.   facility

1.	gravitas	2.	patrimonium
3.	maternitas	4.	vinolentia
5.	unanimitas	6.	turbulentia

7. pestilentia	8. militia
9. latitudo	10. urbanitas
11. humanitas	12. justitia
13. necessitas	14. majestas
15. satietas	16. vicinitas
17. paucitas	18. miseria
19. avaritia (avarus-a-um 'greedy')	20. altitudo
21. proprietas	22. lassitudo (lassus-a-um 'weary, tired')
23. acrimonium	24. sanctimonium
25. magnitudo	26. claritas
27. beatitudo	28. levitas
29. pietas	30. malitia

Exercise II. Form Words

A. From <u>sanctus</u> form:
  1. a place for holy things
  2. three abstract nouns using the new noun-forming suffixes

B. From each of the following, form a noun in-(i/e)ty, -mony, -ice, -(i)tude, or -y. Be sure to use the Latin base. If unsure that your creation is a real word, hunt in the dictionary.

 1. varius
 2. testis
 3. sollicitus (anxious)
 4. efficas, <u>efficacis</u> (accomplishing)
 5. pulcher
 6. longus
 7. parcus (sparing, stingy: base in English is parsi-)
 8. comis (courteous, friendly)
 9. controversus (turned against)
10. fortis
11. heres
12. debilis (weak)
13. unus
14. qualis
15. mendax, <u>mendacis</u> (lying)
16. posterus
17. universus (all together)
18. dignus
19. asper (harsh, bitter, rough)
20. quantus
21. quietus (at rest)
22. celeber
23. amoenus (pleasant) [Note: Latin <u>oe</u> becomes <u>e</u> in English]
24. animosus

25. alacer, <u>alacris</u> (eager, quick)
26. felix, <u>felicis</u> (happy)
27.   gratus
28. liber-a-um
29. brevis
30. clarus
31. deus
32. divinus
33. facilis
34. femininus
35. fraternus
36. humilis
37. mater, <u>matris</u>
38. mortalis
39. par
40. pater, <u>patris</u>

Exercise III. Matching

Match the words in column A with words in column B that have identical (or nearly identical) meanings. In column C form another word from the same base as the word in column A.

<u>A</u>	<u>B</u>	<u>C</u>
1. solitude	1. greediness	
2. liberty	2. mannerliness	
3. avarice	3. righteousness	
4. mendacity	4. wickedness	
5. modesty	5. shortness	
6. turpitude	6. loneliness	
7. justice	7. wretchedness	
8. misery	8. highness	
9. altitude	9. falsehood	
10. brevity	10. freedom	
11. asperity	11. fruitfulness	
12. fecundity	12. hardship	

Exercise IV. Matching Stems

Give the Latin base-word from which each of these pairs is derived. Look up the second member of each pair and see how it got to be that way.

1. piety, pity
2. lassitude, alas
3. propriety, property
4. sanctity, saint
5. majesty, mayor
6. clarity, clear
7. beatitude, beauty
8. acrimony, eager
9. aptitude, attitude
10. hostility, host

EXERCISE V

Use each of the folowing in a sentence:

posterity
debility
sanctimony, sanctity
pulchritude
acrimony
comity
quality
quantity
quiddity
amenity

Exercise VI

Using adjective forming suffixes from previous lessons, form adjectives from the following nouns:
Example: multitude multitudinous

1. pulchritude
2. society
3. parsimony
4. propriety
5. variety
6. sanctimony

7. longitude
8. heredity
9. malice
10. avarice
11. acrimony
12. majesty

Part B

Suffixes Added To Noun Bases To Form Nouns With Various Meanings

-atus becomes English -ATE and means 'office of' (corresponding to some of the meanings of English -hood and -ship)
  E.g. consul 'consul': consulatus, 'consulship': CONSULATE
  princeps, principis ('first man, emperor, prince'): principatus ('office of the emperor', 'emperorhood'): PRINCIPATE

-ium becomes English -Y and denotes act or office, place or position (N.B. -cium, -tium: -CE: -gium: -GE)
  E.g. artifex, artificis 'artisan: artificium 'craftsmanship, art': ARTIFICE
  collega 'comrade in office, colleague': collegium 'colleaguehood, guild, association': COLLEGE
  augur 'interpreter': augurium 'act of interpreting, interpretation': AUGURY

147

-ina becomes -INE 'act, office, condition, characteristic, art'
    E.g. discipulus 'pupil, disciple': <u>disciplina</u> 'the art that relates to pupils': DISCIPLINE

DIMINUTIVES:

    Diminutives are nouns formed from nouns to indicate small size. In Latin they keep the gender of the original full-size noun.

<u>-ulus</u>, <u>-ula</u>, <u>-ulum</u> becomes English -ULE
<u>-olus</u>, <u>-ola</u>, <u>-olum</u> becomes English -OLE (-<u>olus</u> is used instead of
        -<u>ulus</u> after a vowel)
<u>-culus</u>, <u>-cula</u>, <u>-culum</u> becomes English -CLE and sometimes -CULE
For all of these the Latin spelling may be retained.

Examples:
    artus 'joint': <u>articulus</u> 'a little joint': ARTICLE
    forma 'form': <u>formula</u> 'a little form': FORMULA
    calx, <u>calcis</u> 'pebble': <u>calculus</u> 'a little pebble, a counting
        stone': CALCULUS
capsa 'box': <u>capsula</u> 'a little box': CAPSULE

    alveus 'hollow': <u>alveolus</u> 'a little hollow', 'small cavity'
    ALVEOLUS

WORDS TO STUDY   Fill in derivatives

auris, auris, f. ear
castra, castrorum, n. pl. camp
cella, -ae, f. storeroom
cerebrum, -i, n. brain
clavis, -is, f. key
codex, <u>codicis</u>, m. (original spelling: caudex) trunk of a tree,
      book
corona, -ae, f. crown
fatuus-a-um silly
forma, -ae, f. shape, beauty
gladius, -ii, m. sword
globus, -i, m. ball, sphere
granum, -i, n. grain
hostis, <u>hostis</u>, m. enemy
immunis, -e tax-exempt
magister, <u>magistri</u>, m. teacher, master
metus, -us, m. fear
minister, <u>ministri</u>, m. attendant, servant, helper
minor, minus smaller, less
minimus-a-um smallest, least
moles, <u>molis</u>, f. mass, heap, pile (tantae molis erat Romanam

condere gentem)
mus, muris, m/f   mouse
nux, nucis, f.   nut
pars, partis, f.   part
rete, retis, n.   net
sanus-a-um   sound, healthy
scrupus, -i, m.   sharp stone
senex, senis, m.   old man
servus, -i, m.   slave
venter, ventris, m.   stomach
vir, viri, m.   man

EXERCISES

Exercise I

a. divide into parts: base, suffix
b. define
c. give English form

Example:
magistratus: magistr- (base of magister) + atus (suffix meaning
      office of); 'office of a master' MAGISTRATE

1. libellus (from liber, libri)
2. servitium
3. musculus
4. granulum
5. augurium
6. commercium (merx, mercis)
7. pontificatus (pontifex 'high priest')
8. ministerium
9. auspicium (auspex-icis: 'bird-watcher, augur')
10. nucleus
11. tribunatus (tribunus 'tribune')
12. corolla (from corona)
13. senatus
14. castellum (from castra)
15. triumviratus (trium- 'of three')
16. gladiolus
17. formula
18. cerebellum

Exercise II

Take these words apart, remembering adjective forming suffixes from lesson 4. Define each word.

1. granular	15. ventricle
2. particular	16. auricle
3. particle	17. pedicel
4. clavicle	18. muscular
5. libelous	19. cellulose
6. artificial	20. scalpel (scalprum, 'knife')
7. lunule	21. meticulous
8. formulaic	22. codicil
9. corpuscle	23. reticular
10. molecular	24. disciplinary
11. capsular	25. particularity
12. cuticle (cutis: 'skin')	26. minuscule
13. globular	27. majuscule
14. scrupulosity	28. ministerial

Exercise III.   REVIEW of nouns and adjectives

From each of the following, form an English adjective and then form an English noun in-(i/e)ty.

Example: similis – adjective <u>similar</u>; noun <u>similarity</u>

1. spontaneus (sponte 'of one's own accord': cf. non mea sponte)
2. acerbus
3. socius
4. aeternus
5. assiduus (constant)
6. civis
7. proprius
8. facilis
9. gravis
10. pius
11. humilis (humble)
12. sobrius
13. immunis
14. avidus
15. anxius
16. felix, <u>felicis</u>
17. varius
18. liber
19. loquax -acis
20. necesse
21. sanus
22. securus
23. simplex
24. vir
25. mendax, <u>mendacis</u>
26. hostis
27. heres, <u>heredis</u>
28. scrupulus
29. fecundus
30. fatuus

QUISQUILIA

PHONY LATIN WORDS

hocuspocusfiliokus, shortened to hocus pocus is possibly derived from Hoc est Corpus Filii (This is the Body of the Son)

omnium gatherum
eatibus anythingus 'the coyote'

absquatulate 'get up and squat elsewhere'
Others are frequently made up by exuberantly joyful Latin students.

Exercise IV. WORD GAME

Locate the origin of these words. All have something unusual in common.

copper	silk	antimacasser
bedlam	blarney	calico
cambric	currant	damask, damascene
damson	lesbian	guinea
magenta	magnet	donnybrook
limerick	meander	milliner
sardonic	sardonyx	sybarite
peach	denim	(blue) jeans
wiener	hamburger	frankfurter
bologna	pilsner	Bible

bunkum (cf. also hokum, a combination of hocus pocus and bunkum)

SECTION TWO: Chapter Six

REVIEW

Exercise I

Give three English derivatives from each of the following Latin words:

1. via	2. albus	3. finis
4. gratus	5. radix (what is the base?)	
6. radius	7. malus	8. similis
9. modus	10. annus	11. sanctus
12. cella	13. civis	14. lex (what is the base?)
15. mater	16. pater	17. primus

Exercise II. Multiple Choice Questions

1. Which is not an Italic language?
Latin   French   Spanish   Italian   Greek   Rumanian

2. Which of these belongs to the Indo-European family?
Estonian   Turkish   Persian   Basque   Korean

3. Which word is derived from a person's name?
smithy   burke   sweater   cartwright

4. Which pair consists of cognates?
brotherhood-fraternity   brother-brotherhood
brother-frater   brotherly-fraternal

5. Which language did not make a large contribution to modern English?
Latin   Welsh   French   Anglo-Saxon

6. Which Latin suffix means about the same as English -ness?
-osus   -lentus   -arium   -itas   -alis

7. Which Latin suffix means about the same as English -ly (as adjective forming suffix)?
-ous   -ary   -alis   -dom

8. Which is not a common change in the formation of English words from Latin words?
Latin ae becomes e   -ia becomes -y   Latin c becomes s
silent -e is added to the Latin base

9. Underline the words that come from languages other than Latin:
mugwump   floccule   scrupulosity   shibboleth   uncle   bugaboo

10. Underline the words from place-names:
currants antebellum antimacassar magenta partisan portmanteau

11. Underline the words you are sure are native English words:
that were quiddity maxixe motherhood matriculation cilice

12. Underline the Latin noun suffixes:
-itas -ar -ilis -lentus -monium -anus -ia -y

Exercise III. General Vocabulary

1. A 'little ear' is:
a. an earwig b. eerie c. an auricle d. an oracle e. aural

2. Another word for heartiness is:
a. cordial b. coronary c. cordiality d. cardiac

3. Radical and eradicate come from the Latin word meaning:
a. rub out b. pull up c. root d. ray e. radish

4. Onus and onerous and exonerate come from the Latin word meaning:
a. burden b. honor c. reward d. responsibility e. work

5. A small net (or grid) is:
a. rectilinear b. a reticle c. reticent d. reticuloendothelial

6. A rara avis is :
a. a rent-a-car agency that tries harder   b. an uncomon fowl
c. an extinct bee d. an undercooked turkey

7. A synonym for felicity is:
a. beatitude b. pulchritude c. gladsome d. opulence

8. Egregious and gregarious are from a Latin noun meaning:
a. greeting   b. flock c. birth, race or family d. Hellenic

9. A finial would most likely be found:
a. at an Irish wake b. on the back of a fish   c. on an end
d. on the production line of a flax factory e. in Helsinki

10. Sanguine and sanguinary are from a Latin noun meaning
a. bloody b. cheerfulness c. red d. death e. blood

11. A corpuscle is:
a. a division of the Army Corps of Engineers   b. the body of a
pecadillo (shortened from corpusculum delicti) c. a small body
d. a muscle in the heart

154

12. Which word is not from Latin virus ('slime, poison')?
a. virology   b. virility   c. viral   d. virulent

13. Nominal and noun come from the Latin word nomen, meaning:
a. phenomena   b. the absence of males (as among the Amazons)
c. an unfavorable omen   d. a name   e. a part of speech

14. A word meaning the opposite of opulence is:
a. perjury   b. pecuniosity   c. penury   d. infelicity

15. Lucre and lucrative come from a Latin word meaning:
a. profit   b. money   c. usury   d. filth   e. embezzlement

16. Which of these shows a change in spelling from its Latin original:
a. omen   b. via   c. aquarium   c. bonus   d. amenity   e. album
f. simile

17. A fatuous person:
a. should go on a diet   b. is silly   c. is only slightly obese
d. is always making fatal remarks

18. A person who displays comity:
a. brings down the house with his amusing routines and anecdotes
b. would probably be an agreeable companion   c. acts as if he/she
were in a deep sleep   d. comes to dinner and eats enough for two

19. A bilingual parrot:
a. speaks with forked tongue   b. knows Latin, Greek, and Hebrew
fluently   c. speaks in two languages   d. eats twice daily

20. A millennium is:
a. a period of 1000 years   b. the last milestone   c. the war to
end all wars   d. a place to buy hats   e. the end of the world, or
a chiliast's dream come true

21. An ingenuous answer is:
a. suggested by one's protective spirit   b. clever and whimsical
c. cute and cutting   d. frank and forthright   e. inutterably stupid

22. A bona fide agreement is:
a. signed and sealed   b. in good faith   c. dead and buried   d. an
osseous pet   e. concerned with canine amity

23. Which is the meaning of sinecure?
a. absolution from sin   b. an incurable illness   c. a wicked, hedonistic curate   d. without care

24. Major, mayor, majuscule are derived from the Latin word meaning:
a. progeny b. leader c. bigger d. ancestors

25. Lassitude is the state of:
a. being a girl below the age of twelve b. being tired c. being caught with a rope d. being the ultimate man (generically speaking) on earth e. having too many sweethearts

26. The calumniators of Epicurus:
a. burnt down his house b. accused him falsely c. turned his garden into a parking lot d. worshipped him on his birthday (as laid down in his kuriai doxai) e. professed belief in his philosophical system.

27. A facetious remark is:
a. invariably wrong-headed b. cruelly factual c. simply fallacious d. witty

28. A lacuna in the text:
a. can be read only with a magnifying glass b. is black c. is blank d. is all wet

29. Linguini is a type of pasta shaped like:
a. tongues b. worms c. tubes d. flowers e. elbows f. shells

30. To rusticate is to:
a. remove rust b. become rusty c. put on makeup d. live in the country e. bring back to life

31. A silvan nymph:
a. lives in the woods b. is emaciated c. is extremely slender d. roams the mountains e. has silver wings f. is used in trout-fishing

32. A mortuary is:
a. an urn b. a place for burying grindstones c. a place where corpses are prepared for burial d. a pigeon-hole for storing ancient customs or laws

33. Gladiators:
a. fight happily for their freedom b. die saluting c. engage in combat with swords d. do battle with wild beasts e. wear clear cellophane

34. Co-eval things:
a. exist during the same time frame b. are wicked together c. evolved from the same parent d. are eternal

35. A magnum opus could be:
a. Clint Eastwood's hand gun   b. an author's masterpiece   c. a very large bottle of Champagne   d. a graduation honor

36. et al. means:
a. you too, Alvin   b. proof that a person was elsewhere   c. for the sake of example   d. and the others

37. Focal and curfew both stem from the Latin word meaning:
a. center   b. fire alarm   c. threshing floor   d. hearth
e. bedtime

38. Quota, bonus, simile, miser, and album are:
a. English adjectives derived from Latin nouns   b. feminine adjective forms   c. English nouns derived from Latin adjectives with gender endings unchanged   d. words made up by university students.

39. a jejune philosophy is:
a. happy-go-lucky   b. youthful   c. inconsistent   d. insubstantial
e. concerned with dietary laws

40. An example of a sesquipedalian word is:
a. yard-stick   b. foot-pad   c. centipede   d. a size 14 shoe
e. floccinaucinihilpilification
Once you have figured out what sesquipedalian means [use a dictionary] list five additional sesquipedalian words you have learned from lessons one through five.

Exercise IV. Multiple Guess Questions

If you feel satisfied with the results of the review exercises on the previous pages, try the following: a score of two or more correct is outstanding.

1. MAXIXE
a. The condition of feeling excruciating pain in the kidneys (especially of sheep)
b. In architecture, the topmost point of a gable, particularly in French architecture
c. One of several headdresses used in Columbian religious pageantry
d. An herb of the madderwort family, used in flavouring a Flemish liqueur
e. A Brazilian dance, similar to the two-step
f. v., intrans., To sign the name by marking the sign of a large X, said of an illiterate person, as 'Charlemagne, being quite unlettered, maxixed, as did King John when forced to accept the Magna Charta."

157

2. RHOPALIC
a. an R shaped mark or figure on an armorial design
b. of or pertaining to an eolithic member of the rose family, represented in fossils found on the island of Rhodes
c. verses in which each word contains one syllable more than the one preceding it
d. In Etruscan, an R-shaped character, probably used in inventorying
e. adj., member of an obscure religious sect in northern India, the members of which wear red vestments and paint their noses white
f. adj., of or pertaining to an illness (rhopalgia), endemic to peoples in the southern Mediterranean area, a symptom of which is diplopia
g. linguistics, esp. psycholinguistics: a form of mild dyslexia especially common among students of the Hellenic culture and language, suffering from maenadism, in which the sufferer confuses the letters P and R (reading, for example, pose as rose); the opposite of rhotacism (q.v.)

3. CACHELOT
a. a whale having a very large head with small cavities
b. a variety of woodbine native to Brittany
c. a member of the leopard family, found principally in central Anatolia
d. a member of the onion family, found in Poland, Germany and parts of western Russia
e. n., vulgarism, an ugly streetwalker
f. a type of small ceramic jar, commonly seen in Victorian parlors, in which tea or aromatic herbs were kept

4. IGASURIC
a. adj., of or pertaining to a minute Mexican lizard of the family iguanilla igasaurides
b. a geological substratum in which fossils of extinct lizards are found
c. condition of cervical abnormality found principally in females of lower economic strata in rural Transylvania
d. species of medicinal fern found only in the vicinity of Iguassu Falls, used by natives to heal wounds caused by poisoned darts
e. an acid found in small quantities in St. Ignatius' bean
f. characteristic of reptiles with very small gastro-intestinal tracts

5. TAKIN
a. a type of barley grown in India, Indochina, Tibet, and the Bayou
b. Shinto war garment of Japanese antiquity, worn by royalty to ward off evil spirits

c. part of a Bedouin camel harness which fits over the camel's ears

d. adj., [underworld dialect or argot], unseemly, indecorous, low-class, synonym of 'low-rent'; as in 'it's just too takin to serve leftovers to guests, even HRH' [from, "The Poorman's Guide to Entertaining Royalty on a Shoestring"]; whence American 'tacky' (q. v.)

f. a horned ruminant of south-eastern Tibet on the northern frontier of Assam

6. CILICE

a. frosty build-up at the bottom of window frames

b. in architecture, an outer frame for an artificial window

c. a type of lace having floral patterns and no seams, common to the peasantry of Cilicia

d. the sound made by vermin experiencing strong viverine emotions, especially among shrews in heat

e. a coarse cloth, hair cloth made from the hair of goats in Cilicia

f. an herb, the seed of which is used as an ingredient in a type of curry powder prepared in Ceylon

7. MANKEEN

a. pertaining to animals inclined to attack men; savage

b. an especially small or young frequenter of Irish public houses

c. Chinese dish in which marinated shark livers are served

d. an early prehistoric hominid, found in England near Kent and on the isle of Man; a highly intelligent ancestor of Homo Sapiens

e. a Japanese lantern of paper painted with skulls and used in currently illegal ancestor-worship

f. Irish slang, a young woman who models clothes (for formation, see poteen)

ANSWERS to Exercises II, III

II
1. Greek   2. Persian   3. burke   4. brother-frater   5. Welsh
6. -itas   7. -alis   8. Latin c becomes English s is not a common change   9. mugwump, shibboleth, bugaboo
10. currants, antimacassar, magenta 11. that, were, motherhood
12. -tas, monium, ia

III
1. c   2. c   3. c   4. a   5. b   6. b   7. a   8. b   9. c
10. e   11. c   12. b   13. d   14. c   15. a   16. d   17. b   18. b
19. c   20. a   21. d   22. b   23. d   24. c   25. b   26. b   27. d
28. c   29. a   30. d   31. a   32. c   33. c   34. a   35. b   36. d
37. d   38. c   39. d   40. e

And for IV: 1. e 2. c 3. a 4. e 5. f 6. e 7. a

LATIN VERBS BECOME ENGLISH

English verbs are formed from the present base and from the perfect participial base of Latin verbs. Sometimes the two bases have given us two separate verbs and different compounds of the same verb often show different bases. Frequently the simple verb does not enter English but a multiplicity of compounds are formed from the Latin verb base.

Some examples:
        From present base:
            addere: ADD
            solvere: SOLVE
        From perfect participial base:
            actum: ACT
            fixum: FIX
        From both bases: two verbs with different meanings:
            referre, relatum: REFER, RELATE
            inducere, inductum: INDUCE, INDUCT
        Such verbs as ducere (lead), vertere (turn), capere (take) give no simple English verb, but many compounds from each base (including both verbs and other parts of speech).
Ducere, ductum:
        conduce, produce, induce, deduce, seduce, adduce, reduce; conduct, product, induct, deduct, abduct, etc.
Capere, captum (-cipere, -ceptum in compounds):
        receive, deceive, conceive, perceive (under French influence); accept, except, concept, precept, receipt, deceit, etc.
Vertere, versum:
        convert, revert, invert, devert, avert; converse, reverse, diverse, inverse, averse, etc.

When learning Latin verbs, the two forms must be learned: THE PRESENT BASE (found by removing -re from the present infinitive) and THE PERFECT PASSIVE PARTICIPIAL BASE (found by removing -um from the perfect passive participle).

The perfect passive participle is formed, generally speaking, by adding -tum to the stem of the verb. If the verb stem already ends in a dental sound, however, the coming together of the two dentals causes a change to -sum. (Note: since a participle is an adjective, it is declined; but for convenience, only the neuter form in -um, also called the supine, is given here.)

Examples: -tum:
        capere: captum
        ducere: ductum

161

    agere: <u>actum</u>
    scribere: <u>scriptum</u>

In the last two examples certain changes have taken place to make pronunciation easier: before -t-, a voiced consonant changes to its unvoiced equivalent: <u>b</u> changes to <u>p</u>; <u>g</u> changes to <u>c</u>. To better understand why this happens, try saying <u>ag-tum</u> and <u>scrib-tum</u> and compare them to <u>ac-tum</u> and <u>scrip-tum</u>.

    <u>-sum</u>:
    mittere: <u>missum</u>
    vertere: <u>versum</u>
    applaudere: <u>applausum</u>

Although these rules need not be memorized, they will give you a clue of what you may expect in the perfect passive participle. The verb forms should be practiced orally so that your ears will be trained as well as your eyes: both senses together will jar your memory.

    Latin verbs come into English in much the same way as nouns do:
    1. The base alone: cf. revert (from revertere)
    2. The base + silent -e: cf. reverse (from reversum)
    3. Irregular changes, especially because of French influence: cf. receive from recipere; chant from cantare

EXERCISES

Exercise I

    Form English <u>verbs</u> from the following Latin verbs. Comment on the type of change that has produced the English verb (present base, participial base, base + silent -e; other change).

    1. vendere, venditum (sell)
    2. laborare (I) (work)
    <u>I</u> beside a verb indicates that it belongs to the first conjugation and has regular principal parts: laboro, LABORARE, laboravi, LABORATUM.
    3. declarare (I) (make known, express)
    4. eludere, elusum (cheat, frustrate)
    5. parare (I) (prepare, get ready, get)
    6. premere, pressus (squeeze)
    7. curare (I) (take care of)
    8. errare (I) (wander, go astray, make a mistake)
    9. clamare (I) (shout)
    10. servire, servitum (be a slave to)
    11. edere, editum (give out, put forth, publish)

162

12. accipere, acceptum (take to)
13. deferre, delatum (carry away, bring to, submit)
14. impellere, impulsum (drive, push, urge on)
15. cedere, cessum (go, yield)
16. impedire, impeditum (hinder)
17. impingere, impactum (dash against)
18. evocare (I) (call out)

Exercise II. Fill-In

1. A vendor is one who _____.

2. To collaborate is to _____ together.

3. A declarative sentence _____ a statement.

4. An elusive gladiator tends to _____ his opponent's blows.

5. Paring fruits and vegetables is a way of _____ them.

6. Suppression is the act of _____ under.

7. Curative measures _____ the situation.

8. Erroneous answers _____.

9. Acclamation is the act of _____ at.

10. An editor is one who _____.

11. Acceptance is the act of _____ to oneself.

12. Deference is the act of _____ to another's feelings or opinion.

13. An impulse _____ one on.

14. The antecedent generally _____ before the relative pronoun.

15. An impediment _____ one.

16. Impingement is the act of _____.

17. An evocation of memories _____ them _____.

Note: the prefixes and suffixes used in these exercises will be treated in more detail later.

Exercise III

Sometimes the derivatives from participial bases are adjectives (or nouns) since the participle is in fact a verbal adjective.
1. Give the most direct English derivative from the participial base.
2. Mark with v those that are verbs; with adj. those that are adjectives and with n those that are nouns. (Sometimes the same English word may be more than one part of speech.)
3. Use each English derivative in a sentence.

1. abstrahere, abstractum (drag away) ABSTRACT adj. (also, v. or n.)
2. abstrudere, abstrusum (conceal)
3. abrumpere, abruptum (break off)
4. abominari, abominatum (curse)
5. aboriri, abortum (miscarry)
6. accipere, acceptum (take, receive)
7. acuere, acutum (sharpen)
8. affligere, afflictum (dash against)
9. affigere, affixum (fasten to)
10. afficere, affectum (influence)
11. addicere, addictum (award to, sentence to)
12. insecare, insectum (cut in)
13. eximere, exemptum (take out, release)
14. exhaurire, exhaustum (drain off)
15. delēre, deletum (destroy, blot out)
16. devovēre, devotum (vow, dedicate)
17. erodere, erosum (gnaw away)
18. finire, finitum (to limit, end)
19. fallere, falsum (cheat, deceive)
20. tendere, tensum (stretch)

VERBS TO LEARN   fill in derivatives
1. ago: AGERE, ACTUM drive, lead, do
2. cedo: CEDERE, CESSUM go, yield
3. clamo: CLAMARE, CLAMATUM shout
4. duco: DUCERE, DUCTUM lead
5. erro: ERRARE, ERRATUM wander, go astray, make a mistake
6. fero: FERRE, LATUM bear, carry
7. mitto: MITTERE, MISSUM send, let go, throw
8. paro: PARARE, PARATUM prepare, get ready, get
9. premo: PREMERE, PRESSUM squeeze
10. scribo: SCRIBERE, SCRIPTUM write
11. sentio: SENTIRE, SENSUM feel
12. solvo: SOLVERE, SOLUTUM loosen, release, undo
13. vendo: VENDERE, VENDITUM sell
14. verto: VERTERE, VERSUM turn
15. voco: VOCARE, VOCATUM call

164

Exercise IV

Match the following derivatives with the meaning of the base words:

1. deactivate	1. write
2. secession	2 undo
3. errata	3. carry
4. oblation	4. go
5. reclamation	5. squeeze
6. deductive	6. feel
7. missionary	7. get
8. impressive	8. sell
9. reparations	9. lead
10. postscript	10. do/drive
11. insentient	11. shout
12. dissolute	12. turn
13. vendition	13. call
14. conversion	14. send
15. invocation	15. wander

Exercise V

Some unusual changes: guess which of the new verbs have given us these words; check your answers in the dictionary:

1. squat
2. essay
3. ancestor
4. duchess
5. Mass
6. print
7. shrive
8. serif
9. scent
10. prose
11. suzerain
12. vouch

QUISQUILIA

Some Latin abbreviations using verb forms

1. cf.   confer (imperative of conferre) 'compare'
2. et seq. et sequens (participle of sequi) 'and the following'
3. i.e. id est 'that is'
4. loc. cit. (in loco citato) 'in the place cited'
5. N.B. nota bene 'note well'
6. ob. obiit 'he/she died'

7. op. cit. (in) opere citato 'in the work cited'
8. P.S. post scriptum 'written afterward'
9. q.v. quod vide 'which see'
10. Rx recipe 'take' (imperative of recipere)
11. R.I.P. requiescat in pace (let him/her rest in peace')
12. v. vide 'see' (imperative of videre)
13. viz. videlicet [videre licet] 'it is permitted to see': 'to wit, namely'
14. sc. scilicet [scire licet] 'it is permitted to know': 'you may understand'

Explain how each of these expressions is used; or give an example of each abbreviation in a context.

Exercise VI. ENDGAME

Find the hidden animals and herds: each of these words comes from the name of an animal, or a group of animals which is not obvious in the meaning.

bugle
canary
canopy
chivalry
muscle
gregarious
peculiar
purse
cavalcade
caterpillar

SECTION TWO: Chapter Eight

PREFIXES I

The prefixes listed below (unless otherwise noted) are from
Latin prepositions. They are attached to nouns, adjectives and
especially to verbs. When taking apart compound verbs and defin-
ing them, it is usually best to translate the prefix as adverbial
rather than prepositional: that is, abduct divides into ab-
(away) + duct (lead, pp. of ducere) and so means 'lead away' (NOT
'away from leading'!).

Some of the prefixes show different forms depending on the
initial letter of the base to which they are added.   The various
possibilities are given in the list below.   The process of change
in consonant sounds to make them more easily pronounceable with
adjacent sounds is called assimilation and will be described
below.

1.   A-, AB-, ABS- away from, off, badly
     The usual form is ab-; a- is used before m, p, v; abs- before
          c, t.
     E.g.
     abruptum 'broken off' AB- + ruptum (pp. of rumpere 'break'):
          ABRUPT
     avertere 'to turn away' (A- + vertere 'turn'): AVERT
     abstractum 'drawn away' (ABS- + tractum pp. of trahere 'draw,
          drag'): ABSTRACT
     abortum 'miscarried, born badly' (AB + ortum pp. of oriri
          'arise, be born'): ABORT

2.   AD- to, toward, against; intensely
     appears also as AC- (before c or q), AF-, AG-, AL-, AN-, AP-,
     AR-, AS-, AT-, and sometimes as A- (before sc, sp, st, gn)
     E.g.
     adventus 'a coming towards' (AD- + ventus noun from pp. of
          venire 'come'): ADVENT
     ad-curatum 'attended to': accuratum (AD- + curatum pp. of
          curare, 'care for, attend'): ACCURATE
     adnotare 'note to, add notes to' (AD- + notare, vb. from noun
          nota 'mark'): ANNOTATE
     ad-sentire 'feel to, agree' (AD- + sentire 'to feel'):
          ASSENT

3.   AMBI- around, about, on both sides
     Before vowels: AMB-
     Ambi- is an inseparable prefix, i.e. it is not used as a
          separate word.
     E.g.
     ambiguus 'going around, uncertain' (AMB- + -iguus derived
     from agere): AMBIGUOUS

167

4. ANTE- before, in front, ahead of
    E.g.
    antecedere 'go before' (ANTE- + cedere 'go'): ANTECEDE
    ANTE- is used in modern formations such as:
        anteroom, antechamber, antedate
        anticipate is from ante- + capere 'to take before'

5. CIRCUM- around
    E.g.
    circumcisum 'cut around' (CIRCUM- + cisum, from caedere
        'cut'): CIRCUMCISE
    circumflexum '[something] bent around' (CIRCUM- + flexum, pp.
        of flectere 'bend'): CIRCUMFLEX

6. CIS- on this side of (indicates location on the side near)
    E.g.
    Cisalpinus 'on this side of the Alps: i.e., on the Italian
        side': CISALPINE
    cislunar: on this side of the moon (between earth and moon)

7. COM- together, with, very
    COM- before b, p, m; COR- before r; COL- before l;
    CO- before h, gn, and usually before vowels; CON- before all
    other consonants.
    From the preposition CUM 'with'
    E.g.
    corrodere 'gnaw thoroughly' (COM- + rodere, 'gnaw'):
        CORRODE
    colloquium 'a speaking together' (COM- + loquium, a noun form
        from loqui 'speak'): COLLOQUY, COLLOQUIUM

8. DE- down, down from, off, utterly; de- may imply removal or
    cessation, and may also give a bad sense to the word
    E.g.
    deformis (adj.) 'ill-formed' (DE- + forma 'shape'):
        DEFORMED
    devolvere 'to roll down' (DE- + volvere 'roll'): DEVOLVE
    DEFOLIATE (a mod. formation) 'to remove the leaves from' (DE-
        + folium 'leaf')

9. DIS- apart, in different directions, at intervals; dis- can
    also be used with a negative force. Dis- is an inseparable
    prefix. DI- before voiced consonants (as g, v); DIF- before
    f; sometimes became French DE- and so sometimes has this
    spelling in English as in DEFY, DEPART
    E.g.
    digredi, digressum 'step apart, in different directions'
        DIS- (before voiced consonant: DI-) + gradi 'step':

DIGRESS

    differre 'bear apart' (DIS-: before f, DIF- + ferre 'bear, carry'): DIFFER

10. EX, E- out from, out of, off, away, away from; thoroughly, utterly, completely
EX- before vowels and h, c, p, g, t (and in Latin before s; but English drops an s after ex-, as in exspectare 'to await': EXPECT); EF- before f; E- before other consonants. E.g.

    eventum 'out-come' (E- + ventum, pp. of venire 'come'): EVENT

    extollere 'raise out' (EX- + tollere 'lift'): EXTOL

11. EXTRA- outside, beyond
variant: EXTRO-
used mostly with nouns
E.g.

    extraordinarius (adj.) 'beyond the rank' (EXTRA- + ordo, ordinis 'rank'): EXTRAORDINARY
many new (i.e. non-classical) formations, such as extra-Biblical (outside the Bible)

These prefixes may be added not only to verbs (where they are used adverbially) but also to nouns (where they may be used prepositionally). For example: aboral AB- away from + OR- from os, oris, 'mouth' + adjective forming suffix 'having to do with'. We may define aboral as 'away from the mouth' a phrase which can be substituted for the adjective and used predicatively: 'in a small aboral sac' or 'in a small sac away from the mouth' (or 'opposite the mouth'). The OED defines aboral: 'pertaining to the region of the animal body at the opposite extremity from the mouth.'

VERBS TO LEARN   fill in derivatives

cado: CADERE, CASUM (-cidere, -casum) fall
caedo: CAEDERE, CAESUM (-cidere, -cisum) cut
capio: CAPERE, CAPTUM (-cipere, -ceptum) take, seize
claudo: CLAUDERE, CLAUSUM (-cludere, -clusum) close
do: DARE, DATUM (-dere, -ditum) give
facio: FACERE, FACTUM (-ficere, -fectum) do, make
(eo): IRE, ITUM go
jacio: JACERE, JACTUM (-icere, -jectum) throw
pello: PELLERE, PULSUM push
rumpo: RUMPERE, RUPTUM break
teneo: TENERE, TENTUM (-tinere, -tentum) hold, keep [-tain]
venio: VENIRE, VENTUM come

ASSIMILATION: [Ad- 'to' + simil- 'like' + at- verbal suffix + -ion 'act of' (-ation 'act of making'): 'act of making like to']:

169

assimilation is the changing of consonant sounds to make them more like and therefore easier to pronounce with the sounds that follow them. For example, in the word 'assimilation', instead of saying ad-similation, we assimilate AD- to AS-, making the consonant of the prefix like that of the base word.

Rule: when certain prefixes ending in consonants are attached to words beginning with consonants, the consonant with which the prefix ends is often changed. The changes that take place are noted with each prefix: but the following general rule may help you to organize the details:

1. The change may be to the same consonant with which the base (to which the prefix is to be attached) begins:
ad-similation: assimilation
ad-notation: annotation
ad-gressive: aggressive
ad-fect: affect
ad-commodation: accommodation
ad-lege: allege
ad-rogant: arrogant
ad-test: attest
ad-pendix: appendix
The prefixes COM-, DIS-, EX- in this lesson also show assimilation.

2. Or the change may be to another consonant more easily pronounced in combination with the initial consonant of the base to which the prefix is to be attached.
ad-quire: acquire
COM- is used before b, p, as well as m because m, a labial, is easily pronounced with the labials b and p (i.e. m is pronounced in the same part of the mouth as b and p: so that -mp- and -mb- do not require any lingual gymnastics to utter): compute, commute, combine. But CON- is used with most other consonants: content, conduct, convex, concoct, consist, confer, congress, conquest.

Exercise on Assimilation

Give the English spelling of each of the following:
1. ad-glutinate
2. com-nive
3. ad-gravate
4. ambi-ition
5. com-venient
6. com-rode
7. ad-stringent
8. ex-fervesce
9. dis-ferent
10. com-lect
11. ex-sist
12. ex-fect
13. con-laborate
14. ad-finity

170

Take these words apart and give meaning of each part (base words can be found in glossary):

A: from nouns
1. ambidextrous (dexter)
2. antebellum
3. antediluvian
4. circumsolar
5. circumlunar
6. antepenult (paene- + ultima)
7. cismontane
8. disseminate
9. extraterrestrial
10. extramundane
11. circumrotate (-ate: verb-forming suffix)

B: from verbs
1. erupt
2. evolve
3. corrupt
4. expel
5. compel
6. antecede
7. circumvolve
8. convent
9. assent
10. dissent
11. devolve
12. commit
13. evoke
14. dismiss
15. exact
16. deduce
17. ascribe
18. elate
19. convert
20. dissolve
21. extrasensory (-ory: adj. suffix 'of/pertaining to')

VOWEL VARIATIONS

The change in the root vowel of closely related words is called vowel gradation. In English, vowel gradation is most common in strong (or irregular) verbs and words related to them.

E.g.
sing, sang, sung; and the noun song
sit, sat an intransitive verb and its transitive counterpart, set; and the noun seat
lie, lay (intransitive) and lay (transitive)
drink, drank, drunk
do, did, done; and the noun deed
think, thought
rise, rose, risen (intransitive); raise (transitive)
give, gave, given; and the noun gift

Some of these correspond to German strong verbs which have parallel changes:

E.g.
singen, sang, gesungen (sing)
sitzen, sass, gesessen (sit)
liegen, lag, gelegen (lie)

171

trinken, trank, getrunken (drink)
tun, tat, getan (do)
denken, dacht (think)
geben, gab, gegeben (give)

A similar phenomenon may be observed in Latin and Greek and it is reflected in the English derivatives (cf. tegere, 'cover'; toga 'toga').

In Latin, the most common vowel change is the weakening of the stem vowel in compounds (that is, when a prefix is added to a verb or noun). This type of vowel change reflects an ancient pronunciation in which the first syllable of every word was accented, so that unaccented vowels were reduced to -e- or -i-.

E.g.
cadere 'fall' + de: de-cadere, originally pronounced decadere: the unaccented -a- is then reduced to -i-, giving decidere 'to fall down' [from which we get deciduous].
captum 'taken' + con-: con-captum: -a- is reduced to -e-: conceptum [CONCEPT]

RULE: The principles of vowel reduction after a prefix are:

1. Before a single consonant, a or e becomes i
Examples:
capio, capere 'take'
    incipere 'take on, begin': INCIPIENT (beginning)
facio, facere 'do'
    efficere: EFFICIENT (doing thoroughly)
tenēre 'hold'
    continēre 'hold together' CONTINENT

2. Before two consonants, a becomes e
captum 'taken'
    praeceptum 'taken before': PRECEPT
iactum 'thrown'
    abjectum, injectum: ABJECT, INJECT

3. ae becomes i; and au becomes u
caedere, caesum 'cut': decidere: DECIDE
                 incisum: INCISE
                 excisum: EXCISE
claudere, clausum 'close': excludere: EXCLUDE
                 occlusum: OCCLUSION

NOTE:
Many verbs from -TINĒRE (from tenēre) and from -CIPERE (from

172

<u>capere</u>) show <u>-tain</u> and <u>-ceive</u> respectively in the English deriva-
tives (because of French influence).

E.g. retinēre: retain
    continēre: contain
    abstinēre: abstain
    concipere: conceive
    decipere: deceive
    recipere: receive
    percipere: perceive

EXERCISES

Exercise I

Vowel weakening: Change each of these to its proper English
spelling; give the verb from which each is derived with its
meaning. Give the meaning of the prefix, if it is one you have
already had. (note: re-: 'back'; per- 'through'; in: 'in')

1. ad-jactive
2. de-facient
3. circum-caesion
4. ex-clausive
5. re-capient
6. re-captacle
7. con-tenent
8. ex-caption
9. con-jacture
10. ef-fact
11. ef-facient
12. abs-tenent
13. in-caesive
14. de-captive
15. de-jaction
16. per-caption
17. af-fact
18. de-fact
19. in-faction
20. ac-cadent

Exercise II

Take these apart; give Latin verb and meaning of English
word.
Example: retain: re- + -tain; tenere; 'hold back'

1. abstain
2. convent
3. exclude
4. add
5. deceive
6. contain

173

7. abject	8. expel	9. exit
10. affect	11. effect	12. disrupt
13. accident (-nt = -ing)	14. excise	15. except
16. conceive	17. confect	18. adit
19. coitus	20. eject	21. corrupt
22. advent	23. exact	24. access
25. acclaim	26. educe	27. differ
28. defer	29. emit	30. dismiss
31. evoke	32. impress	33. conscript
34. circumscribe	25. dissent	36. absolve
37. dissolute	38. divert	39. averse

Exercise III.

Form words meaning:

1. feel together	2. out-come
3. come together	4. break out
5. throw out	6. send out
7. yield to	8. turn away
9. write around	10. come around
11. cut down	12. lead together (2)
13. lead down (2)	14. lead to
15. feel toward	16. squeeze out
17. taken out	18. cut out
19. take to	20. give out
21. close in	

QUISQUILIA: Some Latin expressions using prepositions AB to EXTRA

ab imo pectore from the bottom of the heart
ab incunabulis from the cradle
ab ovo usque ad mala from the egg to the apples
ab universali ad particulare
ab uno disce omnes from one, learn all
a cruce salus from the Cross, salvation
ad astra per aspera
ad Kalendas Graecas on the twelfth of never (the Greeks did not have Kalends)
ad majorem Dei gloriam
ante victoriam ne canas triumphum before the victory do not sing the triumph
cum grano salis with a grain of salt
Dominus vobiscum
de te fabula narratur the tale is told about you
de minimis non curat lex the law is not concerned with minutiae
de gustibus non est disputandum there is no arguing about tastes
de mortuis nil nisi bonum of the dead, nothing but good

deus ex machina
ex cathedra   from the seat (of authority)
ex oriente lux   light from the east
extra muros
extra ordinem

Figure out any that are not translated. Know how each is used.

Exercise IV. ENDGAME

Some interesting compounds:

factotum: do-all	facsimile	amanuensis
accord	alarm	arrive
annoy	biscuit	cauliflower
accost	combine	apparel
conclave	convey	dismal
mischief	precocious	recalcitrant

Choosing two or three of these, find out what each is combined from.

PREFIXES   II

Learn these prefixes, paying special attention to those that show assimilation.

12.   IN-[1]<u>in</u>, <u>into</u>, <u>on</u>, <u>toward</u>, <u>against</u>; <u>in-</u> also indicates 'to put into', as in <u>imperil</u> 'to put into danger' (from Latin <u>periculum</u>); sometimes <u>in-</u> denotes intensity. Assimilates to: IL- before <u>l</u>; IM- before <u>b</u>, <u>m</u>, <u>p</u>; IR- before <u>r</u>; some words under French influence show EN-. E.g.
incidere, <u>incisum</u> (IN- + <u>cadere</u>) 'cut into' INCISION
impellere, <u>impulsus</u> 'push on': IMPEL, IMPULSE

INDU- (INDI-) an old form and strengthened form of IN- which shows up in a few words: INDIGENT (<u>ind-</u> + <u>egere</u> 'to need') and INDIGENOUS 'native born' from <u>indigena</u> (cf. <u>genus</u>)

13.   IN-[2]<u>not</u>, <u>lacking</u>, <u>without</u> (an inseparable prefix)
Assimilates to I-before <u>gn</u>; IL- before <u>l</u>; IM- before <u>b</u>, <u>m</u>, <u>p</u>; IR- before r
IN- is used mostly with adjectives and adverbs in Latin, sometimes with nouns.
Examples:
ILLEGAL (from <u>lex</u>, 'law')
IGNOMINIOUS [(g) <u>nomen</u>, 'name']
IMPURE (<u>purus</u>)

14. INTER- <u>among</u>, <u>between</u>, at <u>intervals</u>, <u>mutually</u>, <u>each</u> <u>other</u>
INTEL- before <u>l</u>
Examples:
<u>interceptum</u>:   INTERCEPT   take between
<u>intercedere</u>:   INTERCEDE   come between
<u>intellectus</u>:   INTELLECT   understanding: choosing between
<u>internus</u> (English: INTERNAL) is an adjective derived from <u>inter</u> with the Latin adjective forming suffix <u>-nus</u> which usually becomes <u>-nal</u> in English [cf. <u>paternus</u>: paternal; <u>diurnus</u>: diurnal].

15. INFRA- <u>below</u>, <u>beneath</u>, <u>inferior</u> <u>to</u>, <u>after</u>, <u>later</u>
Used in new compounds (not derived from existing Latin words).
INFRARED
INFRASONIC
INFRADIG 'beneath one's dignity' [for Latin <u>infra</u>

dignitatem]

INFRALAPSARIANISM, a doctrine that God allowed the fall of man and elected some from the fallen to be saved by a redeemer [lapsus, 'fall']

16. INTRA- in, within, inside of
Intra- is a Late Latin prefix from the classical Latin adverb intra 'on the inside'
intra- occurs only in modern compounds
E.g.
INTRAMURAL 'within the walls' [murus, 'wall']
INTRAVENOUS 'within the veins' [vena, 'vein']

17. INTRO- in, into, inward
introducere 'lead, bring in': INTRODUCE
introspicere, introspectum 'look inside': cf.
INTROSPECTIVE

18. JUXTA- near, beside
JUXTAPOSE: 'put beside'
JUXTABASAL, JUXTASPINAL, JUXTAMARINE

19. OB- toward, against, across (one's way), opposite to, down, for, out of; intensified action.
OB- in some words is used idiomatically and it is often difficult to show its exact force.
Assimilates: O- before m; OC- before c; OF before f; OP- before p.
E.g.
oblongus 'long crosswise': OBLONG
offerre 'bring for': OFFER
obduratus 'hardened against' OBDURATE

20. PER- through, by, thoroughly, away, badly, to the bad
Assimilates to PEL- before l
E.g.
permeare, permeatus 'pass through' PERMEATE
perfidia, 'bad faith': PERFIDY
per-lucidus 'thoroughly bright': PELLUCID

21. POST behind, after (in time or place)
E.g.
postponere 'put after': POSTPONE
cf. such modern formations as:
POSTNATAL, after birth
POSTORBITAL, behind the socket

VERBS TO LEARN   fill in derivatives
condo: CONDERE, CONDITUM build, store, hide

dico: DICERE, DICTUM say, speak
emo: EMERE, EMPTUM buy, procure
fundo: FUNDERE, FUSUM pour
ludo: LUDERE, LUSUM play
pendo: PENDERE, PENSUM hang, weigh
peto: PETERE, PETITUM aim at, seek
pono: PONERE, POSITUM put
sisto: SISTERE, STATUM set, stand
sto: STARE, STATUM stand
tendo: TENDERE, TENTUM / TENSUM stretch, spread, aim

EXERCISES

Exercise I

1. Take apart and give meaning of each part

1. postponement
2. infer
3. omit
4. postscript
5. invoke
6. intermit
7. oppress
8. intervene
9. introduce
10. antependium
11. indict
12. abscond
13. assist
14. circumfuse
15. postlude
16. confuse
17. erode
18. interject
19. interdict
20. intersect
21. introvert
22. object
23. commute
24. intercede
25. perpetual
26. peremptory

2. Find noun or adjective which is the base of each of these and define each word:

1. juxtamarine
2. inert
3. ineptitude
4. extramural
5. perfidious
6. antepenult
7. cismontane
8. extracellular
9. illegal
10. interregnum
11. extracurricular
12. intranuclear
13. intracostal
14. obvious
15. devious
16. impervious
17. posthumous
18. postnatal
19. intramolecular
20. perennial

3. Make up words meaning

1. bring in
2. lead down
3. turn to the bad
4. write down

5. loosen away
6. send to
7. squeeze against
8. shout out (-claim)
9. go out (go/yield)
10. call on
11. feel apart
12. take between
13. thoroughly made
14. give to
15. give out
16. push in different directions
17. push on
18. break in between
19. cut together (adj.)
20. fall in together
21. come upon
22. go out (use form of ire; lit. 'he goes out')
23. roll in
24. throw against
25. close in
26. close completely (i.e. together)
27. hold (-tain) through to
28. hold off
29. [adj.] put to
30. [adj.] put against
31. put down
32. put after
33. bought off, out
34. speak against [against: CONTRA]
35. come against
36. (something) said out
37. say/speak between
38. stretch to
39. stretch out
40. play out
41. play to
42. (something) played between
43. hide away
44. pour in different directions
45. pour in (syn. 'steep')
46. seek/aim with
47. stand with
48. stand off/down
49. stand out
50. stand through
51. hang down
52. hang to

MORE PREFIXES

22. PRAE- (English: PRE-) before, in advance, in front of, head-first, at the end
E.g.
praecedere 'go before': PRECEDE
praetendere 'spread in front of, give as an excuse': PRETEND

23. PRAETER past, beyond (English: PRETER-)
E.g.
praeterire, praeteritum 'go past': cf. PRETERITE (past tense)
PRETERNATURAL: beyond what is natural (modern formation)

24. PRO- forth, for, forward, in front of, publicly, instead of (in modern formations also: in favor of, as profascist) Before vowels: PROD-
E.g.
proclamare 'shout publicly': PROCLAIM
procedere 'go forward': PROCEED

180

proconsul: PROCONSUL

25. RE-   back, again, against, behind (inseparable prefix)
           before vowels: RED-
           E.g.
           repellere 'drive back': REPEL
           recordari 'bring back to mind': RECORD
           redimere, redemptum 'bring back': REDEEM; cf.
           REDEMPTION

26. RETRO- backwards, behind
           in modern formations
           E.g.
           RETROGRESSIVE 'tending to step backwards'

27. SE-   aside, apart, away (inseparable prefix)
           before vowels, SED-
           E.g.
           securus 'free from care (cura)': SECURE
           seducere 'lead apart, away': SEDUCE

28. SINE- without
           SINECURE 'without care' (not used as a prefix in
           Latin) (rarely used as a prefix in English)
           in French: sans

29. SUB-   under, beneath, inferior, secondary, less than, in
           place of, secretly
           Assimilates: SUC- before c; SUF- before f; SUG- be-
           fore g; SUM- before m; SUP- before p; SUR- before
           r; sometimse SUS- before c, p, t.
           E.g.
           subtrahere, subtractum 'draw away from underneath':
           SUBTRACT
           suffundere 'pour under' SUFFUSE

30. SUBTER- beneath, secretly
           subterfugere 'escape, evade': SUBTERFUGE

31. SUPER- over, above, excessively, beyond
           in words from French, SUR- (as in surcharge, surtax,
           surrealism, surplus)
           E.g.
           superimponere 'place on top' SUPERIMPOSE

32. SUPRA- above, over, greater than, preceding
           in modern formations
           E.g.
           SUPRARENAL 'above the kidney'

33. TRANS- <u>across</u>, <u>over</u>, <u>beyond</u>, <u>through</u>; sometimes as an intensive
   TRA-; TRAN- (before s)

SUMMARY OF PREFIXES

1. <u>Assimilation</u>: the following show assimilation

ad	com-
ex-	in-(1 & 2)
inter-	ob-
per-	sub-

2. <u>Intensity</u>: The following prefixes can be used as intensives: i.e. they can mean <u>very</u>, <u>thoroughly</u>, <u>exceedingly</u>.
   com- [with: <u>altogether</u>]
   de- [down: <u>downright</u>]
   ex- [out from: <u>outright</u>]
   in- (1) [in: <u>inside out</u>]
   ob- [<u>right in the way</u>]
   per- [through: <u>through and through</u>]
   pro- [forth: <u>foremost</u>]
   super- [<u>over and above</u>]
   trans- [<u>across and over</u>]

3. <u>Negativity</u>: the following can be used to imply NOT, BADLY, WITHOUT
   ab- away from, badly (separation)
   de- down from, badly (separation)
   dis- apart (may imply negation, reversal, removal)
   ex- out from, removed from (separation)
   in- (2) not
   per- through, to the bad
   re- back (sometimes in the sense of removing or negating as in REPEAL)
   se- without (by oneself) [related to sine-]

VERBS TO LEARN   fill in derivatives

cano: CANERE, CANTUM sing
cerno: CERNERE, CRETUM sift
cieo: CIĒRE, CITUM move, stir, rouse, call
-clino: CLINARE, CLINATUM turn, bend
curro: CURRERE, CURSUM run
fateor: FATĒRI, FASSUM [-fiteri, -fessum] confess
flecto: FLECTERE, FLEXUM bend
gero: GERERE, GESTUM carry, wage
haereo: HAERĒRE, HAESITUM cling, stick
lego: LEGERE, LECTUM collect, gather, choose, read
porto: PORTARE, PORTATUM carry
prehendo: PREHENDERE, PREHENSUM seize

quaero: QUAERERE, QUAESITUM [-quirere, -quisitum] seek
rogo: ROGARE, ROGATUM ask
scando: SCANDERE [-scendere, -scensum] climb
seco: SECARE, SECTUM cut
servo: SERVARE, SERVATUM save
sumo: SUMERE, SUMPTUM take, take up
traho: TRAHERE, TRACTUM draw, drag
utor: UTI, USUM use
vado: VADERE, -VASUM go, make one's way
vinco: VINCERE, VICTUM conquer, win
vivo: VIVERE, VICTUM live

Exercise II

1. Take apart, define each part (words from new vocabulary)

1. inquire	2. requisite	3. accent
4. concern	5. discrete	6. excite
7. incur	8. concur	9. profess
10. inflect	11. reflex	12. congest
13. adhere	14. decline	15. collect
16. elect	17. support	18. disport
19. apprehend	20. interrogate	21. ascend
22. dissect	23. reserve	24. observe
25. assume	26. presume	27. abstract
28. extract	29. abuse	30. pervade
31. convict	32. convince	33. survive

2. Make up English words meaning:

1. to sing back	2. sifted apart
3. to sift apart	4. to stir out
5. to stir in	6. to run back
7. to run against	8. to acknowledge publicly
9. to bend down	10. to bend back
11. to carry under	12. to stick together
13. to stick in	14. to lean back
15. to choose apart	16. to carry across
17. to carry off (down)	18. to carry together
19. to seize together	20. to ask away
21. to ask down	22. to climb across
23. to climb down	24. to climb down with
25. to cut in	26. to cut between
27. save back	28. save ahead
29. to take-up thoroughly (with)	30. to take-up again
31. draw/drag together	32. draw/drag down
33. use through and through	34. make one's way out
35. make one's way in/against	36. bring/come back to life

183

Exercise III. More Words to Take Apart: REVIEW

Go over verbs from previous lessons. Divide into parts; give meanings.

1. imbibe
2. subtract
3. abscess
4. affirm (firmus)
5. ambitious
6. transcript
7. subsume
8. circumvolve
9. cissolar
10. comfort (fortis)
11. detect (tegere 'cover')
12. dismiss
13. extol (tollere 'raise')
14. extramural
15. impound (ponere)
16. ineptitude
17. conduce
18. obvious
19. pretext (texere 'weave')
19. prescribe
20. pretermit
21. resist
22. retrocede
23. subdue (ducere)
24. superintend
25. surmise (mittere)
26. supralapsarianism (labi, lapsus 'slip, fall')
27. recede
28. repulse
29. introvert
30. transect
31. suffer
32. seduce
33. subvert
34. subscript
35. rescript
36. resolute
37. remit
38. submit
39. repress
40. suppress
41. succeed
42. resent
43. revoke
44. prevent
45. subject
46. recluse
47. seclude
48. repeat
49. subsist
50. insist

QUISQUILIA

Some Latin Expressions using Prepositions

in hoc signo vinces   in this sign you will conquer
in vino veritas   in wine, truth
in nomine Domini
in absentia
in statu quo
inter alia
inter arma silent leges   among arms, the laws are silent
per veritatem vis   through truth, strength
post equitem sedet atra Cura   behind the horseman sits black Care
post hoc ergo propter hoc
mens sana in corpore sano   a sound mind in a sound body
in lumine tuo videbimus lumen   in thy light we shall see the light

pro bono publico
dulce et decorum est pro patria mori   it is sweet and noble to
                                          die for one's native land
Apologia pro sua vita
pro aris et focis   for altars and hearths
pro Deo et ecclesia
sine die
sub specie aeternitatis
nil sine numine   nothing without divine will
palma non sine pulvere   victory (is) not without dust (effort)
super flumina Babylonis   by the waters of Babylon

Figure out or look up the expressions of which meanings have not
been given. Think of ways in which you might use these expressions.

Exercise IV.   END GAME

Which of these are from Latin?

litmus   caucus
bunkum   doldrum
catalpa   buckram
totem

[If you checked any as being from Latin, look them up and be
surprised.]

185

SUFFIXES ADDED TO THE PRESENT BASE OF VERBS

Although there are some suffixes which can be added both to the present base and to the perfect passive participial base, most are added to only one or the other. In this lesson we will treat only those suffixes that are added to the present base, beginning with noun-forming suffixes.

NOUN-FORMING SUFFIXES ADDED TO PRESENT BASES OF VERBS

-or: English -OR (the English form of these nouns is identical to the Latin nominative form, which is also the base)
-or forms abstract nouns meaning ACT or CONDITION OF. E.g.
errare: present base: err-: ERROR 'act or condition of wandering'
terrēre: present base: terr-: TERROR 'condition of feeling or of causing fright'

-ium: English -IUM, -Y
-cium, -tium: CE
-gium: GE
denotes 'the act of' or 'something connected with the act' E.g.
colloqui: 'speak together' present base: colloqu-
colloquium 'a speaking together', 'act of speaking to-gether': COLLOQUY or COLLOQUIUM
refugere 'to flee back': refugium: REFUGE

-io, base -ionis: in English: -ION
used to form action nouns, meaning 'the act or result of'
[-ion is more commonly added to participial base]
legere 'collect': legio: LEGION
opiniari 'think': opinio: OPINION

-men: English, -MEN indicates 'result or means'
acuere 'sharpen' ACUMEN
specere 'look at' SPECIMEN

-mentum: English -MENT or -MENTUM indicates 'result or means of an act'
armare 'to arm or equip': armamenta (neut. pl.): ARMAMENT
impedire 'to hinder': impedimentum: IMPEDIMENT
movēre 'to move': momentum [for 'movimentum']: MOMENT, MOMENTUM

-bulum: English -BULUM, -BLE (also -bula: -BLE)

187

-culum: English -CULUM, -CLE
  Meanings: means, instrument, place
  If an l occurs in either of the two syllables preceding the
  suffix, -brum, -crum are used instead of -bulum and -culum
  Examples:
  currere 'run': curriculum 'a race course': CURRICULUM
  stare 'stand': stabulum 'a standing place': STABLE
  fari 'speak': fabula 'story, play': FABLE
  pascere 'feed' (base: pa-): pabulum 'fodder': PABULUM,
    PABLUM
  fulcire 'prop up': fulcrum 'a means for propping up':
    FULCRUM
  sepelire 'bury': sepulcrum/sepulchre 'a place for burying':
    SEPULCHRE

VERBS TO LEARN   Fill in Derivatives

augeo: AUGĒRE, AUCTUM increase
candeo: CANDĒRE shine, be white
doceo: DOCĒRE, DOCTUM teach
frango: FRANGERE (FRAG-), FRACTUM break
horreo: HORRĒRE shudder, stand stiff
humeo: HUMĒRE be damp
liqueo: LINQUĒRE be fluid, be clear
loquor: LOQUI, LOCUTUM speak
luceo: LUCĒRE shine, be light
rapio: RAPERE, RAPTUM [-ripere, -reptum] snatch
rego: REGERE, RECTUM move in a straight line, direct, rule
specio: SPECERE/SPICERE, SPECTUM look at
studeo: STUDĒRE be diligent, be eager, study
terreo: TERRĒRE, TERRITUM frighten
timeo: TIMĒRE fear
tremo: TREMERE quake, quiver
valeo: VALĒRE, VALITUM be well [valē, valēte 'good-bye']

VERBS TO RECOGNIZE (for exercises)

ardeo: ARDĒRE, ARSUM be on fire, burn
audeo: AUDĒRE, AUSUM dare, be bold
caleo: CALĒRE be warm, glow
doleo: DOLĒRE (DOLITUM) be in pain, grieve
furo: FURERE rave, rage
lino: LINERE, LITUM smear
liveo: LIVĒRE be black and blue
palleo: PALLĒRE be pale, yellow, or faded
(rancens): RANCĒRE be stinking
rigeo: RIGĒRE be stiff
squaleo: SQUALĒRE be rough, stiff, or clotted
stupeo: STUPĒRE be stunned

torpeo: TORPĒRE be stiff, be numb
torreo: TORRĒRE parch, scorch
tumeo: TUMĒRE swell, be swollen
vigeo: VIGĒRE thrive, flourish

Notice that many of these verbs have no perfect passive participle because, being intransitive, they are by nature unable to be put in the passive.

EXERCISES

Exercise I

Divide into (prefix) base and suffix; define:

1. document
2. timorous
3. augury
4. liquamen (a Roman sauce, made from rotten fish)
5. fragment
6. liniment
7. humorous
8. vigorous
9. suspicion
10. caloric

11-22: take apart, give meaning and use each in a sentence

11. rigorous
12. ardor
13. torpor
14. fervor
15. rancor
16. furor
17. squalor
18. tumor
19. lanquor
20. stupor
21. augment
22. ferment (fervēre)
23. tenor
24. miracle (mirari 'wonder at')
25. regiment
26. vocabulary
27. argument (arguere 'make clear')
28. cement (for 'caed-mentum)
29. sepulchre
30. vehicle (vehere 'carry, convey')
31. monument (from monere 'warn')
32. nutriment (nutrire 'nourish')
33. option (optare 'choose')
34. region
35. detriment (terere, tritum 'rub')
36. regimen
37. foment (fovēre 'warm')
38. condiment
39. emolument (emoliri 'accomplish')
40. experiment (experiri 'try, test')

Exercise II

Put together words meaning (consult vocabulary of this lesson):

1. act of shuddering
2. a speaking alone (alone: <u>solus</u>)
3. bird-watching (bird, <u>avis</u>, contracts to <u>au</u>-)
4. condition of being faded, pale
5. act of being eager
6. condition of being fluid, a fluid
7. act of shaking
8. a speaking against (<u>ob</u>-)
9. condition of being white
10. condition of being moist
11. condition of being strong
12. act of wandering

13-18: translate these words or phrases

13. rigor mortis
14. errare est [=<u>is</u>] humanum
15. ad valorem
16. argumentum ad hominem
17. erratum
18. via dolorosa

II ADJECTIVE-FORMING SUFFIXES ADDED TO THE PRESENT BASE OF VERBS

-<u>idus</u> becomes English -ID <u>tending to, of such and such quality</u>
    <u>acēre</u> 'be sour' <u>acidus</u>: ACID
    <u>rigēre</u> 'be stiff': <u>rigidus</u>: RIGID
    <u>turgēre</u> 'swell': <u>turgidus</u>: TURGID

-<u>ilis</u> becomes English -ILE <u>able to be</u> (denotes a passive capacity)
    <u>agere</u>: <u>agilis</u> 'easily moved': AGILE
    <u>docēre</u>: <u>docilis</u> 'easily taught': DOCILE

-<u>bilis</u> becomes English -BLE <u>able to be</u>
    <u>affari</u> 'speak to': <u>affabilis</u> 'able to be spoken to, easy to
        talk to': AFFABLE
    <u>arare</u> 'plow': <u>arabilis</u> 'able to be plowed': ARABLE
        (sometimes joined to participial stem)

-<u>ax</u>, genitive -<u>acis</u> (stem -<u>ac</u>-) becomes English -ACIOUS
    <u>tending to</u>
    <u>vivere</u> 'live': <u>vivax</u> 'lively': VIVACIOUS
    <u>rapere</u> 'snatch': <u>rapax</u> 'ready to snatch': RAPACIOUS

-ulus becomes English -ULOUS <u>tending to</u>
  credere 'believe': credulus: 'tending to believe':
    CREDULOUS
  pendere 'hand': pendulus 'hanging': PENDULOUS

-uus becomes -UOUS <u>tending to</u>
  nocēre 'hurt' nocuus 'hurtful': cf. INNOCUOUS 'harmless'

EXERCISES

Exercise I

1. Define, use in a sentence; give noun form (e.g. of tumid:
TUMOR) of those marked with an asterisk(*)

1. * tumid	2. * facile
3. * docile	4. * audacious
5. perfervid	6. * candid
7. pellucid	8. * rapid
9. * rapacious	10. * humid
11. conspicuous	12. feracious
13. incredulous	14. invalid
15. incredible	16. * languid
17. * placid (placere, 'please')	18. rabid (rabies 'madness')
19. * sensible	20. * fallible
21. fallacious	22. * rigid
23. * timid	24. fragile (also frail)
25. tepid (tepere 'be lukewarm')	26. * capacious
27. rancid	28. tenacious

29. sagacious (saquire 'perceive clearly')
30. pugnacious (pugnare 'fight') 31. tremulous
32. bibulous (bibere 'drink') 33. querulous (queri 'complain')
34. continuous 35. horrible
36. promiscuous (miscere 'mix') 37. insoluble
38. perspicuous 39. perspicacious
40. incongruous (congruere 'come together')
41. voluble (volvere) 42. garrulous (garrire 'chatter')
43. gravid 44. morbid (morbus 'disease')
45. torrid

Exercise II

Give: 1. noun [in -or] meaning 'condition of being'
       2. adjective derived from it 'pertaining to the condi-
          tion...'
       3. adjective 'tending to be'
       4. noun derived from it 'condition of tending to be'

191

Example:
rigēre   1. rigor   2. rigorous   3. rigid   4. rigidity

   1. humēre
   2. timēre
   3. valēre
   4. stupēre
   5. languēre [be droopy]
   6. rancēre
   7. tumēre
   8. liquēre
   9. squalēre
  10. fervēre
  11. torpēre

QUISQUILIA

The word HUMOR is one that has changed considerably in meaning, from 'moisture' to 'the ability to recognize, appreciate, and share what is funny'. In the interim HUMOR referred to the bodily fluid that determined a person's disposition; the four principal humors being blood, phlegm, choler, and black bile which (respectively) produce by the dominance of one or another the sanguine (or cheerful), phlegmatic (or sluggish), choleric (or irascible), or melancholic (or gloomy) personality. For an experience in the history of ideas, look up HUMOUR in the OED and follow up by checking out the various personality types. Or read selections from Burton's Anatomy of Melancholy: of especial interest to students is Part 1, Section 2, Member 3, Subsection 15, "Love of Learning, or overmuch study. With a Digression of the Misery of Scholars, and why the Muses are Melancholy."

PARTICIPLES

English has many words derived from the Latin present participle and from the Latin perfect participle and some from the future participles. A participle is a verbal adjective. Most of
the words derived from present participles are adjectives in English, though some are nouns: but they have lost most of their
verbal nature. From the perfect passive participle we have adjectives, nouns and verbs; from the future participles, adjectives
and nouns.

I - The present participle: formed in English by adding -ing to
the verb stem; in Latin by adding -ns, base -NT- to the PRESENT
BASE of the verb.

Examples: by conjugation:
  I vigilare 'watch, be wakeful': vigilans, base: vigilant-
       'being wakeful, keeping watch': VIGILANT

  II latēre 'lie hidden': latens, base: latent- 'lying hid-
       den': LATENT

  III delinquere 'leave off, be wanting': delinquens, base:
       delinquent- 'leaving off, being wanting': DELINQUENT

  III (i-stem) incipere 'begin': incipiens, base: incipient-
       'beginning': INCIPIENT

  IV salire 'leap, jump': saliens, base: salient- 'leaping,
       jumping': SALIENT

Words of this type, if derived directly from the Latin participle,
will show the stem vowel of the Latin verb: that is, if the Latin
verb belongs to the first conjugation, then the derivative will
end in -ANT; if to the second or third conjugation, then the derivative will show -ENT; if to the fourth conjugation or to the
i-stems of the third then -IENT will occur in the English form.
If, however, the word has come through French, rather than directly from Latin, it will show -ANT whatever its Latin form, because
the present participle in French is in -ant, without regard to
stem vowel. The -ANT is particularly common if the English word
derived (through French) from the Latin present participle is primarily a noun, rather than an adjective:

Examples:
    tenēre: Lat. tenens, base: tenent- 'holding': English
       TENANT (one holding)

but: continēre: <u>continens</u>, <u>continent</u>- 'holding together': CONTINENT (used in English both as a noun and as an adjective)

pendere 'hang': <u>pendens</u>, <u>pendent</u>-: PENDENT (adj., as in 'But this bird hath made his pendent nest.'); PENDANT (noun)

RULE:

The suffix -NT is to be translated:

a) as an adjective: _____ING

b) as a noun: one _____ING <u>or</u> something _____ING

EXERCISES

Exercise I

Form words meaning:

1. one doing (use AGERE)
2. bearing out
3. loosening (or 'something loosening')
4. feeling
5. unfeeling
6. one holding
7. running
8. one shouting (clamare: claim-)
9. something going before (cedere)
10. driving/pushing forward
11. standing in
12. walking (ambulare)

Exercise II

Take these apart and define

1. belligerent
2. intermittent
3. intelligent
4. important
5. recurrent
6. ascendent
7. secant
8. Vincent
9. inherent
10. adherent
11. repellent
12. deficient
13. decadent
14. accident
15. incident
16. translucent
17. prevalent
18. valiant
19. regent
20. exponent
21. descendant

From the present participles, abstract nouns are formed in Latin by adding –ia to the base: giving –ntia, which becomes in English –NCE or –NCY. These nouns express 'quality, condition, state of being _____ '.

Examples:
        vigilare: vigilans, vigilant–: VIGILANCE
        latēre: latens, latent–: LATENCY
        delinquere: delinquens, delinquent–: DELINQUENCY
        incipere: incipiens, incipient–: INCIPIENCE, INCIPIENCY
        salire: saliens, salient–: SALIENCE

Exercise III

    Take apart and define

1. regency
2. diffidence
3. sentience
4. solvency
5. insistence
6. instance
7. circumstance
8. inference
9. difference
10. incompetency
11. agency
12. incumbency (incumbere 'to lie upon')

Exercise IV

    Form words meaning:

1. state of running back
2. result of not making out
3. result of coming together
4. condition of falling in
5. state of bearing between
6. state of clinging to

WORDS TO LEARN

Verbs:

audio: AUDIRE, AUDITUM hear
sum: ESSE, FUTURUM (future active participle) be
for: FARI, FATUM speak
fido: FIDERE, [FISUM] trust, rely on
fluo: FLUERE, FLUXUM flow
jaceo: JACERE lie
maneo: MANĒRE, MANSUM remain
migro: MIGRARE, MIGRATUM change one's place of living, move

mordeo: MORDĒRE, MORSUM bite
nascor: NASCI, NATUM be born
orior: ORIRI, ORTUM rise
paenitet: PAENITERE repent (impersonal verb: used only in third
    person)
placeo: PLACĒRE, PLACITUM please, be agreeable
possum: POSSE (base: POT-) be able
salio: SALIRE, SALTUM leap, jump [-silire]
scio: SCIRE, SCITUM know
sedeo: SEDĒRE, SESSUM sit [-sidere]
sequor: SEQUI, SECUTUM follow
stringo: STRINGERE, STRICTUM draw tight
tango: TANGERE, TACTUM touch
video: VIDĒRE, VISUM see

Adjective:
omnis, -e (base: OMNI-) all

Exercise V

Form words meaning:

1. lying next-to
2. remaining in
3. state of seeing ahead (forth)
4. condition of talking out
5. one not speaking
6. rising
7. state of being born again
8. trusting completely (with)
9. state of flowing together
10. one moving (changing place of living)
11. state of not hanging down (from)
12. feeling regret
13. not being able
14. leaping
15. act of following together
16. drawing tight to
17. touching together
18. condition of flowing in
19. hearing
20. act of hearing

Exercise VI

Take apart and define these words:

1. inconsequential	2. penitential
3. evidence	4. fluency
5. permanence	6. infancy
7. nescience	8. resiliency
9. subsequent	10. omnipotence
11. emigrant	12. diffidence
13. omniscient	14. transcendental
15. nascent	16. residential
17. tangent	18. influential
19. pendant	20. interdependent
21. sequence	22. conscience
23. prescient	24. penitentiary

II - GERUNDIVES

The gerundive ending -ndus, -a, -um is added to the PRESENT BASE: first conjugation -andus; second and third -endus; fourth and -i-stems of third: -iendus. It becomes -ND (-AND, -END) in English or retains the Latin ending, and sometimes adds the adjective ending -ous. The gerundive carries the meaning 'that must be _____, that ought to be _____.'

These forms are derived from the Latin future passive participle (or gerundive) which expresses obligation or necessity, as in the famous remark of Cato the Elder (a.k.a. Cato the Censor):

> Carthago delenda est!
> Carthage must be destroyed

with which he ended every speech he made in the Senate, whether the necessity of wiping Carthage off the map was pertinent to the matter at hand or not.

Examples:
addere 'to add': addendum (neuter) 'that which must be added':
    English ADDENDUM, pl. ADDENDA 'thing(s) to be added'
dividere 'to divide': dividendum 'that which must be divided':
    DIVIDEND
stupere 'to be stunned': stupendus 'to be stunned over':
    STUPENDOUS

Exercise VII

A. form words meaning:

197

1. things (use neuter plural form) that must be corrected (corrigere)
2. the thing to be drawn or dragged under
3. of (something) to be quaked at
4. the thing to be lessened (minuere)
5. a thing that ought to be squeezed back (ends in -and, from French)
6. one to be revered (reverēri)

B. take apart and define:

1. viand (from vivenda)   2. agenda
3. memorandum (from memorare) 4. referendum
5. multiplicand   6. legend
7. horrendous

III - PERFECT PASSIVE PARTICIPLE

The perfect passive participles of Latin verbs give many English adjectives. Those in -atum and -itum form English adjectives in -ATE and -ITE. For those which have bases ending in two or more consonants as well as for some in -itum, the base alone is used to form adjectives in English. A silent -e is frequently added.

Examples:
    finire 'to bound, to limit': finitum: FINITE 'limited'
    rumpere 'break': ruptum 'broken': cf. ABRUPT 'broken off'

Exercise VIII

Take these apart. Tell from what verb they are derived. Define.

1. indefinite   2. prerequisite
3. considerate   4. abject
5. tacit   6. exquisite
7. precise   8. exempt
9. absolute   10. adverse
11. appellate (from appellare 'call, appeal')
12. apposite   13. averse
14. cognate   15. composite
16. discrete   17. contrite (terere, tritus
18. erose   'rub')
19. innate   20. intense
21. irresolute   22. separate
23. obese (edere 'eat')   24. perquisite

198

25. perverse
27. perfuse
29. replete

26. profuse
28. recondite

Exercise IX.   Review of English Words Derived from Latin Participles

1. tell what part of speech
2. define
3. give Latin verb from which it is derived: divide into prefix-(es) and base if it is a compound
4. tell which participle it is from: present, gerundive, perfect passive participle (ppp)

Examples:
exact   1. adj. (or verb)   2. driven out: precise   3. ex + agere
    4. ppp
expediency   1. noun   2. condition of being freed, made ready
    3. ex + pedire   4. present

1. extant	2. agency	3. exigency
4. ardent	5. augend	6. accident
7. cadent	8. incident	9. concise
10. accent	11. incipient	12. except
13. abscess	14. secret	15. claimant
16. recluse	17. recondite	18. current
19. recurrent	20. dictum	21. edict
22. Benedict	23. data	24. indolent
25. exempt	26. erratum	27. inefficient
28. beneficence	29. fact	30. sufficient
31. afferent	32. efferent	33. sufferance
34. different	35. conference	36. reflex
37. refuse	38. affluent	39. influx
40. influential	41. belligerency	42. gerend
43. inherent	44. abhorrent	45. ambient
46. transient	47. subject	48. oblant
49. prelate	50. latent	51. legendary
52. intelligence	53. eloquent	54. translucent
55. intermittent	56. repellant	57. pendent
58. dependency	59. competent	60. component
61. deponent	62. composite	63. importance
64. prerequisite	65. rapt	66. regent
67. recto	68. arrogant	69. ascendancy
70. script	71. manuscript	72. transcript
73. secant	74. sentience	75. sense
76. insistence	77. subsistent	78. solvency
79. dissolute	80. stance	81. instant
82. state	83. student	84. continent

85. tenancy	86. torrential	87. tremendous
88. abuse	89. inadvertant	90. inconvenience
91. adventure	92. future	93. valence
94. reprimand		

Exercise X. END GAME

These words are from Latin verbs, but the bases are hidden because of various changes. Try to match these with the list of Latin verbs. Learn any that are not familiar.

1. obey	a. vidēre (2 answers)
2. quintessence	b. salire (2)
3. ineffable	c. scire
4. defy	d. fari
5. influenza	e. fidere (2)
6. remnant	f. placēre
7. Noel	g. nasci
8. pleasant	h. sequor (2)
9. puissant	i. stringere
10. exultant	j. audire
11. somersault	k. fluere
12. sciolism	l. manēre
13. seance	m. sedēre
14. sue	n. tangere
15. sect	o. sum, esse
16. prestige	p. posse
17. taste	
18. clairvoyance	
19. visa	
20. fiance	

ANSWERS:
1. j 2. o 3. d 4. e 5. k 6. l 7. g 8. f 9. p 10. b 11. b
12. c 13. m 14. h 15. h 16. i 17. n 18. a 19. a 20. e

SUFFIXES ADDED TO THE PERFECT PASSIVE PARTICIPIAL BASE

I - Noun-forming Suffixes:
-or: English -OR is added to the perfect participial base to form
AGENT nouns, meaning 'one who, that which _____'
    This suffix corresponds to English -er.

Examples:
    narrare, narratum 'tell': narrator 'one who tells':
        NARRATOR
    secare, sectum 'cut': sector 'that which cuts': SECTOR

-tio, -sio (genitive (t/s) ionis: base -ion): English -TION,
    -SION. This suffix causes the same changes as those that
    take place in the formation of the perfect passive
    participle: so that, in effect, we add the ending -io,
    -ionis, English -ION to the perfect participial base.
    Meaning: an act, or the state or result of an act (the act
    being named in the verb)

Examples:
    trahere, tractum 'drag, draw: tractio: the act of drawing:
        TRACTION
    imprimere, impressum 'press on, in, upon': impressio:
        'result of pressing on': IMPRESSION

-tura, -sura: -TURE, -SURE: add -URE to ppp base
    meaning: the act or result of

Examples:
    frangere, fractum 'break': fractura 'result of breaking':
        FRACTURE
    premere, pressum 'squeeze': pressura 'act of squeezing':
        PRESSURE
    uti, usum 'use': usura 'act of using': USURY

-tus, -sus (forming fourth declension nouns): in English -t, -s
    (the base alone) or the base + silent -e
    The nominative of these nouns is identical to the masculine
    nominative of the perfect passive participle.
    Meaning: an act or the result of an act

Examples:
    advenire, adventum 'come to': noun, adventus, -us 'a
        coming': ADVENT
    congredi, congressum 'step together': noun, congressus 'a
        stepping together': CONGRESS

cadere, casum 'fall': noun, <u>casus</u> 'a falling': CASE

VERBS TO LEARN (concentrate on those marked *) Fill in Derivatives

imitor: IMITARI, IMITATUM copy
* jungo: JUNGERE, JUNCTUM join
* moveo: MOVĒRE, MOTUM move
* moneo: MONĒRE, MONITUM warn
* pingo: PINGERE, PICTUM mark by incision: tatoo, paint
pungo: PUNGERE, PUNCTUM prick, sting
* reor: RĒRI, RATUM think
stinguo: STINGUERE, -STINCTUM quench
* struo: STRUERE, STRUCTUM pile up, construct
* tego: TEGERE, TECTUM cover
* torqueo: TORQUĒRE, TORTUM twist
tondeo: TONDĒRE, TONSUM shear, clip, shave
* vello: VELLERE, VULSUM pluck, pull
vexo: VEXARE, VEXATUM shake
voveo: VOVĒRE, VOTUM promise, vow

EXERCISES

Exercise I

        Form and define one agent noun in -OR and one action noun in
-ION from each of the following verbs; use ppp base.

1. monēre   [you may use prefixes]
2. movēre
3. imitari
4. struere
5. tegere
6. agere
7. capere

Exercise II

        Take apart and define (from vocabulary of this lesson):

1. premonition   2. contortion
3. conjunction   4. compunction
5. intrusion   6. reconstruction
7. irrational   8. persecution
9. prosecution   10. extortion
11. admonition   12. obstruction
13. emotional   14. pictorial
15. ration   16. destruction
17. execution   18. vexation

202

19. distinction
20. promotion
21. convulsion
22. commotion
23. depiction
24. extinction
25. devotion
26. construction
27. protection
28. revulsion
29. fiction
30. function

Exercise III

Review of earlier verbs: tell what verb each of these is from and define the English word:

1. conversion
2. addition
3. resolution
4. inversion
5. commission
6. oblation
7. reproduction
8. conscription
9. ascription
10. dissolution
11. remission
12. impression
13. suppression
14. aberration
15. vacation
16. deception
17. edition
18. expulsion
19. irruption
20. corruption
21. incision
22. prevention
23. transition
24. elocution
25. evolution
26. ejection
27. inclusion
28. intention*
29. retention
30. inattention
31. exclamation
32. recession
33. avocation
34. juxtaposition
35. redemption
36. diction
37. allusion
38. condition
39. fusion
40. competition
41. station
42. preposition
43. infraction
44. inspection
45. volition (volo, velle: 'wish')
46. auction
47. correction
48. mansion
49. revision
50. audition
51. nation
52. immigration
53. session
54. execution
55. prosecution
56. restriction

* A hint for deciding whether suffixed forms in -tent- are from tendere or tenere: Check whether the unsuffixed form is in -tend (from tendere) or -tain (from tenere)

retain: retention
intend: intention
attend: attention
detain: detention

But: contention: contend or contain?

Exercise IV

Form words meaning: <u>THE ACT OF-</u>

1. turning back
2. sending under
3. bearing back
4. writing down
5. squeezing out
6. calling in/on
7. taking in (=beginning)
8. pushing forward
9. breaking out
10. cutting out
11. coming together
12. coming upon (in)
13. talking around
14. rolling back
15. throwing down
16. closing out
17. shouting forth (or publicly)
18. going apart
19. putting forth
20. speaking against
21. playing on (in)
22. pouring together
23. seeking again
24. over-seeing
25. moving out

Exercise V

Take these apart: explain formation; give meaning

1. capture
2. juncture
3. nature
4. conjecture
5. pressure
6. fissure
7. picture
8. sense
9. habit
10. recess
11. transit
12. egress
13. aperture

Form English nouns from these Latin nouns; tell what verb each is from (consult vocabulary list in second part of this lesson). Give meaning of Latin verb and of English noun:

1. censura
2. cultura
3. structura
4. statura
5. textura
6. tinctura
7. tonsura
8. apparatus
9. circuitus
10. congressus
11. eventus
12. lapsus
13. consensus
14. prospectus
15. tactus

Exercise VI. Agent or Abstract

Tell which each of these is, what verb it is from, and define it. [Remember that agent nouns are built on the participial base and abstract noun in -or are built on the present base.]

204

1. actor	2. agitator
3. captor	4. censor
5. curator	6. doctor
7. horror	8. factor
9. vigor	10. intercessor
11. languor	12. monitor
13. motor	14. pallor
15. pastor	16. possessor
17. valor	18. tumor
19. tenor	20. precursor
21. professor	22. rector
23. rancor	24. rigor
25. author (augere)	26. ardor
27. spectator	28. sponsor (spondere, 'promise')
29. auditor	30. candor
31. clamor	32. error
33. favor (favere 'support')	34. debtor [Lat. debitor]
35. stupor	36. tremor
37. victor	38. narrator
39. furor	40. tutor (tueri 'watch')

II Adjective-forming Suffixes built on participial base:

-tilis, -silis: -TILE, -SILE that is, add -ILE to participial
    base. Meaning: 'able to be _____'

Examples:
    ducere, ductum: ductilis 'able to be lead/drawn': DUCTILE
    mittere, missum: missilis: MISSILE
    'something that can be thrown'

-bilis with -i- as connecting vowel is sometimes added to partici-
    pial base: -IBLE 'able to _____'

Examples:
comprehendere, comprehensum 'understand': comprehensibilis:
        COMPREHENSIBLE
    plaudere, plausum 'clap, approve': plausibilis 'deserving
        applause, able to be approved': PLAUSIBLE

Note: true formations from Latin show -ible, but non-Latin words
made up in English show -able.

-orius: -ORY, -ORIOUS, -ORIAL (formed from agent nouns in -or +
        ius) 'pertaining to'
    audire, auditus 'hear' auditorius 'pertaining to hearing':
        AUDITORY

205

-ivus: -IVE expresses a <u>tendency</u> or <u>quality</u> ("tending to") nasci,
   natus: <u>nativus</u>: NATIVE
   iubere, <u>iussus</u>: <u>iussivus</u>: JUSSIVE

VERBS TO LEARN (concentrate on those marked*)
Fill in Derivatives

aperio: APERIRE, APERTUM open
* censeo: CENSERE, CENSUM assess, reate, estimate
* colo: COLERE, CULTUM till, honor, dwell
* credo: CREDERE, CREDITUM believe
-fendo: -FENDERE, -FENSUM strike, hurt
findo; FINDERE, FISSUM split
* findo:FINGERE, FICTUM form
fugio: FUGERE, FUGITUM flee
fungor: FUNGI, FUNCTUM perform
* gradior: GRADI, GRESSUM [-gredi, -gressus] step, walk
* habeo: HABERE, HABITUM have
labor: LABI, LAPSUM slide, slip
* texo: TEXERE, TEXTUM weave, build
* tingo: TINGERE, TINCTUM dip

Exercise VII

   Find Latin verb from which each is derived. Give meaning of
English word:

1. textile	2. pensive
3. consecutive	4. fissile
5. fictile	6. votive
7. sensory	8. depictive
9. executive	10. disjunctive
11. distinctive	12. convulsive
13. fugitive	14. reptile (repere 'creep')
15. subjective	16. volatile (volare 'fly')
17. comprehensive	18. objective
19. productive	20. repulsive
21. fossil	22. incorruptible
23. impulsive	24. indestructible
25. ablative	26. offensive
27. indefensible	28. restrictive
29. inadmissible	30. incomprehensible
31. dative	32. captive
33. vocative	34. inactive
35. notorious	36. cursory
37. constructive	38. passive
39. missive	40. descriptive

41. deceptive	42. impressive
43. preventive	44. transitive
45. inclusive	46. pretentive
47. prehensile	48. volitive (volo, 'wish')
49. effusive	50. instinctive
51. incisive	52. evocative
53. native	54. cursive
55. transitory	56. declamatory
57. peremptory	

Exercise VIII. END GAME

More surprises: match the Latin verb with the English word.

1. mob
2. monster
3. pinto
4. junta
5. point
6. motif
7. summon
8. pun
9. pimento
10. arraign
11. truss
12. counterpane
13. nasturtium
14. svelte
15. devout
16. apertif
17. miscreant
18. tissue
19. effigy
20. feverfew
21. able
22. feign
23. stain
24. avourdupois
25. prebend
26. degree

a. habēre (3 answers)
b. pungere (3)
c. pingere (2)
d. gradi
e. tingere
f. fugere
g. texere
h. credere
i. aperire
j. movēre (2)
k. monēre (2)
l. vovere
m. rēri
n. jungere
o. fingere (2)
p. vellere
q. torquēre (2)

ANSWERS: 1-j 2-k 3-c 4-n 5-b
6-j 7-k 8-b 9-c 10-m 11-q 12-b
13-q 14-p 15-l 16-i 17-h 18-g
19-o 20-f 21-a 22-o 23-e 24-a
25-a 26-d

VERB REVIEW

EXERCISES

Exercise I

Match words in columns B and C with meanings of the basic verbs in column A; fill in the Latin verb beside the meaning in column A.

Part 1

A	B (present base)	C (participial base)
Ex: 1. drive, lead, do [agere/actum: B-15; C-7]	1. cede	1. arson
2. open	2. aperient	2. precursor
3. burn, be on fire	3. occlude	3. excise
4. hear	4. augend	4. indoctrinate
5. increase	5. abscond	5. errata
6. fall	6. traduce	6. faction
7. cut	7. audience	7. exact
8. sing	8. redeem	8. fate
9. take, seize	9. canorous	9. deductive
10. go, yield	10. colony	10. aperture
11. sift	11. beneficence	11. profess
12. close	12. cadent	12. occasion
13. till, honor, dewll	13. infant	13. oblation
14. hide, build, store	14. confiteor	14. fictitious
15. run	15. agency	15. caption
16. teach	16. capacious	16. reflex
17. lead	17. discern	17. agriculture
18. buy	18. inflect	18. recondite
19. go astray	19. offering	19. auditorium
20. make, do	20. ardent	20. auction
21. speak	21. docile	21. canticle
22. confess	22. decide	22. clause
23. bear	23. err	23. secessionist
24. form	24. figment	24. exemption
25. bend	25. incur	25. secret

A (meaning of basic verb)	B (present base)	C (participial base)
1. flow	1. labile	1. lectionary
2. break	2. pigment	2. fraction
3. flee	3. affluent	3. elusive
4. pour	4. migrant	4. fugitive
5. perform	5. fungible	5. digression
6. carry, wage	6. immanent	6. expensive
7. walk, step	7. mordacious	7. habit
8. have	8. ambient	8. circumlocution
9. cling	9. expel	9. gesticulate
10. go	10. movement	10. missive
11. slide, slip	11. confound	11. influx
12. collect, read	12. nascent	12. hesitate
13. speak	13. interlude	13. commotion
14. play	14. fragment	14. agnate
15. remain	15. fugacious	15. perfunctory
16. move/change one's place of living	16. pendulous	16. impulsive
17. send	17. belligerent	17. transitory
18. bite	18. habeas corpus	18. immigration
19. move	19. orient	19. repetition
20. be born	20. inherent	20. remorse
21. rise	21. intermittent	21. infusorian
22. puch	22. competent	22. picturesque
23. hang	23. retrograde	23. supralapsarian
24. aim at, seek	24. legend	24. abortive
25. paint	25. colloquial	25. mansion

PART 3

A (meaning of basic verb)	B (present base)	C (participial base)
1. put	1. expunge	1. perquisite
2. carry	2. sequel	2. expressionistic
3. seize	3. apprehend	3. supererogatory
4. squeeze	4. regency	4. saltant
5. prick	5. repacious	5. ascension
6. seek, ask	6 astringent	6. adscititious
7. snatch	7. deponent	7. scriptorium
8. rule	8. construe	8. insessorial
9. ask	9. secant	9. retrospective
10. jump	10. presentiment	10. obstruction
11. climb	11. reprimand	11. sector

12.	know	12.	resolve	12.	sumptuary
13.	write	13.	circumstance	13.	executor
14.	cut	14.	distinguish	14.	rectangle
15.	sit	15.	important	15.	apposition
16.	feel	16.	subsume	16.	tactile
17.	follow	17.	descend	17.	prehensile
18.	loosen	18.	contingency	18.	extinction
19.	look	19.	arrogant	19.	sensuous
20.	stand	20.	sediment	20.	absolution
21.	quench	21.	scribble	21.	surreptitious
22.	draw tight	22.	specimen	22.	stricture
23.	construct	23.	salient	23.	stature
24.	take, use	24.	omniscience	24.	punctilious
25.	touch	25.	query	25.	transportation

PART 4

1.	cover	1.	Quo vadis?	1.	contentious
2.	stretch	2.	torque	2.	tortuous
3.	hold	3.	utilitarian	3.	conversion
4.	dip	4.	tinge	4.	victory
5.	twist	5.	valence	5.	victuals
6.	use	6.	vendor	6.	detention
7.	go, make one's way	7.	tegument	7.	vocation
8.	be well/be strong	8.	providence	8.	event
9.	sell	9.	extend	9.	intinction
10.	come	10.	tenement	10.	revisionist
11.	turn	11.	Venite	11.	abusive
12.	see	12.	evince	12.	detective
13.	conquer	13.	invoke	13.	invasion
14.	live	14.	vivacious	14.	valetudiarian
15.	call	15.	invert	15.	vendition

ANSWERS

part 1: 1-15,17; 2-2,10; 3-20,1; 4-7,19; 5-4,20; 6-12,12; 7-22,3;
8-9,21; 9-16,15; 10-1,23; 11-17,25; 12-3,22; 13-10,17; 14-4,18;
15-25,2; 16-21,4; 17-6,9; 18-8,25; 19-23,5; 20-11,6; 21-13,8; 22-
14,11; 23-19,13; 24-24,14; 25-18,16. part 2: 1-3,11; 2-14,2; 3-
15,4; 4-11,21; 5-5,15; 6-17,9; 7-23,5; 8-18,7; 9-20,12; 10-8,17;
11-1,23; 12-24,1; 13-25,8; 14-13,3; 15-6,25; 16-4,18; 17-21,10;
18-7,20; 19-10,13; 20-12,14; 21-19,25; 22-9,16; 23-16,6; 24-22,19;
25-2,22. part 3: 1-7,15; 2-15,25; 3-3,17; 4-11,2; 5-1,24; 6-25,
1; 7-5,21; 8-4,14; 9-19,3; 10-23,4; 11-17,5; 12-24,6; 13-21,7;
14-9,11; 15-20,8; 16-10,19; 17-2,13; 18-12,20; 19-22,9; 20-13,23;
21-14,18; 22-6,22; 23-8,10; 24-16,12; 25-18,16. part 4: 1-7,12;
2-9,1; 3-10,6; 4-4,9; 5-2,2; 6-3,11; 7-1,13; 8-5,124; 9-6,15; 10-
11,8; 11-15,3; 12-8,10; 13-12,4; 14-15,5; 15-13,7.

Exercise II. Verb Review

Column B lists present infinitives: Choose the word from column C that shows the participial base of the same word as given in column B (hint: fill in participle beside infinitive). In column A, fill in meaning of verb in column B.

Part 1

A- Give Meaning	B- Present Infin.	C- word from participial base
	1. agere	1. intercede
	2. audire	2. receptacle
	3. augēre	3. suicide
	4. cadere	4. occasional
	5. caedere	5. auctioneer
	6. capere	6. audience
	7. cedere	7. decision
	8. cernere	8. recluse
	9. claudere	9. augmentative
	10. colere	10. recessional
	11. currere	11. culture
	12. defendere	12. defensive
		13. exclude
		14. discern
		15. discrete
		16. cadence
		17. reactionary
		18. audition
		19. defendant
		20. cursive

ANSWERS: 1-17; 2-18; 3-5; 4-4; 5-7; 6-2; 7-10; 8-15- 9-8; 10-11; 11-20; 12-12

Part 2

A-Give meaning	B-present base	C-word from ppp.
	1. dicere	1. docile
	2. dare	2. redeem
	3. docēre	3. reductive
	4. ducere	4. fiction
	5. emere	5. confection
	6. facere	6. collation
	7. fallere	7. fallacy
	8. ferre	8. doctor
	9. findere	9. reduce
	10. fingere	10. infant

11. fari	11. addictive
12. frangere	12. redemptive
	13. fatality
	14. transfer
	15. false
	16. fissure
	17. efficient
	18. figure
	19. dative
	20. fragile
	21. fracture

Answers: 1-11; 2-19; 3-8; 4-3; 5-12; 6-5; 7-15; 8-6; 9-16; 10-4;
11-13; 12-21.

Part 3

A-give meaning	B-pres. infin.	C-word from ppp.
	1. fugere	1. transition
	2. fundere	2. belligerent
	3. fungi	3. transfusion
	4. gerere	4. gesture
	5. haerēre	5. conjecture
	6. ire	6. subjunctive
	7. jacēre	7. elaborate
	8. jungere	8. legend
	9. labi	9. inherent
	10. legere	10. function
	11. manēre	11. adjacent
	12. migrare	12. collapse
		13. refund
		14. fugitive
		15. adhesive
		16. electoral
		17. immigrant
		18. mansion
		19. refugee
		20. emigration
		21. manumit

ANSWERS: 1-14; 2-3; 3-10; 4-4; 5-15; 6-1; 7-5; 8-6; 9-12; 10-16;
11-18; 12-20

Part 4

A give meanings	B pres. infin.	C word from ppp.
	1. mittere	1. disposition
	2. monēre	2. permutation
	3. movēre	3. removal
	4. mutare	4. commit

213

5. nasci
6. oriri
7. pati
8. pellere
9. pendere
10. petere
11. ponere
12. prehendere

5. enate
6. reprehensible
7. passivity
8. abortive
9. patience
10. repellant
11. depend
12. pension
13. origin
14. dismissal
15. monitor
16. demotion
17. mutant
18. compulsive
19. apprehend
20. competitive
21. petulant

ANSWERS: 1-14; 2-15; 3-16; 4-2; 5-5; 6-8; 7-7; 8-18; 9-12; 10-20; 11-1; 12-6

Part 5

A meaning

B pres. inf.
1. premere
2. pungere
3. quaerere
4. rapere
5. regere
6. rēri
7. scandere
8. scire
9. sedēre
10. sentire
11. sequi
12. solvere

C word from ppp.
1. consecutive
2. corrective
3. irrational
4. science
5. depression
6. condescension
7. plebiscite
8. sessional
9. sedentary
10. sequel
11. resolute
12. inquisition
13. sensitive
14. punctuation
15. rapt
16. expunge
17. querulous
18. regent
19. sententious

ANSWERS: 1-5; 2-14; 3-12; 4-15; 5-2; 6-3; 7-6; 8-7; 9-8; 10-13; 11-1; 12-11

Part 6

A meaning	B pres. inf.	C word from ppp.
	1. specere	1. extinct
	2. stinguere	2. instrument
	3. stare	3. intangible
	4. stringere	4. integument
	5. struere	5. contemptible
	6. sumere	6. suspicion
	7. tangere	7. protectorate
	8. tegere	8. attentive
slight, despise	9. temnere	9. retentive
	10. tendere	10. tactile
	11. tenēre	11. station
	12. texere	12. district
		13. superstructure
		14. suspect
		15. extinguish
		16. consume
		17. pretext
		18. presumptive
		19. extant

ANSWERS: 1-14; 2-1; 3-11; 4-12; 5-13; 6-18; 7-10; 8-7; 9-5; 10-8; 11-9; 12-17

Part 7

A meaning	B pres. inf.	C word from ppp.
	1. tingere	1. votive
	2. torquēre	2. intrusive
	3. trahere	3. avulsion
	4. trudere	4. reconvene
	5. tundere	5. subversive
	6. uti	6. evidence
	7. vellere	7. contusion
	8. venire	8. conviction
	9. vertere	9. counterrevolution
	10. vidēre	10. tinge
	11. vincere	11. distinctive
	12. volvere	12. unadvisedly
	13. vovēre	13. invert
		14. intractible
		15. conventional
		16. abusive
		17. intruder
		18. contortion
		19. invincible

215

ANSWERS: 1-11; 2-18; 3-14; 4-2; 5-7; 6-16; 7-3; 8-15; 9-5; 10-12; 11-8; 12-9; 13-1

SECTION TWO: Chapter Fourteen

VERB-FORMING SUFFIXES; VERBS DERIVED FROM NOUNS

I Verbs derived from other verbs:

A. FREQUENTATIVES
Frequentatives express <u>constant</u>, <u>repeated</u>, or <u>intensified</u> <u>action</u>. They are formed from the perfect participial stem by the addition of the first conjugation endings: <u>-are</u>, <u>-atum</u>; sometimes <u>-itare</u>, <u>-itatum</u> is added instead.

Examples:

dicere, <u>dictus</u>: ppp. base: <u>dict-</u>: frequentative:
   <u>dictare</u>, <u>dictatum</u> 'keep saying, say intensively or repeated-
ly': DICTATE
vidēre, <u>visum</u>: ppp. base <u>vis-</u>: frequentative:
   <u>visitare</u>, <u>visitatum</u> 'go to see': VISIT
canere, <u>cantus</u> 'sing': ppp. base <u>cant-</u>: frequentative: <u>cantare</u>,
   <u>cantatum</u> 'keep singing': CHANT, INCANTATION
Frequentatives may be recognized usually by the presence of -A-,
or -AT-, or -IT- attached to the participial base.

Some frequentatives are irregularly formed:
agere: <u>agitare</u>: AGITATE
cogere: <u>cogitare</u>: COGITATE (cf. <u>cogito ergo sum</u>)
   Both <u>agitare</u> and <u>cogitare</u> are formed from the present base.

B. INCHOATIVES (or INCEPTIVES)
Inchoatives mean 'begin to'. They are easy to recognize because of the presence of -<u>sc</u>- added to the present base. The new
verb belongs to the third conjugation.

Examples:
florēre 'to flower': efflore<u>sc</u>ere 'to begin to flower out':
   EFFLORESCENT
alere 'nourish, grow': coale<u>sc</u>ere 'to begin to grow together':
   COALESCE
adolēre 'increase': adole<u>sc</u>ere 'begin to increase': ADOLESCENT
creare 'form': cre<u>sc</u>ere 'begin to be formed, increase, grow':
   CRESCENT
Note that (g)no<u>sc</u>ere is an inchoative literally meaning 'begin to
know' and is cognate to English 'know'.

VERBS TO LEARN

alo: ALERE, ALTUM grow, nourish
candeo: CANDĒRE glow, be white

217

creo: CREARE, CREATUM cause to grow, create
      cresco: CRESCERE, CRETUM 'grow, increase' (inchoative of
      creare)
ferveo: FERVĒRE boil, ferment
floreo: FLORĒRE thrive, bloom
      [from flos, floris flower]
memini: MEMINISSE remember (verb found only in perfect active)
soleo: SOLĒRE, SOLITUM be accustomed

EXERCISES

Exercise I

Divide into parts; define; mark those derived from frequentatives (F), and those derived from inchoatives (I); and give original verb.

1. excrescence
2. efflorescent
3. conversation
4. incandescence
5. habitation
6. fervent
7. dictate
8. spectator
9. effervescent
10. candor
11. expectation
12. hesitate
13. gestation
14. florid
15. tractate
16. coalesce
17. reminisce
18. result
19. quiescent
20. visitation
21. crescent
22. convalesce
23. annotate
24. agitation
25. obsolescent

C. SUFFIXES DERIVED FROM VERBS

1. -ficare (from facere) becomes English -FY 'to make, to cause'
     adjective: -FIC 'making, causing'
     noun: -FICATION 'act of making or causing'
     TERRIFY 'cause fright'
     TERRIFIC 'causing fright'
     MORTIFICATION 'act of causing death'

2. -igare (from agere) becomes English -IGATE 'drive, cause to be'
     NAVIGATE: 'drive a ship'

3. -iscere (from inchoative suffix) through French influence gives
     rise to the English verbal suffix -ISH
     FINISH, FLOURISH

4. -plicare 'fold' becomes English -PLY, -PLICATE
     as an adjective: -PLY, -PLEX (-PLEX also as a noun) 'fold,
     folded'

218

5. -fer (from ferre, 'bear') becomes English -FER, -FEROUS
   -FER 'that which bears'
   -FEROUS 'bearing'
   CONIFER 'cone-bearer'
   CONIFEROUS 'bearing cones'

6. -vorare 'to eat' -VOROUS 'eating'
   -VORE 'eater of'
   CARNIVORE, CARNIVOROUS 'eater of flesh', 'flesh-eating'

7. -cida, cidium from caedere ('kill'): -CIDE
   from -cida, -CIDE means 'a killer of'
   from -cidium -CIDE means the killing of'
   HOMOCIDE is either 'one who kills a human being' or 'the
        killing a human being'

II - VERBS MADE FROM NOUNS

   Verbs can be made from nouns in Latin as in English (cf. to
stonewall, to table a bill, to chair a meeting, to bottle up one's
emotions, to pig out, to parrot back, to cup one's hands). Verbs
are made from nouns, adjectives, and adverbs in Latin by adding
the first conjugation endings to the base. These usually come into English from the past participial base and end in -ATE. [Some
Latin verbs derived from nouns belong to the fourth conjugation,
e.g. finire, from finis: FINISH; vestire from vestis: to VEST.]

Examples:
vestigium 'footprint, track': vestigare 'to track': cf.
      INVESTIGATE
vox, vocis 'voice': vocare 'to use the voice', 'call': cf.
      VOCATION
anima 'breath, spirit, mind': animare 'give a certain frame of
      mind to': ANIMATE
os, oris 'mouth': orare 'use the mouth, beg, speak': ORATE
donum 'gift': donare 'to make a gift': DONATE

WORDS TO LEARN

alter-a-um   other
anima, -ae, f.   breath, mind
animus, -i, m.   mind, soul, spirit
castus-a-um   pure
cavus-a-um   hollow
culpa, -ae, f.   fault, blame, guilt
labor, -oris, m.   work, exertion
linquo: LINQUERE, -LICTUM   leave, quit
littera, -ae, f.   letter
locus, -i, m.   place

219

(g)nosco: (G)NOSCERE, NOTUM know
novus-a-um new
nuntius, -ii, m. messenger, message
plecto: PLECTERE, PLEXUM weave, plait
    PLICARE plait, fold
plenus-a-um full
radix, <u>radicis</u>, f. root
ruga, -ae, f. wrinkle, fold
sterno: STERNERE, STRATUM spread
templum, -i, n. sanctuary
terminus, -i, m. boundary, limit
vermis, -is, m. worm
vestigium, -ii, n. track, footprint
verus-a-um true
vestis, -is, f. clothes
alienus-a-um belonging to another

Exercise II

Find the noun, adjective, or adverb that forms the base; give
its meaning; give the meaning of the compound:

1. renovate	2. oration
3. consummate	4. ameliorate
5. enunciate	6. emendation
7. elaborate	8. alleviate
9. adulterate (alter)	10. obliterate
11. eradicate	12. corrugate
13. contemplate	14. decapitate
15. exculpate	16. pejorative
17. graduate	18. excavate
19. evacuate	20. castigate
21. circumnavigate	22. illuminate
23. procrastinate (cras, adv. 'tomorrow')	
24. equate	25. exaggerate (agger 'heap')
26. relocate	27. verify
28. animation	29. transliterate
30. relinquish	31. exterminate
32. generation	33. confirmation
34. comfort	35. alienation

Make up words using the bases given below:

1. alienus: 'to make to belong to another':
2. cumulus 'heap': 'to heap on <u>to</u>':
3. decimus 'tenth': 'to (kill every) <u>tenth</u> (man)':
4. fluctus 'wave': 'to move in waves':
5. germen, germin- 'sprout': 'to produce sprouts':
6. corium 'hide': 'to take the hide off':

220

7. lacer 'mangled': 'to mangle':
8. liber: 'to set free':
9. littera: 'to rub off the letters':
10. nomen, nomin-: 'to name':
11. numerus: 'to number out':
12. opus, oper-: 'to work':
13. radius: 'to emit rays on':
14. robor 'oak, strength': 'to strengthen thoroughly/together':
15. socius: 'act of joining as allies':
16. stimulus 'goad, spur': 'act of goading'
17. stirps 'stock, stem': 'to pluck out the stock':
18. unda 'wave': 'to cover with waves (on)':
19. asper 'rough' 'to make thoroughly rough (out)':
20. frustra 'in vain': 'to make to act in vain':
21. iterum 'again': 'to go back over again':

Exercise III

a. Whom or what does each kill:
1. fratricide
2. parricide
3. infanticide
4. genocide
5. tyrannicide
6. regicide
7. deicide
8. suicide
9. matricide
10. patricide
11. atavicide
12. novercicide
13. pesticide
14. vermicide

b. what is eaten:
1. omnivore
2. herbivore
3. carnivore
4. vermivorous
5. avivorous
6. insectivorous

c. what do these bear:
1. aquifer
2. bacciferous plants
3. crucifer
4. conifer

d. give Latin noun or adjective from which each of the following is derived:
1. culprit
2. transvestite
3. bilocation
4. alternate
5. comfortable
6. animadversion
7. alliteration
8. locative
9. magnanimous
10. determine
11. travesty
12. vermiculation
13. investigation
14. contemplation
15. corrugate
16. innovation
17. replenish
18. aver

e. take these apart: define each part; define whole:
1. justify
2. nullify
3. stratify
4. modification
5. notify
6. qualification
7. rectify
8. vivify
9. mollify (mollis 'soft')
10. apply
11. complication
12. implicate
13. supplication
14. replicate

f. find bases, give meanings (the dictionary may be necessary for some of the etymologies and meanings, especially of those marked*)
1. * altruism
2. * subaltern
3. unanimous
4. * pusillanimous
5. chastise
6. laboratory
7. literatim (adv.)
8. delinquent
9. derelict
10. locum tenens
11. locus classicus
12. * acquaint
13. * quaint
14. * connoisseur
15. notorious
16. notion
17. * novel
18. * novacain
19. annunciation
20. nuncio
21. perplex
22. plenum
23. plenary
24. plenipotentiary
25. plenitude
26. * supple
27. * radish
28. radicle
29. radicand
30. rugose
31. substratum
32. consternate
33. prostrate
34. term
35. terminology
36. terminate
37. * vermeil
38. * vermillion
39. vermicelli
40. vestigial
41. invest
42. very
43. verily
44. veracity
45. verism
46. veridical
47. cavity
48. cavern
49. * cage
50. concave
51. * decoy
52. * jail
53. terricolous

Exercise IV. Verb Review: Productive Verbs

Take one of the following and try to find <u>fifty</u> or more English derivatives. Use an etymological dictionary such as Partridge's <u>ORIGINS</u>.

1. ago: agere/actum
2. facio: facere/factum
3. duco: ducere/ductum
4. capio: capere/captum
5. mitto: mittere/missum
6. gero: gerere/gestum
7. venio: venire/ventum
8. dico: dicere/dictum

9. teneo: tenēre/tentum
11. lego: legere/lectum
13. jungo: jungere/junctum
15. paro: parare/paratum
17. verto: vertere/versum
19. rapio: rapere/raptum
21. puto: putare/putatum
23. video: vidēre/visum

10. tendo: tendere/tentum, tensum
12. iacio: jacere/jactum
14. pello: pellere/pulsum
16. porto: portare/portatum
18. vinco: vincere/victum
20. sto: stare/statum
22. rego: regere/rectum

SECTION THREE: Chapter One

PRACTICAL WORD STUDY: GREEK
GENERAL REMARKS & SIMPLE CHANGES: TRANSLITERATION

I - INTRODUCTION: General Remarks on Greek[1]

Greek, like Latin, is a highly inflected language. Nouns, pronouns, and adjectives are declined according to number (singular, plural, and even in a few instances, a dual, for two[2]), gender (masculine, feminine, neuter) and case (nominative, genitive, dative, accusative). There are three declensions of nouns and adjectives in Greek and these become easily recognizable for the student of Greek grammar because they follow certain patterns. As in Latin, each noun is listed in two forms, the nominative and the genitive because these two forms establish the pattern that the noun follows. Along with the two noun forms that show the declensional pattern, the definite article is given to show gender. Here Greek differs from Latin since Latin has no definite article, no article of any kind in fact. The expression hoi polloi ('the many', 'the common people': looked at from a snob's exculsive vantage point) shows the Greek definite article hoi ('the', in the nominative plural, masculine form to show that the expression refers to human beings) with the adjective polloi, the masculine nominative plural of polus meaning 'much, many', which gives us many English derivatives in poly- (as, for example, polyhedron, polysyllabic, polymorphous, polychrome, polyglot, polygon, polygraph, polysyndeton, polypody).

But, since the definite article is not otherwise used in English derivatives from Greek, the reader of this book will not be burdened with learning it. A second form of the noun, furthermore, will be given only when the base of the noun differs from the base of the nominative, as occurs frequently in the third declension of Greek nouns (as it does in Latin too).

Examples of Greek nouns and adjectives and how to find the bases:
Declension

I   archē 'beginning, rule': base: arch- archangel
     hōra 'hour, period of time': base: hor- horoscope
     politēs 'citizen': base polit- politics

---

1. For more information on inflection, see Section Two, Chapter One.

2. The dual was almost obsolete in Classical Greek, surviving primarily for natural pairs, such as hands, feet, a team of horses or oxen.

The nominative endings of the first declension are -e, -a, -es, and -as: the base is found by removing the nominative ending. Note: the -o- in horoscope and other examples is a connecting vowel.

II dēmos 'the people': base: dem- democracy
    metron 'measure': base: metr- metronome

Adjectives:
    mikros 'small': base: mikr- which becomes micr-: microscope
    megas (fem. megale) 'big': bases: mega-, megal-: megabucks, megalomorph [megas is an irregular adjective]

In the second declension, the nominative endings are regularly -on and -os which are removed to find the base.

III A- combining base found by removing nominative ending
     basileus 'king': combining base: basil-: basilica
     genos 'race, kind': base: gen-: genotype

B-   second base needed for combining form:
     pragma, pragmatos 'deed, thing done': base: pragmat-: pragmatic
     mētēr, mētros 'mother': base: metr-: metropolis
     sarx, sarkos 'flesh': base sark- which becomes in English sarc-: sarcophagus
     iris, iridos 'rainbow': base irid-: iris, iridescent

Adjective:
     pas, gen. pantos, neuter nom. pan 'all, every': bases: pan, pant-: panacea, pantograph

Greek Verbs
    Greek verbs are conjugated in general according to two patterns, thematic and athematic. The changes in form show person, number, tense (present, imperfect, future, aorist, perfect, pluperfect, future perfect), voice (active, middle, passive), and mood (indicative, optative, subjunctive, imperative, infinitive, participle). The Greek verb system is complex and very subtle. The tenses show not only the time of the action but its aspect (that is, whether it is a simple, single action or a continuous action, or a completed action). The voices show degrees of intimacy between the subject and the action of the verb: if the subject of a transitive verb simply performs the action on an object, then the active voice is used; if the action is performed on the subject, then the verb is passive; but if the subject is intimately involved in the action or does it for his, her, its, or their own benefit, then the middle voice is used.

In the vocabularies, Greek verbs will be given in the infinitive form. The following chart will explain the different infinitive endings.

I Thematic Verbs   --ein (active)

--esthai (middle: this form will be given for deponent verbs, verbs with no active)

-an (active for -a- stems)

II Athematic Verbs

--nai (active: the vowel preceding this ending varies)

--sthai (middle, for deponents)

Usually the present infinitive will be given, unless another form is used for the English derivatives.

In their various tenses, Greek verbs sometimes show several different stems: these will be given beside the infinitive form.

ballein 'throw' stems: ball-, blē-, bol-: ballistics, problem, diabolical

tithenai 'put' stem: thĕ: theme, thesis

EXERCISES

Exercise I

Nouns: give an English derivative of each of these: if there are two bases, give a derivative of each base. Learn these words: they will be used again. If no derivative occurs to you look in an English dictionary for words beginning with the base.

1. theos   God
2. logos   word[1]
3. metron   measure
4. bios   life
5. aēr   air

---

1. logos: To Aristotle, logos was what separated man from the animals. There is no simple way to define logos, a shortened list of its meanings may give the reader some idea of its use in Greek: computation, reckoning, account, relation, correspondence, ratio, proportion; explanation, plea, case, statement of a theory, argument, thesis, reason, formula, law, rule of conduct, debate, reason, abstract reasoning, talk, saying, oracle, proverb, subject matter, language, the Word or Wisdom of God, the person of Christ [cf. en archē(i) ēn ho logos].

6. sophos   wise
7. philos   beloved, dear, loving
8. phōs, phōt-   light
9. chrōma, chrōmat-   color
10. anthrōpos   human being

Verbs: give an English derivative of each. Find the base by removing the infinitive ending. For practice in recognizing verbs, identify which type of infinitive each is:

1. schizein 'split'
2. archein 'begin, rule' (cf. arche 'beginning, rule')
3. baptein 'dip'
4. dran 'do, act, perform' (base: dra-)
5. graphein 'write'
6. mainesthai: base: man- 'rage, be mad'

II - Changing Greek into Latin

Although there are some exceptions, Greek words usually pass through the intermediate step of Latin before being adopted by English. That is, in general, Greek words are made to conform to Latin spelling after being transliterated into the Roman alphabet. The Greek words given in this book in the vocabulary lists and examples have of course been transliterated into the writing system which we use (the Roman alphabet). But in many instances additional spelling changes must be made.

Consonants:
    k becomes c

Vowels:
    u becomes y   (unless used in a diphthong)

Diphthongs:
    ai becomes ae or e
    ie becomes e or i
    ou becomes u
    oi becomes oe or e or i

Endings:
    -os becomes -us
    -on becomes -um
    -ōn sometimes becomes -o   Kritōn: Crito
    -ē sometimes becomes -a   numphē: nympha

Note: there are two separate letters for -e- and for -o- in Greek e (short 'e') is epsilon; ē (long 'e') is eta; o (short 'o') is omicron; ō (long 'o') is omega. See appendix on the transliteration of Greek.

Exercise II

Change these transliterated Greek words into their Latin spellings. Give one English derivative of each. If necessary remove ending, add silent -e, or add a suffix.

1. krisis 'judgment'
2. kuklos 'circle'
3. ainigma 'riddle'
4. haima, haimat- 'blood'
5. daimōn 'a divinity'
6. dunamis 'power'
7. akros 'topmost'
8. korōnē 'anything curved: ring, crown'
9. Mousa one of the goddesses who sponsor the arts
10. oikos 'house'
11. peiratēs 'one who attempts'
12. phainomena 'things appearing' (participle, neuter plural)
13. papuros a writing material
14. phoinix a fabulous bird
15. psuchē 'soul'
16. skēnē 'tent, hut, stage-building'
17. thēsauros 'store, treasury'
18. krokodeilos 'lizard'
19. kalux 'cup of a flower'
20. gumnasion 'place for exercising'

Some place names:
21. Delphoi
22. Assuria
23. Thermopulai
24. Surakousai
25. Kithairōn (a mountain near Thebes)

Exercise III. Literary Figures

Change to their Latin spellings. If any are unfamiliar to you, find out what they wrote (and read it!).

1. Aischulos
2. Thoukudidēs
3. Platōn
4. Epikouros
5. Kallimachos
6. Hippokratēs
7. Isōkratēs
8. Sophoklēs
9. Theokritos

Exercise IV   Heroes, Heroines, Victims, Villains, and Monsters

Find out what weird and wonderful things these mythical figures did. Change to common spellings.

1. Klutaimnēstra
3. Oidipous
5. Kuklōps
7. Phoibos
9. Peirithōos
11. Tundareōs
13. Puthōn

2. Mēdeia
4. Phaidra
6. Apollōn
8. Chimaira
10. Aineias
12. Astuanax

SECTION THREE: Chapter Two

SIMPLE CHANGES IN FORMING ENGLISH WORDS FROM GREEK NOUNS

1. Direct entries with no change, or with only the changes required to standardize spelling. This is especially common with technical words in various fields, where the concept is taken directly from Greek and the word brought in unchanged.

> E.g.
> agapē 'love': English AGAPE
> Sometimes these words retain the direct transliterations,
>   without the Latin changes:
> dikē 'justice': used when writing of the Greek concept of
>   justice;
> hubris 'insolence, arrogance'

2. The base alone: the Greek word transliterated, but with the ending dropped:
> dikastēs 'member of the jury': DICAST

3. The base of the Greek word with silent -e added:
> tupos 'mark': TYPE
> metron 'measure': METRE (British spelling); METER

4. Common changes, following Latin:
> -eia becomes Latin -ia, English -Y
> politeia 'the relation of the citizen to the state':
>   POLITY
> -tia becomes -CY
> dēmokratia 'rule by the people': DEMOCRACY

5. Various and irregular changes:
> aēr: AIR (but cf. aero- as a prefix)
> eleēmosunē: ALMS (but cf. eleemosynary)
> thēsauros: TREASURE (but cf. thesaurus)

EXERCISES

Exercise I

1. Following the rules for changes, give the commmon spellings of Each of these proper nouns:

1. Aiguptos	2. Homēros
3. Eukleidēs	4. Hēsiodos
5. Aisōpos	6. Bakchos
7. Helenē	8. Dionusos
9. Troia	10. Kroisos

11. Aristotelēs   12. Boiōtia
13. Apollōn

2. Give a simple English derivative from each of these (do not add prefixes or suffixes). Then try to add a second derivative from the same Greek word: this may be a compound. * means that the word shows irregular change.

1. ergon   'work, deed'
2. therapeia 'service, treatment'
3. stoa 'porch'
4. Akadēmeia "Plato's school" [named after Akademos, a legendary Attic (i.e. Athenian) figure]
5. thumos (an aromatic herb)
6. theatron 'place for viewing'
7. metron 'measure'
8. sukophantēs 'informer'
9. kuklos 'circle'
10. puxos 'boxwood: box'
11. ōdē 'song'
12. agora 'marketplace'
13. aiōn 'age'
14. angelos 'messenger'
15. aspis 'shield, snake'
16. aithēr 'upper air'
17. astēr 'star'
18. athlētēs 'contestant'
19. axiōma 'that which is thought worthy'
20. baktērion 'staff, cane'
21. biblion 'book'
22. chaos 'empty space'
23. choros 'dance'
24. chrōma, chromat- 'color'
25. daimōn 'a divinity'
26. despotēs 'master, lord of the house'
27. * diakonos 'servant, attendant'
28. diaita 'way of living'
29. diskos 'a round plate'
30. * drakōn 'serpent'
31. ēchō 'sound'
32. eikōn 'image'
33. eirōneia 'dissimulation, purposely affected ignorance'
34. prosēlutos 'one who comes to a place'
35. ēthos 'custom'
36. historia 'inquiry'
37. *hōra 'period of time'
38. humnos 'song'
39. * kamara 'vaulted chamber'
40. kanōn 'rod, rule, standard'
41. kosmos 'order, universe'

42. ekleipsis 'a leaving out, failing'
43. lura 'stringed instrument'
44. mimos 'imitator'
45. pompē 'a sending: a solemn procession'
46. phōnē 'voice'
47. *scholē 'leisure'
48. sphaira 'a ball'
49. thronos 'a seat'
50. tupos 'mark'
51. * turannos 'ruler who comes to power by means other than
        rightful succession'
52. * zēlos 'eagerness'
53. phialē 'vessel, bowl' (2 simple derivatives: one regular,
        one showing irregular change)
54. papuros

Exercise II

A. Answer these questions, using a dictionary:

1. What have the Stoic philosophers to do with a porch (stoa)?
2. Explain the difference between cosmology and cosmetology.
3. See if you can find a theory explaining what a sycophant has to
do with a fig (sukon).

B. Using a dictionary, find the Greek base word of each of these
(all are in the exercises above): Find meanings of any that are
unfamiliar.

 1. jealousy
 2. atmosphere
 3. chum
 4. canonical hours
 5. story
 6. catechism, catechumen
 7. desk
 8. tarragon
 9. gas
10. echolalia
11. dais
12. anechoic
13. pendragon
14. choir
15. tragedy
16. allegorical
17. category
18. evangel
19. aspidistra

20. aspic
21. box
22. bushel
23. vial
24. paper

Vocabulary: Learn these Words   Fill in Derivatives

astēr (base: aster or astr-) star
axios   worthy
biblion   book
chrōma   color (base: chromat-)
daimōn   a divinity
eikōn   image
ergon   work, deed
ēthos   custom
hōra   period of time
kosmos   order, universe
kuklos   ring, circle
metron   measure
mimos   imitator
phōnē   voice
scholē   leisure
tupos   mark

Exercise III

Using a dictionary, give base word of each of these and give the meaning

1. disaster
2. chronaxy
3. chromium
4. pandemonium
5. iconostasis
6. argon
7. encyclopaedia
8. isometric
9. mimosa
10. saxophone
11. scholia
12. timbre
13. bibliotheca

QUISQUILIA

Words from myths and legends: find meanings, origins, and stories behind these words:

234

1. hermetic
2. panic
3. palladium
4. chimerical
5. gigantic
6. harpy
7. mentor
8. stentorian
9. mosaic
10. peony
11. phoenix
12. satyr
13. siren
14. sibyl
15. typhoon
16. tantalize
17. titanic
18. cyclopean
19. atlas
20. hydra
21. labyrinth
22. narcissistic
23. hector
24. phaeton
25. polyphemus moth
26. morphine
27. ocean
28. python
29. amazon
30. arethusa (orchid)
31. arctic
32. aegis
33. daedal
34. lethal
35. calliope
36. gorgon
37. ambrosia
38. Procrustean bed
39. Pandora's box (or jar)
40. Achilles' heel (tendon)
41. Midas' touch
42. Cadmean victory
43. a sop to Cerberus
44. to pile Pelion on Ossa
45. sow Dragon's teeth

SECTION THREE: Chapter Three

WORDS MADE FROM TWO NOUN BASES

Ancient Greek is a language rich in compounds. The extensive vocabulary of Greek is one of the delightful features of the language and has given rise to the much used expression, 'the Greeks had a word for it.'

The easiest formations derived from Greek for the student of English vocabulary to learn to use and recognize are those compounded from two bases: two nouns, an adjective and a noun, a verb and a noun. Because Greek itself is so fond of compounding and the methods of compounding in Greek are set out already, many modern terms (especially technical words) for things and concepts which the ancients did not know, are formed on the analogy of Greek.

Compounding nouns and nouns: connecting vowel:
Nouns of the <u>first</u> declension when forming the first element of a compound show -a- or -o- as the connecting vowel. Most modern formations use -o- on the analogy of the second declension. Nouns of the <u>second</u> declension usually use -o- to connect the first element of a compound to the second. Nouns of the <u>third</u> declension may show their own stem vowel or drop the ending and add -o- to the base.

The list below gives words commonly used as an element in compounds: most are derived from nouns, though some are verbal. Learn these well.

As first element:

PHILO- (before vowel phil-)   from <u>philos</u> 'loving, dear': indicates
love of : PHILOLOGY 'love of logos'
as the second element:
  -PHILE 'one loving'
  -PHILOUS or -PHILIC 'tending to love'
  -PHILIA (from <u>philia</u> 'love') 'tendency toward' or 'abnormal attraction to'

MISO-   (before a vowel, <u>mis</u>-) from <u>misos</u>, 'hatred': indicates
<u>hate</u> of: MISOLOGY 'hatred of logos'

As second element:

-METER from <u>metron</u>, 'measure' indicates 'an instrument for measuring' as THERMOMETER 'an instrument for measuring heat'

(<u>thermos</u>: 'hot')

-PHONE from phōnē 'voice': indicates 'sound or sound-emitting device' as TELEPHONE (<u>tele-</u> 'from afar')
-PHONY 'sound of a specified type'

-LATRY from <u>latreia</u> 'service for pay': indicates 'worship of' as IDOLATRY 'the worship of idols' (from <u>eidolon</u>, 'idol')

-LATER (from -<u>latrēs</u>) 'one who worships'
-LATROUS 'tending to worship'

-LOGY from Latin -<u>logia</u>, from Greek <u>logos</u> 'word': indicates 'discourse, speech' or 'the science, theory or study of' as ANTHROPOLOGY 'the study of mankind'

-PHOBIA from <u>phobos</u> 'fear' indicates 'fear of', as AGORAPHOBIA 'the fear of the marketplace, fear of open places'
-PHOBE indicates 'one who fears' as AGORPAPHOBE

-NOMY from <u>nomos</u> 'law, custom, usage': indicates 'systematized knowledge of or laws concerning' as ASTRONOMY

-SCOPE from <u>skopein</u> 'to look': indicates 'an instrument for observing, as TELESCOPE
-SCOPY indicates 'a viewing of'

-SOME from <u>sōma</u> 'body' : indicates 'body', as CHROMOSOME 'color-body'

-GONY from <u>goneia</u> 'generation' from <u>gonos</u> 'offspring, seed': indicates 'production of' as COSMOGONY 'the production of the universe'

-GENESIS from <u>genesis</u> 'birth, origin': indicates 'generation, birth' as PARTHENOGENESIS 'virgin-birth' (<u>parthenos</u> 'virgin')

-ONYM from <u>onoma</u> 'name' indicates 'name', as PSEUDONYM 'false name, pen name'

-MANCY from <u>manteia</u> 'prophecy' (from <u>mantis</u> 'seer') indicates 'telling the future by', 'divination by', as NECROMANCY 'telling the future by dead bodies'

-CRACY from <u>kratia</u> from <u>kratos</u> 'strength, power' indicates 'government or rule' as DEMOCRACY 'rule by the people'
-CRATIC 'having to do with government or rule'
-CRAT 'one participating in or supporting a form of government'

238

-IATRY   from <u>iatreia</u> 'healing' from <u>iatros</u> 'physician' indicates 'medical treatment' as PSYCHIATRY 'treatment of the soul/ mind'

-GRAPHY   fron <u>graphein</u> 'to write' indicates 1. a method of writing or drawing' as ICONOGRAPHY 'the drawing of images' or 2. 'a descriptive science of' as GEOGRAPHY 'the descriptive science of the earth'
-GRAPH   indicates 1. 'a means of drawing or writing' or 2. 'something drawn or written'
-GRAPHIC 'having to do with 1 or 2 above'
-GRAPHER 'a person who writes about a specific field or one who employs a specific means of writing or drawing."

-ARCHY   from <u>archia</u> from <u>archē</u> 'rule' indicates 'government or rule', as MONARCHY 'rule by one'
-ARCH   as first element indicates highest rank, as ARCHDEACON

-MANIA   from <u>mania</u> 'madness' indicates 'a madness for' or 'an exaggerated craving for' as BIBLIOMANIA
-MANIAC 'one displaying such an excessive desire for'

EXERCISES

Exercise I

Using vocabulary from the previous lessons with the compounding elements given above, take apart and define:

1. astrology	2. axiology
3. bibliography	4. chromatography
5. demonology	6. iconolatry
7. ergophobia	8. ethology
9. horoscope	10. cosmography
11. cyclometer	12. metronome
13. mimeograph	14. phonophobe
15. misology	16. philology
17. astrogenesis	18. bibliomania
19. demonocracy	20. iconology
21. ethography	22. cyclolatry
23. metroscope	24. phonograph
25. scotophobia	26. chromatophilia
27. aerometer	28. agoraphobia
29. archangel	30. choreograph
31. aeronomy	32. historiography
33. hymnody	34. hymnology
35. papyrology	36. ergonomy
37. horologiography (horologion 'a timepiece')	

38. cosmophonography (a proposed method of writing all the world's languages in one phonetic alphabet)
39. mimography (the art of writing gesture languages)
40. axioscotic (skotos 'shadow, darkness')

Exercise II

Make up words meaning:
1. systemized knowledge of the stars
2. a lover of books
3. morbid fear of [certain] colors
4. worship of demons
5. the method of drawing images
6. generation by work
7. an instrument for measuring the hours
8. an instrument for viewing the universe
9. telling the future by means of rings
10. the science of measurement
11. the study of sound
12. the theory of colors

NEW VOCABULARY   Learn these as you do the exercise to follow
Fill in Derivatives

aitia   cause
algos   pain
anemos   wind
anthrōpos   human being
anēr, andr-   man
atmos   steam, vapor
bios   life
chronos   time
dēmos   the people
dendron   tree
ethnos   nation, people
gamos   marriage, sexual union
gē   earth (geo- combining form)
glōtta/glōssa   tongue
gunē, gunaik(o)-   woman
haima, haimato-   blood
hēlios   sun
histos   web, tissue
hudor; hudro-   water
hupsos   height
ichthus   fish
karpos   fruit
kephalē   head
kruos   frost
lithos   stone

lukos   wolf
martur   witness
mētēr, mētro—   mother
morphē   form, shape, outward appearance
muthos   speech, story
naus   ship: nautes sailor   —naut 'sailor'
nekros   corpse
nephos   cloud
oikos   house (oeco—, eco—)
ornis, ornitho—   bird
oros   mountain
osteon   bone
pais, paido—   child
patēr, patro—   father
pathos   suffering, experience   —pathy illness'
petra   rock
phōs, phōto—   light
ploutos   wealth, riches
polis   city, city-state
pous, pod—   foot
psuchē   soul, breath, life
pur   fire
rhiza   root
skia   shadow
sōma, sōmat(o)—   body
stēthos   chest
stichos   line, verse
taphos   tomb
tektōn   worker, carpenter, builder
technē   art, skill
telos   end
theos   God
therapōn/theraps   attendant   therapeia treatment
tokos   birth
topos   place
xenos   foreigner, stranger
xulon   wood
zōon   living thing, animal

Exercise III

(taking the words in the order given above):   define the
words and answer the questions:

1. etiology
give an example of an etiological myth or story.

2. algometer
-ALGIA as a suffix indicates 'pain in a specified area' as NEURALGIA: gives three additional -algias.

3. anemometer
Give an example of an anemochore (a plant with seeds or spores dispersed by the wind). What is another name for windflowers?

4. misanthrope
What do you call a person who loves his fellow human beings?
What is the science that studies human beings?
Give an example of anthropomorphism.

5. androgenous
Explain the word philander and how its modern meaning developed.

6. atmosphere
What is an instrument for measuring vapor called?

7. biography
Give ten additional words from bios.

8. Chronology
give a word meaning an instrument to measure time.

9. democracy
give a word for 'one who fears the people'.

10. dendrology
Name a 'tree-loving' plant.
Name the science that is concerned with the age (i.e. TIME) of trees.

11. ethnology
Find out what an ethnarch is.
Give an example of ethnocentric behavior.
Give an example of ethnogamy.

12. misogamy
Look up the etymology of gamete: what has it to do with gamos?

13. geology
What is the etymological meaning of geometry? What does this tell you about the origin of the science of geometry?
Look up geodesy/geodesic and explain why a geodesic dome is so called.
Give ten words using GEO- as a prefix.

14. glossary
From what language is the suffix of glossary?

242

Find out what a <u>bugloss</u> is: animal, vegetable, or mineral?
What is a <u>gloss</u>?
Give a synonym for <u>gloze</u>.
Define <u>glossalalia</u> and tell where it occurs.

15. gynandry
How (if at all) does <u>gynandry</u> differ from <u>androgyny</u>?
The <u>gynaeceum</u> was a feature of an ancient Greek house: what was it?
What is <u>gynecocracy</u>? Do you know a place, real or fictitious where it is practiced?

16. hemophilia
What is a <u>hematozoon</u>?
What is the science that studies blood called?

17. heliograph
Why was the gas <u>helium</u> so named?

18. histogenesis
Give a word meaning 'the study of tissue'.
Give a word meaning 'the study of tissue disorder (suffering)'.

19. hydrometer
Why is rabies called <u>hydrophobia</u>?
Look up <u>clepsydra</u> and give its meaning.
What is <u>dropsy</u> and why is it so named?
What have these words to do with water:

hydrogen	carbohydrate
hydra	hydrochloric
formaldahyde	hydrangea
hydrocephaly	hydromancy?

20. hypsography
What does an <u>hypsometer</u> measure when it can get up that high?

21. ichthyornis
The symbol of the fish with the Greek letters IXΘYΣ in it is an acronym for <u>Iēsous Christos Theou Huios Sōtēr</u>: translate.
What does an <u>ichthyopolist</u> sell and an <u>ichthyophagist</u> eat?

22. carpolith (or carpolite)
What is a <u>carpel</u>? Where does the diminutive -el come from?
If a plant had <u>carpomania</u>, what would its problem be?
Greek <u>karpos</u> is cognate with English <u>harvest</u> and Latin <u>carpere</u>: can you give a derivative of Latin carpere?

23. cephalopod
Does <u>hydrocephalous</u> correctly describe a condition?

24. cryogenics
What might cryotherapy be good for?
Give words meaning 'an instrument for measuring frost' and an 'instrument for examining frost'.

25. lithography
Define: lithology,   lithosphere,   lithostratigraphy,   lithopone.
Which of these is part Latin?
Look up and define litharge and chrysolite.

26. lycanthropy
A lycanthrope would most likely be seen on   a) the six o'clock news   b) a soap opera   c) a crime drama   d) creature features
What is a lycopodium?

27. martyrology
What would you call a 'writing about witnesses'?

28. metropolis
Do you know of any culture where metronyms are employed?
The name of the goddess Demeter has been interpreted as meaning 'earth-mother': can you think of any attributes of Demeter that would make this title appropriate?

29. geomorphology
The study of a language is often divided into morphology and syntax: explain why this is so.
Look up and define morpheme.

30. mythology
give five other words derived from muthos:

31. cosmonaut
What does each of these sail in or on or among?
          astronaut
          aeronaut
          aquanaut
          Argonaut

32. necrology
Cut out the necrology section of your local paper.
Use each of these in a coherent sentence:
          necromancer
          necropolis
          necrophilia
          necroscopy
Where would you be least likely to meet a necrophobe: a) at Madison Square Garden   b) at tea   c) on a train   d) at a mortuary

33. nephelometer
Make up five other words using nephalo- and define each.
Find out why nepheline is so named.

34. ecology
Find out what each of these has to do with oikos (house):
economy, parish, diocese, ecumenism, ecospecies, ecosystem

35. ornithocracy
Who might advocate such a system of government [if interested,
read Aristophanes' BIRDS]?
What is the science that studies birds?

36. orogeny
What is a treatise on mountains called?
What is an oread and where does one live?

37. osteopathy
What is a teleost?

38. pediatry
Look up and give the meaning and derivation of pedant.

39. patriarch
Do you know anyone who uses a patronymic?
What does patriot have to do with pater?

40. pathogenesis
What is wrong with a psychopath?
What is the study of diseases called?
What language is the first element of sociopath from?

41. petrology
Look up the derivations of: Peter
                             parsley
                             petroleum

42. photography
What is a person who cannot stand light called?
What would you call a person with an inordinate craving to turn on
lights? Why is phosphate so named?

43. plutocracy
plutodemocracy
plutomania: can you think of any person, real or fictional, who
suffers from this particular madness?
plutology & plutonomy: explain why these have been used as alter-
native names for the science of political economy.

44. necropolis

245

Name a city that has an acropolis.
What is the etymological meaning of metropolis?
Give the meanings of these words derived from polis:
     policlinic, cosmopolis, megalopolis, Decapolis, Naples (what
     do you call a native of Naples), propolis.

45. Antipodes
What is the medical treatment of feet called?
Look up pew and find out what it has to do with feet.

46. psyche
Divide and define the parts of psychedelic.
Give five additional words from psychē.

47. pyre
Look up and define empyreal.
What is an informal synonym for pyromaniac?
What is pyrography?
How does a person practicing pyromancy operate?

48. rhizobium
Give the etymology of licorice.
Take apart and define: rhizomorph, rhizopod, rhizocephalan,
rhizogenic.

49. skiaphobe
Divide and define and use in a sentence: skiascope and skiagra-
phy. Look up squirrel and explain what it has to do with a
shadow.

50. chromosome
Take apart and figure out the meaning of somatoetiological.
How does the meaning of somatopsychic differ from that of psycho-
somatic?

51. stethemia
What do you call 'an instrument for examining the chest'?
an instrument for measuring the chest?

52. stichometry
Find an example of stichomythia in a literary work.

53. architect
technocracy

54. teleology
What is a talisman and by what steps does it come from telos?

55. theosophy (-SOPHY from sophia 'wisdom')
Give five additional words with their meanings from theos.

Look up the following and define their elements:
Theodicy, theophany, theomachy.
Find the origin of enthusiasm.
What is Hesiod's Theogony about?

56. heliotherapy
Make up five words ending in -therapy and tell what they are good
for.

57. tocology
Explain the meaning of Theotokos.

58. toponomy
What would a person about to be tested on the topography of Athens
have to know about?
What do these mean: topic, topical, toponym, topiary, topotype?

59. xenophobia
Explain how xenogamy is a synonym for cross-fertilization.
Describe the habits of one suffering from xenomania.
What is xenoglossy?

60. xylophone
Give another name for engraving (i.e. drawing or writing on wood).

61. zoology
Explain the ending of zoon. What is the plural?
Make up words with the following meanings:
a. the description of animals
b. the description of the distribution of animals on the surface
   of the earth
c. animal worship
d. measurement of animals
e. systemized study of or laws relating to animals
f. something shaped like an animal
g. animal lover (or a plant whose seeds are disseminated by
   animals)
h. fear of animals

REVIEW OF NOUNS

Match each word with the meaning of the first element of the compound; give meanings of other elements. Try to do this without
looking up the words: study any that you have to look up.

247

I

1. etiology	a. fish
2. hypsolatry	b. wind
3. pedophobia	c. head
4. patriarch	d. height
5. ichthyomancy	e. universe
6. algogenesis	f. fruit
7. anemophile	g. father
8. carpolith	h. human being
9. pathosocial	i. rock
10. anthropology	j. pain
11. androgenous	k. voice
12. cephalalgia	l. cause
13. petroleocrat	m. man (male)
14. phonoxenograph	n. suffering
15. cosmography	o. child

II

1. photolithotype	a. ring
2. cryotherapy	b. stone
3. astrophobia	c. city-state
4. atmoscope	d. star
5. cyclography	e. wolf
6. plutogenous	f. soul
7. bibliolater	g. frost
8. lithosphere	h. light
9. politarch	i. witness
10. podomania	j. color
11. bionomy	k. steam, vapor
12. lycolatry	l. book
13. psychopomp	m. life
14. chromatonomy	n. foot
15. martyrdom	o. wealth

III

1. pyrotechnics	a. time
2. metropolis	b. divinity
3. metronome	c. shape
4. chronoscope	d. body (living)
5. rhizopod	e. tree
6. demononomy	f. body (dead)
7. morphonomy	g. mother
8. demophile	h. measure
9. mythophile	i. the people
10. dendrogeography	j. fire
11. somatochrome	k. speech, story
12. aeronaut	l. chest
13. necroscopy	m. image
14. iconoscope	n. air
15. stethemia	o. root

IV

1. stichography	a. house
2. ergomania	b. end
3. nepheloscope	c. mountain
4. technocracy	d. nation
5. ecology	e. tongue
6. ethnodicy (dike 'justice')	f. cloud
7. ethography	g. earth
8. ornithographer	h. custom
9. teleozoon	i. bone
10. orogeny	j. line
11. gamogenesis	k. God
12. osteopathy	l. marriage
13. geomorphology	m. bird
14. glossography	n. skill
15. theomania	o. work

V

1. gynandromorph	a. birth
2. hematozoon	b. wood
3. tocology	c. hatred
4. toponomy	d. place
5. osteopathy	e. web
6. heliotype	f. foreigner
7. histopathology	g. animal
8. horography	h. blood
9. xenomorph	i. sun
10. xylophobia	j. water
11. zoocracy	k. hour
12. hydrometer	l. name
13. philanthropy	m. love
14. misogyny	n. woman
15. onomatomancy	o. bone

ANSWERS

I 1-l; 2-d; 3-o; 4-g; 5-a; 6-j; 7-b; 8-f; 9-n; 10-h; 11-m; 12-c; 13-i; 14-k; 15-e

II 1-h; 2-g; 3-d; 4-k; 5-a; 6-o; 7-l; 8-b; 9-c; 10-n; 11-m; 12-e; 13-f; 14-j; 15-i

III 1-j; 2-g; 3-h; 4-a; 5-o; 6-b; 7-c; 8-i; 9-k; 10-e; 11-d; 12-n; 13-f; 14-m; 15-l

IV 1-j; 2-o; 3-f; 4-n; 5-a; 6-d; 7-h; 8-m; 9-b; 10-c; 11-l; 12-i; 13-g; 14-e; 15-k

V 1-n; 2-h; 3-a; 4-d; 5-o; 6-i; 7-e; 8-k; 9-f; 10-b; 11-g; 12-j; 13-m; 14-c; 15-l

QUISQUILIA: words from Greek history and geography
Find the meanings of these as common nouns or adjectives and explain how the modern meanings relate to the original meaning.

1. marathon (and various -thons): from Marathon, a place in Attica
2. solecism: from Soloi, a place in Cilicia colonized by Athenians
3. currant: from Corinth
4. laconic: from Lakōn, 'Spartan'
5. attic: from Attikos 'of Attica', the hinterland of Athens
6. magnet: from Magnēs ('of Magnesia')
7. copper: from Kuprios 'from Cyprus'
8. meander: from Maiandros, a river in Phrygia
9. mausoleum: from Mausolos, satrap of Caria in the fourth c. B.C.
10. parchment: from Pergamenos 'of Pergamum', the center of a Hellenistic kingdom in Asia Minor
11. pheasant: from Phasis, a river in the Caucasus
12. caryatid: from Karuai, a village in Laconia
13. philipic: from Philip, Macedonian king
14. pyrrhic victory: from Pyrrhus
15. byzantine: from Byzantium
16. colossal: from Colossos, a giant statue of Apollo in the harbor at Rhodes
17. sybarite: from Sybaris, a city in southern Italy

Other words and expressions having to do with Greek history and politics: find out what they refer to in classical culture and what they mean now:
1. ostracize
2. draconian
3. solon
4. ephebe
5. ephor
6. amphictyony
7. 'as rich as Croesus'
8. 'the sword of Damocles'
9. 'owls to Athens'

SECTION THREE: Chapter Four

WORDS MADE FROM ADJECTIVE AND NOUN BASES

Study this list of Greek Adjectives and then work on the exercises. The combining form is given in upper case.

akros   topmost: ACRO-
allos   other: ALLO-
aristos   best, most fit: ARISTO-
autos   self: AUTO-
barus   heavy: BARY-, BARI-, BARO-
bathus   deep: BATHY-, BATHO-
brachus   short: BRACHY-
etumos   true: ETYMO-
eurus   wide: EURY-
gumnos   naked: GYMNO-
heteros   one of two, other: HETERO-
hieros   holy, sacred: HIERO-
holos   whole: HOLO-
homos   one and the same: HOMO-
homoios   like HOMEO-, HOMOIO-
hugros   wet, moist: HYGRO-
idios   one's own, peculiar: IDIO-
isos   equal ISO-
kainos   new: CENO- CAENO-; as second element -CENE
kakos   bad, ugly: CACO-
kalos   beautiful: KAL-, CALO-; CALLI-
kenos   empty CENO-, KEN-
koinos   common: CENO-, COENO-
makros   long: MACRO-
megas, base: megal- big, large, great MEGA-, MEGALO-; as second
        element: -MEGALY 'enlargement'
mikros   small, little: MICRO-
monos   alone, only, single MONO-
murios   countless, 10,000: MYRIA-
neos   new: NEO-
oligos   few, little: OLIGO-
orthos   straight, right, correct: ORTHO-
oxus   sharp: OXY-
palaios   old (from palai, adv. 'long ago'): PALEO-, PALAEO-
pas, neuter pan; base: pant- all: PAN-, PANTO-
platus   wide, broad: PLATY-
polus   much, many: POLY-
        comparative: pleion 'more, greater' PLIO-, PLEO-
        superlative: pleistos 'most, greatest': PLEISTO-
prōtos   first: PROTO-
pseudēs   false: PSEUDO-
sophos   wise, clever: SOPHO-

251

as second element, from <u>sophia</u> 'wisdom': -SOPHY
stenos narrow: STENO-
stereos firm, solid: STEREO-
tele (adverb) far away: TELE-
thermos warm, hot: THERMO-
trachus rugged, harsh: TRACH-, TRACHY-
xēros dry, harsh: XERO-

EXERCISES

Exercise I

Practice the new vocabulary by working on these: Fill in meaning of each Greek adjective.

1. AKROS
Take apart and define:
acronym
    Give some examples of acronyms:
acrophobia
acrocarpous
acromegaly
acrodont (odont- 'tooth')
What is the upper, fortified part of a city called?

2. ALLOS
form words meaning:
a. the name of one person assumed by another [i.e. 'other-name']
b. a signature made by one person for another [i.e. 'other-writing']
Take apart and define parts:
    allogamy
    allometry
    allopathy
    allophone
Look up and give origin and meaning of:
    agio
    allegory

3. ARISTOS
    Give a word meaning: 'government by the best'
Take apart and define:
    aristotype
    aristocrat
N.B. ARISTOS is not to be confused with ARISTON 'breakfast': <u>Aristology</u> is 'the science of dining'.

4. AUTOS
Divide into parts and define:

autonomy
autocracy
autograph
autoecious
autogamy

Give antonyms for: autograph and autogamy
Make up or find ten additional words beginning with AUTO-, and
give their meanings.
Give meanings of the following and use each in a sentence:
autochthonous (chthon 'earth')
autacoid (akos 'remedy')
autarky (arkein 'suffice')

5. BARUS Take apart and define:
barysphere
baryon
barium: why was this element so named?
baritone (tonos: accent, tone)
isobar
barometer: for what is this instrument used?

6. BATHUS
1. What is bathos? Explain how it differs from pathos. Which is
proper to tragedy and which to soap-opera or melodrama?
2. Take apart and define:
bathysphere
batholith
bathometer
bathymetry
3. Look up bathyscaph.

7. BRACHUS
1. Define brachylogy and give an example.
2. Take apart and define:
brachydactylia [daktulos 'finger']
brachypterous [pteron 'wing, feather']
brachycephalic

8. ETYMOS
Give the etymological meaning of ETYMOLOGY
Explain why the etymological meaning of a word does not always
conform to usage.
What is an ETYMON?
What is etymography? Do you think it is an efficient system, or
do you find it cacographic?
Do you regard an etymologicon as a valuable resource for use with
this book?

9. EURUS
Eurydice: who was she and what does her name mean?

Take apart and define:
    eurypterid
    eurycephalic
    eurybathic
    eurythermal
    eurygnathous [gnathos: jaw]

10. GUMNOS
Take apart and define:
    gymnobiblism
    gymnosperm [sperma, spermat- 'seed']
    gymnosophist: what is the modern counterpart?

11. HETEROS
Take apart and define:
    heterology
    heteronomous
    heteromorphic
    heterography: can you think of a language that exhibits
        heterography?
    heteromerous [meros 'part']

12. HIEROS
Take apart and define:
    hierocracy [can you give an example of this form of govern-
        ment?]
    hierodule [doulos 'slave']
    hierarchy
Look up the name Jerome and find its original spelling and etymo-
    logical meaning.

13. HOLOS
Take apart and define:
    holograph
    holotype
    holozoic
    Holocene (kainos)

14. HOMOS
    homogeneous: define and give an antonym
    homogamy: define
    homograph: define and give three examples
    homologous: define and use in a sentence
    homonym: give three examples of homonyms

15. HOMOIOS
Take apart and define:
    homeopathy
    homoiothermous
    homeomorphism

254

16. HYGROS
Give words meaning:
    a. an instrument for measuring humidity.
    b. an instrument for examining humidity.
    c. an instrument that records humidity.

17. IDIOS
Why is a disease of unknown cause called idiopathy?
A thing that has its own shape or form is called an _____.
Take apart and define:
    idiolatry
    idiograph
    idiobiology
    idiochromosome
    idiometer
Look up idiot and give its etymology. Explain how it got the meaning it has today.

18. ISOS
Take apart and define:
    isosceles [skelos: leg]
    isotope
    isotherm
    isogloss
    isomer
    isochronal
    isotone

19. KAINOS
Take apart and define:
    cenogenesis
    Cenozoic
    pliocene
    pleistocene
What is kainite and why is it so named?

20. KALOS (KALLOS 'beauty')
Take apart and define:
    kaleidoscope [eidos 'form': 'that which is seen']
    calligraphy
    callisthenics [sthenos 'strength']
After what mythical person was the Calliope named?

21. KAKOS
Take apart and define:
    cacophony
    cacography
    caceconomy

cacoepy (epos: word)

cacology: do you know anyone who practises cacology?

caconym: find an example of a caconym in scientific terminology.

cacoethes: give an example.

   N.B. the particularly bad habit of constantly finding fault is called cacoethes carpendi: avoid it!

22. KENOS
Take apart and define:
   cenotaph [taphos 'tomb']
   cenosphaira
Look up and give meaning of kenosis. What term is used by the Western Church to express the same act?

23. KOINOS
Take apart and define:
   cenobium
   What is the ruler or leader of a cenobium called?
   coenopsyche
   coenosarc [sarx, sarkos 'flesh']
   coenotype
   coenosome

24. MEGAS [MEGA-, MEGALO-]
Take apart and define:
   megalomania
   megalith
   omega
Make up or find ten additional words using mega-, megal(o)-, or -megaly.

25. MIKROS
Take apart and define:
   microbe
   microcosm
   omicron
Give ten additional words and their meanings, using micro-.

26. MAKROS
Take apart and define:
   macron
   macrocephaly
   macrocosm
   macromolecule
Give five additional words with their meanings using macro-.

27. MONOS
Look up minster and give the original Greek word and its closest

English derivative.
Give the Greek original of <u>monk</u>.
Take apart and define:
    monocracy
    monarch
    monoecious
    monomer
Give ten additional words using <u>mon(o)</u>-.

28. MURIOS
Take apart and define:
    myriopod
    myriameter

29. NEOS
Explain the ending of <u>neon</u> and find out why the gas is so named.
Take apart and define:
    neology
    Neocene

30. OLIGOS
Define: Oligocene
What is government by the few called?

31. ORTHOS
Take apart and define:
    orthodox
        What is the opposite of orthodoxy?
    orthoepy
    orthostichy
    orthoscope
Give a word meaning 'correct-writing' (i.e. 'proper spelling').

32. OXUS
Take apart and define:
    oxytone
    oxymoron (<u>mōros</u> 'foolish, dull'): give an example of an
        <u>oxymoron</u>.
Find out why <u>oxygen</u> was so named and explain why the name is inappropriate.

33. PALAIOS
Take apart and define:
    paleobotany [<u>botanē</u> 'pasture, herb, grass']
    palaeography
Give ten additional words using <u>paleo</u>-, <u>palaeo</u>- with their meanings.

34. PAS [PAN-, PANTO-]

Take apart and define:
    pantheon
    pantomime
    pancreas [kreas 'flesh, meat']
Look up and give meanings and use in sentences:
    panoply
    panegyric
    panacea

35. PLATUS
Trace the derivation of: place, plaza, piazza, plate, plateau, platitude.
Describe a platypus.

36. POLUS
Take apart and define:
        polyhistor
        polyglot
        polyphone
What is the state of having more than one husband called?
And the state of having more than one wife?
Use hoi polloi in a sentence.

37. PRŌTOS
Look up and explain the etymology of:
        protein
        protocol (Explain how kolla 'glue' is attached to the
                    meaning.)
Give five additional words beginning with proto

38. PSEUDĒS
Give three examples of pseudonyms.
Find or invent five words using pseudo- and give their meanings.

39. SOPHOS
Sophomore: look up this word and trace the steps in its spelling.
(Contrary to pupular opinion, sophomore does not combine the two
elements sopho- + moros 'fool'.)
What does a gymnosophist wear?
Divide and define:
        philosophy
        theosophy

40. STENOS
Explain parts and give meanings of:
        stenography
        stenotype

41. STEREOS
   What is <u>stereo</u> short for?
   What is a <u>steropticon</u>?
   Give a five letter word for 'one cubic meter'.
Divide and define: <u>stereoscope</u>.
Look up <u>cholesterol</u> and explain its parts.

42. TELE
Take apart and define:
   telepathy, telegony
Give ten additional words using <u>tele-</u> with their meanings.

43. THERMOS
Take apart and define: <u>isotherme</u>.
What is an instrument for measuring heat?
What is a written record of such an instrument?

44. TRACHUS
Why is the <u>trachea</u> so named?
Take apart and define:
   Trachyglossa
   trachycarpous

45. XĒROS
Explain why the <u>xerox</u>-process was so named.
Take apart and define: <u>xerography</u>.
Look up, give etymology and meaning of:
   elixir
   phylloxera
What kind of plant might be called a <u>xerophil</u>?

List of new nouns from previous exercises: Fill in Derivatives

chthŏn earth
daktulos finger
dikē right, law, justice
epos word
gnathos jaw
kreas flesh, meat
meros part
mōros fool (as adjective, foolish, dull)
odous (or odōn), base: odont- tooth
pteron feather, wing
sarx, sark- flesh
skelos leg
sperma, spermat(-o-) seed
sthenos strength
tonos accent, tone
taphos tomb

QUISQUILLIA: WORDS FROM GREEK PHILOSOPHY

A. words used in everday speech: find out where these come from, what they mean, and how they apply to Greek philosophy or philosophers.

academic
epicure
platonic love
stoical
Socratic irony
cynical
skeptical
peripatetic
sophistry
dialectic

B. other words from the Greek philosophers and words used to describe philosophical schools: find out what these mean and what schools or philosophers they are associated with:

eidos: theory of 'ideas'
Heraclitean flux (panta rhei)
lyceum
neoplatonism
ataraxia
metempsychosis
entelechy
demiurge
eudaimonia
acrasia
mimesis
hylozoism
presocratic
Milesian school
Eleatics
isonomia
apatheia
anamnesis
Orphism

PART TWO: WORDS FROM NUMBERS

Learn these Greek numbers and related words and their Latin counterparts:

ENGLISH	GREEK	LATIN
half	hēmisus: HEMI-	semi-
one	heis, mia, HEN	unus (I)
first	prōtos	primus
single	monos	singuli-ae-a
two	duo (DI-, DY-)	duo (II)
second	deuteros	secundus
double	diploos	duplex
in two	dicha (DICHO-)	
three	treis, tria (TRI-)	tres, tria (III)
third	tritos	tertius
triple	triploos	triplicus
four	tessares (TETRA-)	quattuor (IV)
five	PENTE	quinque (V)
six	HEX	sex (VI)
seven	HEPTA	septem (VII)
eight	OKTŌ	octo (VIII)
nine	ENNEA	novem (IX)
ten	DEKA	decem (X)
hundred	HEKATON	centum (C)
thousand	CHILIOI	mille (M)
number	ARITHMOS	numerus
angle	GŌNIA	angulus
plane	HEDRA ('seat')	planum
line	GRAMMĒ	linea

Notes: with Greek numbers, the suffix -AD means 'a group of': TRIAD. NANO- indicates very small size or 'one billionth', from Greek nannos, 'dwarf' as in nanoplankton, nanosecond.

EXERCISES ON GREEK NUMBERS

Exercise I

Take these words apart and give meanings:

1. trilogy
2. chilometer (give alternate spelling)
3. logarithm
4. icosahedron (from eikosi, 'twenty')
5. hemistich
6. diplopia (-opia refers to a condition of the eyes)

7. dichogamous
9. octameter
11. goniometer
13. dyad
15. henotherm
17. pentateuch (teuchos, 'tool, case, writing materials: volume')
18. arithmomancy
19. decathlon (athlon 'prize: contest')

8. tetrarchy
10. polygon
12. pentagon
14. diplodocus (dokos, 'beam')
16. tetrahedron

20. tripod

21. orthagonal
23. octahedron
25. polyhedron
27. pentagram
29. enneagon
31. hexahedron

22. triad
24. polygon
26. dipody
28. enneaeteric (etos, 'year')
30. decalogue
32. hendecasyllabic
(syllabic='of syllables')

33. distich
35. heptagon
37. octopus (give plural)
39. dichotomy (-tomy from temnein 'to cut')

34. pentad
36. ennead
38. tetralogy

40. hemipterous

41. hexagram
43. Heptateuch
45. monograph
47. tricycle
49. octomerous
50. Hexteuch

42. chiliad
44. pentathlon
46. monostichous
48. enneastyle (stulos:
'column')

Exercise II

ARITHMOS/NUMERUS: fill in the numbers: (words are from Greek and Latin)

1. September, October, November, and December were originally _____the, _____, _____, and _____months in the old Roman calendar which began in March.

2. A millennium is a period of _____ _____s.

3. A kilogram weighs_____ grams.

4. A hectare is a unit of area equal to _____ ares (or 2,471
acres).

5. A tetrapod has _____ _____.

6. A dodecahedron has _____ _____s.

7. A unicorn is a fabulous beast that has_____spiraled_____ projecting from its forehead.

8. A monochrome print has_____ _____.

9. A triglyph is an ornament in a Doric frieze having_____ parallel vertical channels on its face.

10. A triptych is a tableau (used as an altarpiece) consisting of _____folding panels (from ptuche, 'fold')

11. A trimester is a period of_____months.

12. In the book of Deuteronomy, the ___of Moses is stated a _____ time.

13. A pentestich is a poem or stanza consisting of ____ _____s.

14. Primogeniture is the right of the_____-born son to inherit the entire estate of his parents.

QUISQUILIA: Find the numbers in each of these words & give
         meaning

1. hyphen
2. hendiadys
3. kilo
4. hecatomb
5. dean
6. tessara
7. trapezoid
8. diploma
9. dimity
10. hebdomad
11. Pentecost
12. Tetragrammaton
13. trivet
14. tetra (fish)
15. diphthong
16. dilemma

SECTION THREE: Chapter Five:

GREEK SUFFIXES

I- General noun and adjective forming suffixes

-ic and -tic 'pertaining to, having to do with'
                    ETHNIC, STATIC

-ac (used instead of -ic if an -i- immediately precedes)
                    CARDIAC

-ics 'things having to do with': 'art science, study of' (used
        with singular verb) from -ika (neuter plural)
                    POLITICS

-ical 'pertaining to' (-ic + -al from Latin)
                    POLITICAL

-oid 'resembling, like, -shaped'
                    ANDROID

-ite 'one connected with, inhabitant of'; also 'a
        commercial product   SYBARITE, LUCITE

-ism 'the belief in, profession of, practice of'
                    HYLOZOISM

-ist 'one who believes in, professes, or practices'
                    PLATONIST

-ast 'one who does'   DICAST
-isk, iscus 'little'   ASTERISK

-ia, -y abstract noun-forming suffix, 'act, state of'
                    POLITY

-sis abstract noun-forming suffix, 'act, state of'
                    METEMPSYCHOSIS

-ma (base: -mat-), -m, -me 'result of'
                    THEOREM, THEME, DOGMA

EXERCISES: Take these words apart and give meanings:

1. scholasticism   2. misoneism (neos)
3. chiliast   4. henotic
5. android   6. asterism
7. gynobiblism   8. macrobiotic

9. pandemonium
10. demotics
11. Georgics (ergon)
12. gynandromorphism
13. theism (how does theism differ from deism)
14. sophist
15. kenosis
16. archetypical (use in a
  sentence)

17. onomastic
18. misogamist
19. philanthropic
20. papyrologist
21. chiliastic
22. goniometrical
23. hemimorphic
24. etiological
25. anthropocentric
26. philandry
27. goniometrical
28. axiomatic
29. biologist
30. bionomics
31. chromatics
32. demoniac
33. pandemic
34. demotist
35. dendroid
36. iconic
37. ethnodicy
38. ethnocentrism
39. ethnotechnics
40. ethicality
41. geotectonic
42. geoponic
43. gamic
44. gynecocratic
45. hemophiliac
46. heliotherapeutic
47. heliocentric
48. histopathologist
49. horologic
50. hypsographic
51. ichthyic
52. carpolithic
53. orthocephalic
54. cosmological
55. cryogenics
56. cycloid
57. monolithic
58. lithostratigraphical
59. lycanthropic
60. martyrologist
61. metronymic
62. isometrics
63. mimetic
64. morphosis
65. nautical
66. necrosis
67. nephologist
68. autoecious
69. osteoid
70. orthopedist
71. allopatric
72. protopathic
73. petrographic
74. phoneme
75. plutocratic
76. photographic
77. polotics
78. psychic
79. pyrotechnics
80. rhizomorphic
81. skiagraphic
82. somatopsychic
83. stichic
84. polytechnic
85. teleological
86. theological
89. paleozoic
90. zodiac (zodion: diminutive
  of zoon)

91. acrophobic
92. allomerism
93. aristocratic
94. autobiographical
95. baryspheric
96. batholithoid
97. brachycephalic
98. etymological
99. eurypterid
100. eurybathic
101. gymnastics
102. hierarchic
103. holographic
104. homocentric

105. homeomorphism
106. hygroscopic
107. idiomatic
108. isometric
109. callisthenics
110. caconymic
111. cenobite
112. macroscopic
113. megalocephalic
114. monochromatic
115. neologism
116. oligarchical
117. orthodontist
118. polydemic
119. protagonist
120. deuteragonist
121. tritagonist
122. pseudonymous
123. sophistic
124. stenotopic
125. stereoscopic
126. telepathic
127. xerosis
128. botanist
129. autochthonous

Make up words meaning:

1. one who studies causes
2. one who studies winds
3. human-like
4. a little star
5. having to do with the globe of vapor
6. one who studies what is worthy (i.e. value judgments)
7. one afflicted with a mad desire for books
8. one who studies small life
9. having to do with many colors
10. having to do with time
11. things having to do with written records concerning the people
    (i.e. populations)
12. one who studies trees
13. having to do with nations
14. things having to do with customs
15. one who studies customs (i.e. animal behaviour)
16. earthlike
17. one who studies tongues
18. one having many marriages
19. one who studies women
20. one who studies blood
21. blood-like
22. study of tissue
23. fish-like
24. having to do with the universe
25. having to do with rings
26. stone-like
27. things having to do with measures
28. having to do with shape
29. one who studies stories
30. one who writes about corpses
31. one who studies birds
32. having to do with the birth (formation) of mountains
33. having to do with bone suffering (disease or disorder)

34. things having to do with the healing of children
35. having (to do with) one's father's name
36. of the study of the soul
37. root-like
38. belief in many gods
39. belief in the naked Book
40. of/having another form
41. of recent life
42. of beautiful writing
43. having solid voice
44. of the earth
45. of the finger
46. of the word
47. toothlike
48. fleshlike
49. one who does justice
50. of marriage

NEW VOCABULARY

agros   field, land
angos   vessel
anthos   blossom, flower
chēmeia 'art of alloying metals' CHEMO-
chlōros light-green
chrysos gold
deinos   terrible
ēlektron amber
erēmos   lonely, desert
gala, galakt(o)-   milk
hēlix, hēlik-   spiral
hippos   horse
hoplon   armor
hugiēs   healthy
hulē   forest, material, matter as suffix: -YL
hupnos   sleep
husteros   later, behind
katharos   clean, pure
keras   horn
kolla   glue
kuōn, kuno-   dog
magos   enchanter, wizard
mēchanē contrivance, machine
mitos   thread
oura   tail
pelagos sea
phrēn   diaphragm, midriff, mind (some derivatives show fren-)
phulē   tribe

```
phullon      leaf
polemos    war
potamos      river
rhētōr    orator
rhodon    rose
sauros    lizard
sklēros    hard
sēma, sēmeion    sign, signal
stear    fat
toxon    bow, bow and arrows
zumē    leaven, yeast
```

EXERCISE

Take these apart:
1. agronomic
2. angiology
3. anthesis
4. chemotherapy
5. chlorosis
6. chrysolite (lite=lith)
7. dinornis
8. electric
9. eremite
10. galactic
11. helicoid
12. hippopotamus
13. hoplite
14. hygiene
15. hylozoism
16. hypnosis
17. hysteresis
18. catharsis
19. ceratoid
20. colloid
21. cynic
22. magician
23. mechanics
24. mitosis
25. uropod
26. pelagic
27. phrenetic
28. phylogeny
29. phyllome
30. polemicist
31. rhetorician
32. rhododendron
33. dinosaur
34. schlerosis
35. semantic
36. stearic
37. toxic
38. zymogenic
39. agrology
40. angiosperm
41. anthology
42. alchemist(al-from Arabic 'the')
43. chlorophyll
44. chrysanthemum
45. dinoceras
46. electrotype
47. eremitic
48. polygala
49. helicopter
50. hipparch
51. eohippus (eo-'dawn')
52. panoply
53. hypnopompic
54. cathartic
55. collagen
56. archimage
57. cynosure
58. phrenology
59. phylum
60. phylloid
61. polemics
62. rhodolite
63. sauropod
64. scleroderma
65. semiology
66. toxemia
67. zymoscopic

QUISQUILIA

Some interesting words from the new vocabulary and some unusual
    entries: find meanings and explain

1. onager
2. stavesacre
3. anthemion
4. alchemy
5. chryselephntine
6. hermit
7. galaxy
8. Mt. Helicon
9. hippocampus
10. Philip
11. hylozoism
12. hysteresis
13. hysteron proteron: give an example
14. Katharevusa
15. protocol
16. Cynic
17. Magi
18. mēchanē: what was this used for in the Greek theatre?
        theos apo mēchanēs = deus ex machina.
19. mitochondrion
20. cynosure
21. archipelago: what was the original archipelago?
22. chervil
23. Polemarch: what did the Polemarch do in Athenian politics?
24. Mesopotamia: why is it so named?

PART II: SOME MEDICAL SUFFIXES AND VOCABULARY
        OF BODY PARTS

-itis   inflammation
-oma   tumor
-osis   abnormal condition

SENSES

-acousia, -acousis   hearing (also: acusia, acusis)
-aphia   touch
-geusia, geusis   taste
-odia, -osmia, -osphresia, -osphresis   smell
-opia, -opsia, -opsy   vision

Various Aches and Pains:
-agra   violent pain
-algesia   excessive sensitivity to pain
-asthenia   loss of strength
-cele   herniation
-ectopia, -ectopy   displacement, malposition
-edema   swelling

```
-malacia     softening
-odynia     pain
-oncus      tumor
-penia      deficiency
-phyma      swelling
-ptosis     sagging, prolapse
-sclerosis    hardening
-sepsis     infection
-spasm      spasm, twitching
```

Exercise 1:   review: special meanings of words from previous when used as techical suffixes: MATCH

1. -algia (from <u>algos</u>)   a. condition of the blood
2. -be (<u>bios</u>)   b. formation, development
3. -col (<u>kolla</u>)   c. process of recording
4. -emia, -hemia (<u>haima</u>)   d. pain
5. -genesis   e. instrument for recording
6. -genic   f. life, organism
7. -gram   g. forming, producing
8. -graph   h. glue, jelly
9. -graphy   i. record
10. -stenosis   j. narrowing, stricture

B.

1. -iatrics   a. enlargement
2. -lite, -lith   b. instrument for measuring
3. -mania   c. treatment
4. -megaly   d. healing, medical art
5. -meter   e. abnormal fear
6. -pathy   f. stone
7. -philia   g. disease
8. -phobia   h. madness, insane craving
9. -therapy   i. love, affinity for
10. -scope   j. instrument for visual
                                          examination

Answers (for both sets):
1-d; 2-f; 3-h; 4-a; 5-b; 6-g; 7-i; 8-e; 9-c; 10-j

Exercise: review of body parts & processes from previous lessons

Match the words with the part they refer to
1. bacteremia   a. tongue
2. dactylic   b. foot
3. somatic   c. body
4. osteopath   d. tooth

5. sarcoma
6. tripod
7. gnathic
8. glossalgia
9. stethoscope
10. orthodontics
11. isosceles
12. creosote
13. histogenesis

e. bone
f. flesh (use twice)
g. blood
h. jaw
i. leg
j. tissue
k. finger
l. chest

VOLCABULARY: BODY PARTS

adēn   gland
arthron   joint
brachion   arm
bronchos   windpipe
bursa   hide, wineskin, pouch, sac
cheilos   lip
cheir   hand
cholē   bile, gall
chondros   cartilage
derma, dermat-   skin
enkephalos   brain
gaster, gastr-   belly,, stomach
gonu   knee
genus   cheek
hēpar, hēpat-   liver
humēn   membrane
hustera   womb
iris, irid-   rainbow, iris
ischion   hip, thigh
kardia   heart
karpos   wrist
kolpos   bosom, womb
kondulos   knuckle
kranion   skull
kustis   pouch, bladder   CYST- = cell
kutos   hollow vessel: -CYTE, CYTO- = cell
mastos   breast
metopōn   forehead
mus, mu-   mouse, muscle
muxa   mucus, slime
nephros   kidney
neuron   sinew; pl. nerves
ōmos   shoulder
ōon   egg
ōps   eye,, face
omma   eye

272

ophthalmos   eye
opsis   face   (literally, 'sight, view')
pharunx   throat
pleura   rib
pneumōn   lung
prōktos   anus
rhis, rhin-   nose
sphuron   ankle
sternon   breast
stŏma, stŏmat-   mouth
thŏrax   thorax
thrix, trich-   hair
tracheia   windpipe

Exercise 1: WHAT HURTS?

1. podagra
2. neuralgia
3. hepatitis
4. sarcoma
5. chilocace (-cace' canker' from kakē, fem. of kakos)
6. phlebostenosis
7. proctalgia
8. dactylasthenia
9. ischiectopy
10. dermatalgesia
11. cytopenia
12. nephrosis
13. arthritis
14. pneumodynia
15. pleurisy
16. phrenitis
17. iritis
18. rhinitis
19. neurosis
20. myxedema
21. mastitis
22. colpitis
23. hysteria
24. chondroma
25. cholecystitis

If they all hurt, take a panacea.

Exercise 2: Form words meaning:

1. gland-like

2. inflammation of the joints
3. arm-foot
4. instrument for measuring the windpipe
5. palmistry: divination by the hand
6. study of the skin
7. inflammation of the brain
8. belly-foot
9. having to do with the liver
10. having to do with the heart
11. knuckle-like
12. the study of cells
13. breast-tooth
14. of the forehead
15. mucus-tumor
16. kidney inflammation
17. study of nerve disease
18. examination of the nose
19. one who studies eyes
20. throat inflammation

Exercise 3: take apart and define these words:

1. adenoncus
2. adenocystic
3. adenalgy
4. adenomyxosarcoma
5. arthritic
6. Arthropoda
7. arthragra
8. arthropathy
9. Brachiopoda
10. brachionoid
11. bronchiostenosis
12. bronchitic
13. bronchoscope
14. bronchadenitis
15. bursalogy
16. bursary
17. burse
18. chiloma
19. Chilopoda
20. Chilobranchidae (branchion
21. chilognathomorphous
22. chironym (meaning: 'unpublished name of a plant or animal')
23. Chiroptera
24. chiropodist
25. chironomy
26. cholelithiasis
27. cholecystitis
28. cholemic
29. chondriosome
30. chondrocranium
31. chodrarthrocace
32. chondrodynia
33. dermatosis
34. dermatodynia
35. dermoid
36. dermatomere
37. encephlasthenia
38. encephaloid
39. encephalomeric
40. encephalometric
41. gastrostomy
42. gastronome
43. gastroadenitis
44. gastrocystic
45. Genyornis
46. gonyalgia
47. hepatica
48. hepatogastric
49. hepatotoxemia
50. hymenography

51. hymenopteran	52. hysteroid
53. hysteromyoma	54. hysterogenic
55. iridomalacia	56. ischiagra
57. ischialgia	58. ischiognathite
59. cardiophonia	60. cardiopneumograph
61. cardiostenosis	62. carpognathite
63. colpitis	64. colpostenosis
65. carpitis	66. condylarthrosis
67. Condylopoda	68. craniosclerosis
69. craniscopy	70. craniolith
71. craniotopography	72. cystozooid
73. cystodynia	74. cytomicrosome
75. cytoderm	76. cystocyte
77. mastoid	78. mastadon
79. metopic	80. metopomancy
81. mopathy	82. myocardiogram
83. myxocyte	84. myxoadenoma
85. nephritic	86. myxopod
87. nephrogenous	88. neurotic
89. neurasthenia	90. neuropathology
91. omodynia	92. o-oecium
93. oo-angium	94. o-oidocephalic
95. autopsy	96. ophthalmologist
97. optophone	98. ophthalmomyitis
99. pharyngobranchial	100. pharyngopatheia
101. pleural	102. pleuropneumonia
103. pneumonocace	104. pleurosteon
105. pneumotherapy	106. pneumomalacia
107. proctology	108. proctodynia
109. rhinoceros	110. Rhinanthus
111. rhinodynia	112. rhinopharynx
113. sternoglossal	114. sternomastoid
115. sternodynia	116. stomatocatharsis
117. stomatonecrosis	118. stomatopod
119. thoracoscopia	120. thoracomyodynia
121. trichomania	122. trichome
123. trichocystic	124. tracheobronchial
125. tracheophony	126. sternotracheal
127. triceratops	128. oligocytemia

QUISQUILIA: LITERARY TERMS

1. Genres:

POIĒTES: from Greek POIEIN 'to make': the POET is maker, creator, at best, imitator of the Divine.

Most of the names for the types of poetry come from Greek:

Epic (from _epos_, 'word'): name several Greek and Roman epic poets and their works. What are some of the later European epic poems? Name one Near-Eastern epic?

Tragedy: look up the etymology of TRAGEDY
Name the three great Athenian tragedians and list three or more plays of each. Who are some Renaissance and Modern writers of tragedies?

Comedy (from kōmos 'revel'), who were the two most famous Greek writers of comedy?

Lyric (from lura, 'lyre': lyric poetry was sung to the lyre) Name some Greek lyric poets.

Bucolic (from bous 'cow": boukolos 'herdsman': in bucolic poetry, the characters are herdsmen: it is a very sophisticated genre, but in a naive setting). Find the names of three Greek bucolic poets. For a more modern 'bucoloic lament', read Shelley's Adonais a lament for John Keats.

Other genres derived from Greek:
elegiac, parody, melodrama, didactic poetry, idyll dithyramb, gnomic verse, epithalamion, paeon, epigram, ode, drama

2. Meters

dimeter, trimeter, tetrameter, pentameter, hexameter, heptameter, octameter: these words tell how many feet to a line

Feet are the arrangements of long and short syllables (or in Modern verse of stressed and unstressed syllables) in the metrical pattern.

For example:
A dactyl is a long syllable followed by two short, from DAKTULOS 'finger': the arrangement is like the joints of a finger, a long and two shorts.

Other feet: find out what these are and why they are so named:
spondee, iamb, trochee, anapestic, dochmiac, choriamb, glyconic, pherecratic, Sapphic, Alcaic, epitrite, tribrach

Other words used in discussing metrics:
catalexis, catalectic, acatalectic, caesura (from Latin), diaeresis, thesis, arsis, syncopation, synizesis

Other TERMS from Greek used in Literary Criticism:

strophe   antistrophe   episode   stasimon   parodos   exodos
prologue   epilogue   monody   palinode   choral ode

anaphora	allegory	metaphor
litotes	synechdoche	rhapsode, rhapsody
epithet	orchestra	anagnorisis
catastrophe	hamartia	'hero'

276

hubris   pathos-- pathetic fallacy
criticism   prosody   anthology
mythopoesis   Muse

GREEK PREFIXES

A- (before a vowel, AN-):   inseparable negative prefix (called
        alpha privative): not, un-.-less

AMPHI-: both, on both sides, around, about

ANA-: Before a vowel, AN-): up, back, again, according to;
        sometimes, ana- carries a reversing force

ANTI-: instead, against, in opposition to

APO- (AP-): from, away from, off, utterly, completely, lack of

DIA- (Di-): through, across, over, assunder

DUS-: in English, DYS- ill, un, mis- difficult, bad, unfortunate
        (inseparable prefix, opposite to eu- 'well')

EK-, EX-: in English, EC-, EX-, out, from, off

EKTO-: in English, ECTO- on the outside, without

EN-: in

ENANTIO-(en- + anti-): opposite

ENDO-: within, inside, internal

ESO-: inward, within

EXO-: outside, external

EPI- (EP): upon, over, at, near

EU-(rarely, EV-) (adverb): well

KATA-: English, CATA- (CAT-): down, against, completely;
        opposite to ana-

META- (MET-): among, between, alteration, change, behind
        (Anatomy) later

PALIN-, PALI- (adverb): back, again, once more, backwards

PARA- (PAR-): beside, beyond, alongside, near, incorrectly,
        resembling

PERI-: <u>around</u>, <u>about</u>

PRO-: <u>before</u>, <u>forward</u>, <u>for</u>

PROS-: <u>to</u>, <u>toward</u>, <u>besides</u>, <u>in</u> front

SUN-: in English SYN- (shows assimilation: SYM-, SYS-)
<u>with</u>, <u>together</u>

HUPER-: in English HYPER- <u>over</u>, <u>above</u>, <u>beyond</u>, <u>exceedingly</u>
(cognate with Latin <u>super</u>)

HUPO-: in English, HYPO- (HYP-) <u>under</u> (cognate with Latin <u>sub</u>)

Exercises: **take these words apart; answer any additional
questions**

1. anonymous
   Give an example of an <u>anonymous</u> work.
2. eponymous
   Give two examples of eponymous heroes, one ancient, one
   modern.
   Find out what <u>archon eponymous</u> means.
3. paronymous
   Give an example of <u>paronymous</u> words.
4. metonymy
   Distinguish <u>metonymy</u> from <u>metaphor</u> and give examples of
   each.
5. synonymous
   Give four pairs of <u>synonyms</u>.
6. antonym
   Give four pairs of <u>antonyms</u>.
7. Give four additional words ending in -<u>onym</u>, -<u>onymy</u>, or
   -<u>onymous</u>
8. symbiosis: take apart, define and give an illustrative
   example
9. enantiobiosis
   Give an antonym for <u>enantiobiosis</u>
10. enchiridion
    Find a book title using the word <u>enchiridion</u>.
11. enantiosis
    A synonym for <u>enantiosis</u> is <u>litotes</u>. Give an example.
12. Catholic
    Notice that the final vowel of many prefixes drops out
    before <u>h</u>, as well as before a vowel: this is called
    elision.

13. cathedral

What does the expression ex cathedra mean?   Use it in a sentence.

14. palinode

Try to find an example of a palinode, or think of an occasion when one might be suitable.

15. analogy

Give an example.

16. anarchic

Give an example of an anarchist or an anarchic group.

17. dialogue

Name a philosopher who wrote in the dialogue form.

18. parody

Name an example of a literary parody.

19. prosody

What are some of the things that would be a concern to a student of prosody?

20. epode

Give three additional words from ode

21. antagonist: name three other -agonists

22. Look up category and trace its etymology

23. paregoric

24. analgesic

25. sympathy

26. empathy

27. parasympathetic

28. parallel [allelon '(of) each other', from allos]

29. parallelepiped [ped, from pedon 'plane, ground']

30. Evangel

Use Evangel in a sentence.

31. dianthus

32. antibiotic

33. amphibian

Name some amphibious animals.

34. exobiology

35. achromatic

36. eudemonia

37. epidemic

38. endemic

Explain the difference between 37 and 38:   use each in a sentence.

39. syndic

Give two derivatives of syndic.

40. catechism

41. anechoic

42. aniseikonia

43. energy

44. hypogeal

45. apogee
46. epigeal
47. perigee
48. epigene
49. epiglottis
50. diagonal
51. perigynous
52. epigyny
53. hendiadys
54. anthelion
55. aphelion
56. parhelion
57. perihelion
58. anomaly
59. anhydrous
60. exocarp
61. epicene (<u>koinos</u>)
62. collenchyma (<u>kuma</u>, wave)
63. encyclical
64. encyclopaedia
(<u>paideia</u> 'education'
from <u>pais</u>, <u>paido-</u> 'child)

65. symmetry
66. amorphous
67. endodontist
68. diocese
Look up etymology
of <u>parish</u>.

69. euonymous
70. endosteum
71. exostosis
72. periostem
73. synostosis
74. anurous
75. paroxysm
76. eupatrid
77. sympatric
78. antipathy
79. apathetic
80. apteryx
81. aphonia
82. diaphony
83. symphony
84. euphony
85. antiphone
86. propolis
Look up the etymology of anthem.
87. apodal
88. pseudepigrapha
89. epigraphy
90. metempsychosis
91. perisarc
92. ectosarc
93. proscenium
94. endosperm
95. asthenia
96. epitaph: find or write an appropriate epitaph for some
person or pet, real or fictitious.
97. apotheosis
98. atheism
99. antitoxin
100. enzyme
101. dysophonia
102. dysteleology
103. diameter
104. apology
105. anagram: give example
106. anachronism
107. anabiosis
108. amphitrichous
109. amphibrach (in metrics v-v)
110. amphimacer (makros v-v)
111. antinomy
112. antipodes
113. antonmasia; give an example
114. parabiosis
115. paranoia (<u>nous</u> 'mind')
116. metamorphosis
117. palingenisis
118. hyperbaric
119. hyposthenia
120. diachronic
121. parapsychology
122. dianoetic (<u>nous</u>)

Look up:
1. hypocorism: give meaning and example
2. paragon: give meaning and etymology
3. diaper: give etymology
4. diapason: give meaning and etymology

Exercise II: Make up words meaning:

1. an instrument for looking around
2. a measure around
3. lack of marriage
4. one who advocates unrule
5. creature having feet on both sides
6. a part opposite
7. a mark (writing) beside
8. relating to change in shape
9. fore-brain (in front of the brain) [neuter: ends in -on]
10. (pertaining to) under the skin

Exercise III: Take these apart and give meanings (Medical)

1. diarthrosis
2. periodontics
5. hypochondriac
7. encephalodialysis (lysis from luein 'loosen')
8. epigastrium
10. perimysium
12. metanephros
14. pronephros
16. pharyngoepiglottic
18. anastomosis
20. anemia
22. hypermetropia
2. synarthrosis
3. periotic
6. epidermal
9. carpometacarpal
11. epimysium
13. perinephrium
15. aponeurosis
17. sternopericardial
19. ancyclostomiasis
21. hypercholesterolemia

NEW VOCABULARY

charis   grace, favor
hēmera   day
hodos   eos, way
horkos   oath
horos   boundary
nux, nukt- night
phulax, phulakt- guard
posis   a drink
sitos   grain, food

thanatos   death
zōnē   belt, girdle
enteron   intestine
stulos   column, pillar

Exercise IV: Take apart these words and give meanings:

Take apart these words and give meanings:

1. Eucharistic
2. ephemeral
3. exodus
4. exorcist
5. aphorism
6. empirical
7. prophylaxis
8. symposiarch
9. parasitic
10. euthanasia
11. evzone (ev- = eu)
12. thanatopsis
13. charisma
14. Decameron
15. phylactery
16. dysentery
17. amphiprostyle
18. peristyle
19. hypostyle
20. parasitology
21. hemeralopia [-al from alaos 'blind'; -opia 'eye condition']
    What is the word for 'night blindness'?
22. anode
    Give a word meang 'a road down'

Take apart and define these other words from hodos:

method	episode
period	synod
stomodeum	electrode
hodograph	odometer

END GAMES

1.   What are these crazy about?

1. acromaniac
2. agoramaniac
3. ailuromaniac
4. anthomaniac
5. automaniac
6. bibliomaniac
7. choromaniac
8. cynomaniac
9. gymnomaniac
10. gamomaniac
11. hedonomaniac
12. heliomaniac
13. hippomaniac
14. hypnomaniac
15. megalomaniac
16. mythomaniac
17. necromaniac
18. ochlomaniac
19. onomatomaniac
20. pathomaniac
21. sitomaniac
22. xenomaniac
23. zoomaniac
24. zymomaniac

2.   What frightens people suffering from these:

1. triskaidekaphobia
2. photophobia
3. stearophobia
4. agoraphobia
5. ergophobia
6. demophobia

7. saurophobia	8. anthropophobia
9. gynecophobia	10. skiaphobia
11. cosmophobia	12. trichophobia
13. pyrophobia	14. anemophobia
15. nyctophobia	16. clerophobia
17. iatrophobia	18. hemerophobia
19. astrophobia	20. hematophobia
21. myophobia	

3. Some psyche words: PSYCHE: "spirit, soul, life force: the conscious self, personality: the individual's mind"

psychology psychologist psychiarty psychiatrist psychotherapy psychoanalysis psychasthenia psychosomatic somatopsychic psychosis psychotic psychopathy psychodrama psycheometry psychostatics psychosophy psychogenesis psychodynamics psychomachy psychoneurology psychophysics psychophysiology psychoplasm

4. Pitfalls and pratfalls: Which of these are from Greek?

1. air	2. catalpa
3. gas	4. catamaran
5. school	6. toll
7. catawampus	8. catamount
9. catalo	10. copper
11. sock	12. pepper
13. kirk	14. catenary

[All except those beginning with cata- or cat-]
Catalpa is from Creek, not Greek: kutuhlpa, meaning 'head with wings', from the shape of the flowers.
Catamaran (a boat with two parallel hulls) is from Tamil (a language of southern India and Ceylon) kattumaram (kattu 'to tie' + maram 'tree, timber').
Catamount (a wild cat) is short for catamountain, i.e. cat of the mountains.
Catalo is a portmanteau word for a hybrid: CATtle + buffALO.
Catenary is from Latin catena 'chain'.
Catawampus is of uncertain origin.
Catamite is from Latin Catamitus, from Etruscan Catmite, from Greek Ganumedes (Ganymede, the cupbearer of Zeus, carried off because of his good looks).

Real words from KATA- include: catabolism, catabolize, catachresis, cataclysm, catafalque, catalase, catalectic, catalepsy, catalogue, catalysis, catamenia, catalyst, catalyze, cataphoresis, cataphyll, cataplasia, cataplasm, catapult, cataract, catastasis, catastrophe, catatonia, catechesis, catechism, catechize, catechumen, categorical, categorize, category, catoptric, catheter, cathexis, cathode, catholic, cation.

For fun: take one of the other prefixes [ana-, dia-, epi-, meta-, para-, peri-, syn-, hyper-, hypo-] and find thirty or more derivatives, watching out for pitfalls.

QUISQUILIA: ALBS & CASSOCKS: Some Words about Religion

Alb: from Latin albus-a-um 'white'
Cassock: Old French casaque from Persian kazagand 'padded jacket'

1. Kurios 'Lord' (from a root meaning 'swollen: strong, powerful'): Kyrie eleison
   Church from Kuriakon (doma) 'the Lord's house,' kirk
2. chriein 'anoint': Christ, christen, chrism; and cream
3. klēros 'lot, legacy' (from a root meaning 'cut': klēros, 'that which is cut off')
   The reference is to the Levites, whose portion (klēros) is the Lord: see Numbers 18. 20-24: from klēros come: Clergy, cleric, clerk, clerisy.
4. laos 'the people': laity, laic, laicize; and liturgy (the work for the people; in classical Athens, a leitourgia was a public service which the wealthy were called upon to perform for the polis, such as training a tragic chorus, outfitting a warship).
5. muein 'close, be shut' (close the lips: close the eyes): mystery, mystic, mysticism; mystagogue
6. presbus 'old': presbyter, presbytery, priest, Presbyterian

For an interesting discussion of the influence of the early translations of the Bible on the English language, read Bradley, The Making of English p. 219 ff.

GREEK VERBS

Verbs in Greek often show a multiplicity of stems in the six principal perts that a Greek verb has. Here only the present infinitive will be given, along with any stems that appear in English derivatives.

Vowel gradation is a characteristic of Greek verbs and this accounts for much of the variation in the stems. Other variations are mostly attributable to assimilation of the final consonant before a suffix.

Some examples:
    legein 'to speak, to gather'
        stems: leg- PROLEGOMENON
                lex- represents leg- + s- of a suffix: DYSLEXIA
                log- (as in logos) in the noun form and its
                derivatives: ANALOGUE (-gue ending shows French
                influence)
    ballein 'to throw'
        stems: ball-: BALLISTICS
                bol-: PARABOLA
                blē-: PROBLEM

Learn these verbs as you do the exercises: study various stems and learn meanings.

                                  fill in derivatives
agein   to lead, bring AG-
        -agogue (from -agogos) 'one leading' as PEDAGOGUE
           or (from -agogē) 'a leading' as SYNAGOGUE
aisthanesthai to feel, perceive AESTH-, ESTH-
akouein   hear ACOU- ACU-
bainein   to go, step, walk BA-, BĒ-
ballein   to throw BALL-, BLE-, BOL-
chorein 'move' CHOR-
        the suffix -CHORE is used to indicate a plant distribut-
        ed by a specific agency: ANEMOCHORE.
        relatd to chorein is choros 'place'
didonai   to give DO-
dokein   seem, think DOC-, DOG-, DOX-
        doxa opinion, praise, reputation
dramein   to run DROM-
dran   to do, act, perform DRA-
dunasthai   to be able, be powerful DYN-
         dunamis power

echein to have, hold HEK- (HEX-), SCHĒ-, OCH-, -UCH-
       related is <u>scholē</u> 'leisure: school' which means
       etymologically 'a holding back'
ienai go I-
einai be [stem <u>es</u>-] participial stem -<u>ont</u>-, -<u>ous</u>- 'being'
gignōskein know GNŌ- [cognate with English <u>know</u> and Latin
      <u>cognoscere</u>]
gluphein carve
graphein draw, write GRAPH- GRAM-
histanai stand STA- STĒ-
kalein call CLE-
kinein move, set in motion
klinein bend, make to slope, recline
koptein cut COP-, COM-
krinein separate, decide, judge CRIN-, CRI-
kruptein hide CRYPT- CRYP-
lambanein take, seize LAB-, LEP-, LEM-
legein gather, say LEG-, (LEX-), (LECT-), -LOG-
luein loose, break, destroy LY-
mathein (aorist infinitive) learn MATH-
nemein assign, allot NEM-, NOM-
      cf. <u>nomos</u> 'portion, custom, law'
pauein cease, stop PAU- [-POSE with meaning influenced by Latin
      <u>ponere</u>]
phagein eat:
      -phage 'one eating'
      -phagous 'eating'
      -phagy 'habit or tendency to eat'
phainein show, make appear; appear: PHAIN- (PHEN-), PHAN-
phanai speak PHA-, PHĒ-
      <u>phēmē</u> a saying
pherein bear, carry PHER- PHOR-
phuein make to grow PHY-
poiein make, do POIE- (POE-)
pōlein sell
prattein do PRAG-, PRAK- (PRAC-)
rhein flow RHE(U)-, RHY- RHO-
schizein split SCHIZ-, SCHIS-
skopein examine SKOP- (SCOP-), SKEP- (SCEP-)
stellein make ready, send STOL- STAL-
strephein turn, twist STREP-, STROPH-
tattein array, assess, assign, set in order, arrange: TAK- (TAC-)
temnein cut TMĒ-, TOM-
trephein feed, nourish TROPH-
trepein turn TROP(H)-
teinein stretch out, strain TEN-, TA-, TON-
tithenai put, place THE-

Exercises: fill in meaning of Greek verb, learn Greek verb and its various stems; answer questions.

1. agein
Take apart and give meanings:
    demagogue
    pedagogue
    mystagogue
    synagogue
    anagoge
    choragus
Make up a word meaning 'tending to bring sleep.'
Look up pedant and find its origin; use it in a sentence.
Strategy comes from strategos 'general' from stratos 'army +
    agein. What is a strategem?
Give a word meaning 'rule by the army.'

2. aisthanesthai
Define and explain:
    aesthete
    aesthetics
    anesthesia

3. akouein
    What is the acoustic nerve?
    If you hear voices and there is no one there, or things that
go bump in the night, you may be suffering from pseudacousis:
what is it?
    What is a word meaning 'scientific study of sound' or 'things
having to do with hearing'? Use it in a sentence.

4. bainein
Take apart and define:
    amphisbaena
    basis
    diabase
    diabetes
    stylobate
    stereobate
    catabatic
Make up a word meaning 'tending to go up'
What do you call one walking on tip-toe?

5. ballein
Take apart and define:
    amphibole
    hyperbole
    metabolism
    catabolic

discobolus
emboly
symbol
emblem

Give a word meaning 'the result of throwing forward'.
    diabolic, devil from diabolos 'the slanderer' from dia +
    ballein Explain what parable and parabola have in common

Also from parabole (parable) come: French parler 'to speak';
    parley, parole, parliament, parlor

6. chorein
take apart and define:
    anchorite
    zoochore
give six additional words ending in -chore (describing the distri-
    bution of plants)

7. didonai
take apart and define:
    dose
    epidote
    apodosis
    anecdote
What is 'a thing given against' (as to counteract a poison)?
the names Dorothy and Theodore are from doron 'gift' (a derivative
of didonai): what is the meaning of the other part of the names?

8. dokein
Take apart and define:
    dogma
    doxology
    paradox: give an example of a paradox
    heterodox: give an antonym for heterodox
Explain what Docetism is.

9. dramein
Take apart and define:
    dromedary
    hippodrome
    anadromous: give an antonym for anadromous.
    acrodrome
    palindrome
Give a word meaning 'a running together'.

Some PALINDROMES: (read these backwards)
    MADAM I'M ADAM [the earliest known palindrome is our progeni-
    tor's introduction to his wife in the Garden of Eden]
    ABLE WAS I ERE I SAW ELBA [equally famous is the exiled

Napoleon's lament from his island home]
A MAN A PLAN A CANAL PANAMA

10. dran
Take apart and define:
    drama
    melodramatic
    drastic
    dramaturgy (-urgy from ergon)

11. dunasthai [dunamis]
Explain these formations and give meanings:
    dyne
    dynamo
    dynamite
    dynamic
    dynast
    aerodyne
What is an instrument for measuring power called?

12. echein
Explain these formations and give meanings:
    cachexia
    epoch
    eunuch (eune 'bed')
    scheme
    entelechy
    hectic

13. ienai
    ion ('going': 'a going particle'): the form ion is a participle: the most common active participial ending in Greek is -on [m.], -ousa [f], -on [n.] with the m. & n. stem in -ont- (see under 14 below).
Form words meaning '[particle] going up' and '[a particle] going down'

14. einai (participial base: ont- 'being')
Take apart and define:
    ontic
    biont
    schizont
    paleontology
    ontological
    ontogeny
ousia: 'being' (noun) Explain and define:
    Homo-ousian
    Homoicusian
    Heterousian

15. gignōskein
Explain formations and define:
    gnostic
    Gnosticism
    prognosis
    prognosticate
    physiognomy
    gnomic
    diagnosis
Give a word meaning 'tending not to know'

16. gluphein
Explain formations and define:
    petroglyph
    glyptic
    glyptograph
    anaglyph
What are 'sacred carvings' called?

17. graphein
Explain formations and define:
    grapheme
    graphite
    seismograph (seismos 'a shaking, an earthquake')
    cacography
Give ten additional words ending in -graphy .
Take apart and define:
    diagram
    telegram
    anagram
    epigram
    program
Look up glamour and give its origin.
What are graffiti? (What is the singular form?)

18. histanai
Explain formations, define, answer questions:
    apostate
    apostasy
    Give a word meaning 'the act of standing out'.
    rheostate: -stat indicates an instrument for stopping/making
    to stand still. Give five additional words ending in -stat.
    hypostasis: what adjective is formed from hypostasis?
    iconostasis
    system
    static

292

19. kalein
Explain formations and define:
    paraclete
    ecclesiastic
    epiclesis

20. kinein
Explain formations, define; answer questions:
    cinema (short for <u>cinematograph</u>)
    telekinesis
    Give a word meaning 'tending to move.'
    kinesthesia
    hyperkinesia

21. klinein
Explain formations, define, answer questions:
    enclitic
    Give a word meaning 'tending to lean forward.'
    climate
    synclinal
    matriclinous
    patriclinous

22. koptein
    syncope
    Give a word meaning 'a cutting off/away'.
    Give a word meaning 'a cutting around'.
    sarcoptic
    comma

23. krinein
    crisis
    one tending to judge is a _____.
    criterion (-<u>erion</u>: 'a means of')
    diacritical
    endocrine
    hypocrisy

24. kruptein
    apocryphal
    crypt
    hidden writing = _____
    hidden name = _____
    krypton
    cryptogam
    Find the origin of <u>grot</u>, <u>grotto</u>, <u>grotesque</u>.

25. lambanein
    astrolabe   dilemma   epilepsy

syllable   cataleptic   prolepsis
narcolepsy (narkē 'numbness, cramp')

26. legein
    prolegomenon [the ending -menos, -e, -on is a middle or pas-
    sive participial ending: cf. phenomenon, ecumenical]
    epilogue: what is found at the other end of a play or story?
    analects
    Give a word meaning 'tending to choose out.'
    dialect   lexicon   dyslexia   catalogue
27. luein
    paralysis
    Give nouns meaning 'a breaking up, a breaking down, a break-
    ing through'; give an adjective for each.
    lysis   lysergic   lysogenesis
    lysophilic   lysophobic

28. mathein
    mathematics
    What do you call a person of much learning?
    chrestomathy [chrēstos 'useful']: a chrestomathy is a selec-
    tion of literary passages used in studying literature or a
    language.

29. nemein
    nemesis   nomarchy   nomad
    anomy   nome
    Give twelve words using -nomy/-nomer/-nomic(al)/-nomous

30. pauein
    pause   diapause   menapause (give antonym)
    Words in -pose such as compose, propose, suppose, repose are
derived indirectly from pauein: in late Latin the word pausare
'to cease' was adopted from Greek and in the spoken language
pausare took over the meaning of Latin ponere/positum 'to place'
[M.E. posen O.F. poser L.L. pausare pausa Gk. pausis Gk.
pauein.]

31. phagein
    esophagus   sarcophagus   dysphagia
    phagophobia   phagocyte
What's Cooking: in the following list, find out what is for dinner for those eating in the custom described by these words in
-phage and -phagous:
    anthropophage   ichthyophage   aerophagous
    pyrophage   cryophage   botanophage
    rhizophage   anthophagous   xylophagous

294

xenophage   papyrophagous   ornithophage
bacteriophage   phyllophagous
Add to the list to your stomach's content.

32. phainein
    sycophant   phantasy   phantom
    phenomenon (for -menon ending see # 26 in this exercise)
    phantasmagoria   phosphene   epiphany
    Theophany   emphasis
    'showing through' = .

33. phanai
    blasphemy [blas- from blaptein 'to harm']
    prophesy   one speaking forth =
    euphemism: give three examples.
    aphasia: difficulty in speaking is _____
    Look up the etymology of blame.

34. pherein
    euphoria: give an antonym
    metaphor   phosphorescent   anaphora: give example
    paraphernalia [pherne 'dowry: that which is brought by the
    bride']

35. phuein   phusis 'nature'
    peri phuseos [genitive of phusis] was a standard title for
    philosophical works on cosmology
    The study of things in nature is _____
    The study of things beyond nature is _____
    neophyte   symphysis   hypophysis
    diaphysis   epiphysis   Monophysite
    euphuism: give an example

36. poiein
    onomatopoeia: give an example
    What is the adjective form of onomatapoeia?
    'the result of making':
    'one who makes':
    pharmocopoeia [pharmakon 'drug']
    mythopoiesis
    Look up: poetaster

37. pōlein
    monopoly   oligopoly
    What is for sale by these vendors:
    ichthyopolist   bibliopole   papyropolist
    oenopole [oinos 'wine'; cf. oenologist]

aeropole   carpopolist   pharmacopole
sitopole

38. prattein
    pragmatic   practical   apraxis
    Look up the origin of <u>barter</u>.

39. rhein
    catarrh   diarrhoea   logorrhoea
    rheostat   rheumatism   rheology
    rhyme   rhythm   hemarrhoid

40. schizein
    schism
    'one who advocates splitting':
    'split foot'
    'split fruit'
    'birth by splitting'
    chiloschisis   schizophrenia   schizoid

41. scopein
    scopophilia   spectroscope
    Give five other <u>scopes</u>
    Look up <u>bishop</u> and show its descent from <u>episkopos</u>

42. stellein
    epistle: give an adjective meaning 'having to do with letters'
    'one sent away/off is an _____
    'having to do with those sent off': _____
    peristalsis   systalic

43. strephein
    strophe   apostrophe
    a turning down:
    a turning up:
Look up boustrophedon and write a few lines 'as the ox turns'.

44. tattein
    tactics   paratactic   hypotactic
    syntax   taxonomy   ataxia   eutaxy

45. temnein
    entomology   anatomy   epitome
    tmesis   diatom   dichotomy
    microtome (-<u>tome</u>: 'an instrument for cutting')
    What is wrong with the name of the <u>atom</u>?
    -<u>tomy</u> 'the surgical cutting of'

-ectomy 'the surgical removal of'
Give six words ending in -tomy and six ending in -ectomy.

46. trephein
     eutrophic   polytrophic
     lack of nourishment:

47. trepein
     tropic   entropy
     A plant that turns toward the sun is _____.

48. teinein
     protasis: write a conditional sentence, and mark the
     protasis and apodosis
     tone: having a single tone is _____
     hypotenuse (-use, from -ousa, see # 13 of this exercise)

49. tithenai
     parenthesis
     Give words meaning:
     a putting under
     a putting together
     a putting in reverse
     a putting through
     a putting forward
     a putting against
     epithet   theme   anathema
     bibliotheca   narcosynthesis
     Look up the origins of bodega and boutique.

Review: match the words with the meanings of their base verbs:

A	
1. metathetical	a. feel
2. demagogic	b. turn
3. Epiphany	c. feed
4. anesthesiologist	d. lead
5. scepticism	e. loosen
6. monotony	f. cut
7. acoustician	g. show
8. tropics	h. go
9. apostasy	i. examine
10. polytrophism	j. hear
11. probatic	k. throw
12. paralyze	l. put
13. dichotomous	m. arrange
14. problematic	n. give
15. anecdotal	o. stand
16. tactician	p. stretch

17. zoochore	a. flow
18. catastrophic	b. hold
19. dogmatics	c. make
20. apostolic	d. run
21. catadromous	e. split
22. schizophrenic	f. grow
23. rheumatism	g. know
24. pragmatism	h. move
25. polypoly	i. bear, carry
26. dramaturgical	j. sell
27. dynode	k. be
28. schematic	l. send
29. ion	m. go
30. palaeontological	n. be able
31. onomatopoetic	o. do (2)
32. phytography	p. seem
33. periphery	q. turn
34. Gnosticism	

C

35. hieroglyphics	a. bend, slope
36. stenographer	b. take
37. apostasy	c. call
38. ecclesiology	d. speak
39. kinematics	e. eat
40. pericline	f. move
41. syncopation	g. hide
42. criticism	h. assign
43. apocryphal	i. learn
44. polysyllabic	j. cut
45. dialectical	k. loose
46. mathematician	l. scratch
47. nomadic	m. judge
48. pause	n. stop
49. phagocyte	o. carve

PART II: MORE VERBS: with each verb, several derivatives are listed: take these apart and give their meanings; answer any other questions.

1. AEIREIN lift, raise up
   aorta   meteor   meteorite   meteoric
   What does a meteorologist study?
   Why is Meteora (in Greece) so named?

2. ARCHEIN be first/begin, rule; adj. ARCHAIOS 'old'
   archaeology   archaic   archaism   archdiocese

298

Give twenty additional words from archein, using arch-, -archy, -arch.

3. ASKEIN exercise
   ascetic   phonascetics

4. BAPTEIN dip
   act of practice of dipping:
   a place for dipping:
   advocate of re-dipping:

5. BRUEIN grow
   embryo   embryology

6. CHARASMEIN engrave, mark
   character   characteristic

7. DEIKNUNAI show [DEIK-, DEIG-]
   deictic   apodictic   paradigm

8. DEIN bind, tie
   diadem   anadem   asyndeton (give an example)

9. DIDASKEIN teach [DIDAK-]
   didactic: name three didactic poems
   Didachē

10. ELAUNEIN drive [ELA-]
    elastic   elater (a type of beetle)
    elasmobranch (certain fish such as sharks, rays, skates)

11. ERAN love
    Eros   erogenous   erotic   erotomania

12. HAIREIN take, choose, grasp
    heretic   heresiarch
    Explain how heresy relates to the meaning of hairein.

13. HARMOZEIN fit together, join
    harmony; name two musical instruments from harmozein

14. HEURISKEIN
    heuristic   Eureka (perfect tense)

15. HIENAI send, throw [HE-]
    catheter   diesis   enema   paresis   synesis

16. HORAN see
    panorama   ephor

17. KAIEIN   burn, kindle [KAU-]
    caustic   holocaust   cautery   encaustic
    Look up ink and find out what it has to do with kaiein.

18. KALUPTEIN   conceal
    apocalypse   eucalyptus   calyptra

19. KENTEIN   stab, pierce
    center (look up steps in etymology)   eccentric

20. KERANNUNAI   mix [KRA-]
    crasis   idiosyncrasy   dyscrasia
    crater: the Greeks served wine in a crater: what has wine
    to do with mixing?

21. KLAN   break [KLA-, KLĒ-]
    iconoclast   clastic
    klēma 'twig': clematis
    klōn 'twig': clone

22. KLEPTEIN   steal
    biblioklept   clepsydra
    What do you call a person with a passion for stealing?

23. KLUZEIN   wash
    cataclysmic   clyster

24. KUBERNAN   steer
    cybernetics   govern   gubernatorial

25. LEIPEIN   leave, be wanting
    ellipse   ellipsis   elliptical   eclipse

26. MNASTHAI   remember [MNĒ-]
    amnesia   amnesty   anamnesis
    Name (if you can remember it) one mnemonic device you have
    used or heard of.
    Who is Mnemosyne and who are her daughters?

27. PERAN   pass through   POROS   ford
    emporium   porosity   aporistic   aporia

28. PHLEGEIN   burn
    phlegm   phlegmatic
    Where is Phlegethon and what is it?

29. PHRAZEIN show, tell
   paraphrase   phraseology   holophrastic   metaphrase
   periphrasis: give a synonym using Latin parts
   periphrastic

30. PIPTEIN fall [PET- PTŌ-]
   symptomatic ptomaine   peripeteia   proptosis
   ptosis: using your list of body parts, form four kinds of
   -ptosis.

31. PLANASTHAI wander
   planetarium Explain why planets are named "wanderers".

32. PLASSEIN mold, form
   plasma   metaplasm   anaplasty   dysplasia   plastic
   -PLASTY as a suffix indicates plastic surgery on some part;
   using your list of body parts, make up five words using
   -plasty.

33. PLESSEIN beat, strike [PLEG- PLEK-]
   apoplexy   paraplegia   hemiplegia   quadriplegic
   [-plegia as a suffix indicates paralysis]

34. PNEIN breathe, blow [PNE-, PNEU-]
   PNEUMA, PNEUMAT- breath, wind, spirit
   pneumatology pneumatic   pneumococcus pneumoconiosis
   apnea   dyspnea (give an antonym) hyperpnea   hypopnea

35. RHAPTEIN sew together, unite
   rhapsode   rhapsody   raphe   raphide
   -RRHAPHY indicates surgical suture: using your list of body
   parts, make up five words ending in -rrhaphy.

36. RHĒGNUNAI break [RHAG-]
   hemorrhage
   Find out what -rrhagia means as a suffix and form five words
   using it.

37. SBENNUNAI quench, extinquish [SBE-]
   asbestos

38. SĒPEIN make rotten
   septic   antiseptic   septicemia

39. SŌZEIN save
   soteriology   creosote

40. STALASSEN drip [STALK-, STALAG-]
    stalagmite   stalactite

41. STIZEIN tatoo, mark STIG-
    stigma: give plural
    astigmatism

42. THEASTHAI behold, view
    theatre   amphitheatre   theorem   theory
    metatheatre

End Game: What's the good word: EUONYMY
eucalyptus 'well-covered'
Eucharist 'thanksgiving' (charis: grace, favor)
eudemon 'a good spirit'
eudemonia means 'happiness, well-being'
eudemonics is the 'art or theory of happiness'
eudemonism is a 'system of ethics that evaluates actions in terms
    of their capacity to bring happiness'
Eugene 'well-born'
eugenics is the 'study of hereditary improvement'
Euglena 'of good eyeball': a type of water organism with a red
    eyespot
eulogy 'a good saying'
Eumenides 'well-minded ones' a euphemism for the Furies
Eunice 'good victory'
euonymous 'good name' (refers to various plants)
eupatrid 'of good father'
eupepsia 'of good digestion'
euphemism 'use of good words'
euphony 'good sound' [also: the tendency to change speech
    sounds for easier pronunciation]
euphoria 'good bearing: feeling of well-being'
euphotic of 'good light' (referring to the upper layer of a body
    of water)
Euphrosyne 'cheerfulness, good disposition' (one of the Graces)
eurythmy 'harmony of proportion, graceful movement'
eutectic 'easily melted' (tēkein, 'melt')
euthenics 'the study of improvement of the human condition
    through improvement in environment' (euthenein 'to
    flourish')
eutropic 'well-nourishing'
euxenite 'kind to strangers' [a mineral which contains many rare
    or strange elements]
Evangel 'the Gospel or glad-tidings'

Many more words that give us little to complain about can be added
to this list. If you feel grouchy look up words beginning with

caco-; or add to this list of hates and hatreds:
misobasilist: hater of kings
misocapnist: hater of tobacco smoke
misoclere: hating priests
misogrammatist: hater of letters
misomusist: hater of culture
misoscopist: hater of sights
misopogonistically: with hatred of beards
misoxeny: hatred of foreigners

APPENDIX I HOW TO PRONOUNCE LATIN

Vowels: use the standard European Vowels:
a: long as in father
    short as in but
e: long as in made
    short as in led
i: long as in machine
    short as in tin
o: long as in bone
    short as in obey
u: long as in hoot
    short as in foot

Diphthongs:
ae: as in aisle [as English long i]
ei: as in weigh
oe: as in toy
au: as in cow

Consonants:
c is always hard (k sound) as in coarse
g is always hard as in go
s is hissed as in see (never as sh or z)
t is always dental as in to (never as sh)
j (which is not distinguished in ancient orthography from i) is
    pronounced as y (as in yet). j is a consonantal i.
v (which is not distinguished from u in ancient orthography) is
    pronounced as w (as in wine). v is consonantal u.
The remaining consonants may be pronounced in the same way as English pronounces them.

Every Latin word has as many syllables as it has vowels or diphthongs: that is, there are no silent letters in Latin.

Accent: the accent falls on the penult (next to last syllable) if it is long. Otherwise it falls on the antepenult (the third from last). A word of only two syllables is accented on the penult. A syllable is long if it contains a long vowel or diphthong, or if it contains a short vowel followed by two or more consonants. Quantities are marked in the glossary where useful for accentuation.

APPENDIX II: SUMMARY OF SUFFIXES FROM LATIN

[Note: Prefixes from Latin can be found in Chapters 8 and 9 of Part II; Suffixes from Greek are in Chapter 5 and Prefixes from Greek in Chapter 6 of Part III.]

[Numbers refer to chapters in Part II.]

-acious (10) from -ax, -acis, 'tending to' forms adjectives, added to present stems of verbs

-al (4) from -alis 'of, pertaining to' forms adjectives from noun bases

-alia, -ilia (4) neuter plural of -alis, -ilis 'things pertaining to' forms nouns from adjectives in -alis, -ilis

-ance, -ence (11) from -antia, -entia 'act, state, condition of --ing' forms nouns from present participles of verbs

-ane, -an (4) from -anus 'of, pertaining to' forms adjectives (and nouns) from noun bases

-ant, -ent (11) from -ns, -ntis '--ing' (present participle) forms adjectives (and nouns) from present base of verbs

-ar, -ary (4) from -aris 'of, pertaining to' forms adjectives from noun bases

-ary, -arious (4) from -arius 'of, pertaining to' forms adjectives from nouns bases

-ary (4) from -arius (masculine form) 'of, pertaining to: a person concerned with' forms nouns from adjectives in -arius

-ary, -arium (4) from -arium (neuter form) 'a place for, a place of' forms nouns from adjectives in -arius

-ate (5) from -atus 'office of' forms nouns from noun bases

-ate 'possessing': forms adjectives from nouns: Examples, affectionate, delicate, dentate, fortunate, illiterate, pinnate, pennate, serrate

-ble (able, ible) (10) from -bilis 'able to be', 'able to' forms adjectives from verb bases, present or ppp

-ble (10) from -bulum, -bula 'instrument or place for' forms nouns from the present base of verbs

-cide (14) from -cida 'one who kills;' from -cidium 'the killing of'

-cle, -culum (10) from -culum 'place or instrument for' forms nouns from the present bases of verbs

-ence see -ance

-ent see -ant

-eous (4) from -eus 'of, pertaining to' forms adjectives from noun bases

-ernal (4) from -ernus 'of, pertaining to' forms adjectives from noun bases

-fer (14) from ferre 'bearing, producing,' 'that which bears'

-ferous (14) 'bearing, producing'

-fic (14) from facere 'making, causing' forms adjectives

-fy (14) 'to make' forms verbs

307

-ic (4) from -icus 'of, pertaining to' forms adjectives from noun bases

-ice (5) from -itia 'quality, state, condition, or character of being' froms nouns from adjective bases

-id (10) from -idus 'tending to, of a quality' forms adjectives from present bases of verbs

-il, -ile (4) from -ilis 'of, pertaining to' forms adjectives from noun bases

-ile (10) from -ilis 'able to be' forms adjectives from either verb base

-ine (4) from -inus 'of, pertaining to' forms adjectives from noun bases

-ion (10, 12) from -io, -ionis 'act, state or result of an act' forms nouns from ppp base of verbs, sometimes from present base

-ity, -ety, -ty (5) from -itas, -etas, -tas 'quality, state, condition or character of being' forms nouns from adjective (and noun) bases

-itude (5) from -itudo (base: -itidin-) 'state, quality, condition or character of being' forms nouns form adjective bases.

-ive (12) from -ivus 'tending to, having the quality of' forms adjectives from ppp. base of verbs

-lent (-olent, -ulent) (4) from -lentus 'full of, disposed to' forms adjectives from noun bases

-men (10) from -men (base: -min-) 'result, means of' forms nouns from present base of verbs

-ment (10) from -mentum 'result, means of' forms nouns from present base of verbs

-mony (5) from -monium, -monia 'quality, state, condition or character of being' forms nouns from adjective bases

-nal (4) from -nus + -al 'of, pertaining to' forms adjectives from Latin adjectives in -nus

-nd- (11) forms gerundives from present base of verbs 'that must be'

-or (10) from -or 'act, state, result of' forms nouns from present base of verbs

-or (12) for -or 'one who, that which' forms nouns from ppp. base of verbs

-orious, -ory (12) from -orius 'tending to, pertaining to' forms adjectives from ppp base of verbs

-ose, -ous (4) from -osus 'full of, having, tending to be' forms adjectives from noun bases

-ous (3) forms English adjectives from Latin adjectives in -us, -a, -um

-tic (4) from -ticus 'of, pertaining to' forms adjectives from noun bases

-tude see -itude

-ty see -ity

-ulous (10) from -ulus 'tending to' forms adjectives from present base of verbs

-uous (10) from -uus 'tending to' forms adjectives from present
base of verbs

-ure (12) from -ura 'the act or result of' forms nouns from ppp
base of verbs

-urnal (4) from -urnus (+ -al) 'of, pertaining to' forms adjectives from noun bases

-y (5) from -ia 'quality, state, condition or character of being'
forms nouns from adjective bases

-y (5) from -ium 'act, office, place, or position' forms nouns
from noun bases

-y (10) from -ium 'act state, instrument, result' forms nouns from
present bases of verbs

APPENDIX THREE: TRANSLITERATION OF GREEK

The Greek Alphabet

Greek Character	Name	Transliteration	Pronunciation
α A	alpha	a	short: cup; long: father
β B	beta	b	b
γ Γ	gamma	g [ng]	hard g go; ng before palatal
δ Δ	delta	d	d
ε E	epsilon	e	short e: bet
ζ Z	zeta	z	sd wisdom; [or dz, adze]
η H	eta	ē	long e: ate
θ Θ	theta	th	thing [or t-h]
ι I	iota	i	short: tin; long: teen
κ K	kappa	k, c	k
λ Λ	lambda	l	l
μ M	mu	m	m
ν N	nu	n	n
ξ Ξ	xi	x	ks, x
o O	omicron	o	short o: pot
π Π	pi	p	p
ρ P	rho	r, rh	trilled r
σ , ς Σ	sigma	s	say
τ T	tau	t	t
υ Y	upsilon	u, y	u
φ Φ	phi	ph	as f [or p-h]
χ X	chi	ch	loch [or k-h]
φ Ψ	psi	ps	ps
ω Ω	omega	ō	long o: go

Practice:
Transliterate these Greek words:

ξενος   φαλμος   θεος   φιλανθρωπια

τεχνολογια   συμβιωσις   ζωδιακος   μητροπολις

Transliterate into Greek:
zōon   barbaros   psychē   potamos
scēnē   mikros   agora   apotheōsis

Diphthongs:

Greek	Transliteration	Pronunciation
αι	ai, ae, e	aisle
αυ	au	house
ει	ei, e, i	sleigh
οι	oi, oe, e, i	coin

311

| ου | ou, u | s<u>ou</u>p |
| ευ | eu | e + u |

Breathing marks:

There was no letter for the sound <u>h</u> in Greek. Instead, a mark, called the breathing mark was used over every initial vowel (over the second member of an initial diphthong) to indicate the presence or absence of the h-sound.

The smooth breathing mark means there is no <u>h</u>: ʼ
The rough breathing mark means there is an <u>h</u>: ʻ

εἰς   <u>eis</u>
ὁδος   <u>hodos</u>

Words beginning with <u>rho</u> and <u>upsilon</u> always have the rough breathing.

ῥοδον   rhodon ʼroseʼ
ὑπερ   hyper ʼoverʼ

Nasal Gamma:

A gamma coming before gamma, kappa, chi, or xi (the palatal sounds) is pronounced as an <u>ng</u> and transliterated as <u>n</u>.

ἀγγελος   angelos ʼmessengerʼ
ἀναγκη   anankē ʼnecessityʼ
συγχορος synchoros ʼpartner in the chorusʼ
Σφιγξ   Sphinx ʼSphinxʼ

Practice:
Transliterate these Greek words:

δαιμων	ὑστερος	Αἰσωπος	φαινομενον	συνταξις
αἰθηρ	ἐγκωμιον	οἰκονομικος	εἰρωνεια	ὑποκριτης
Εὐριπιδης	Οἰδιπους	αἰνιγμα	πειρατης	Ἰφιγενεια

Transliterate these into Greek:

angos	bronchos	chimaera
haima	hēdonē	heteros
hippos	idios	ichthys
pharynx	pseudēs	technē
astēr	Aeschylus	Thucydidēs
Sōcratēs	Theocritus	Clytaemnēstra
Phaedra	Astyanax	Antigonē

For more words to practise transliterating, use the Greek glossary.

GLOSSARY OF BASE WORDS: LATIN

* Words in lesson vocabularies

A

* acer, ACR- sharp
acerbus bitter, sour
* aequus even, equal
aeternus immortal, everlasting
aevum age, eternity
ager, AGR- field
* AGere/ACTum drive, lead, do
alacer, alacr- eager, quick, brisk, cheerful
* albus white
aliēnus belonging to another (adj.)
alius other (of more than two)
* ALere/ALTum grow, nourish
alter other (of two)
altus high, deep
ambitio, AMBITION- a going around
ambulāre go, walk
amīcus friend
amita aunt
amo: AMāre love
amoenus pleasant, delightful
* amplus large, spacious
ancilla maidservant, handmaiden
* anima breath, spirit, soul
* animus reason, mind, soul, life
* annus year
* antīquus old, ancient (former)
anxius troubled
aperio: APERIre, APERTum open, uncover
appello: APPELLāre address, entreat, appeal, call
* aptus fitted to, fit
* aqua water
aquila eagle
arbiter witness, judge
arcus bow
ardeo: ARDēre/ARSum be on fire, burn
arguere make clear, demonstrate
arma (n. pl.) arms
* ars, ART- art, skill, craft
artus joint
asper rough, bitter, harsh
assiduus busy, constant
audeo: AUDēre/AUSum dare
* audio: AUDIre/AUDITum hear
* augeo: AUGēre/AUCTum increase
aura breeze

313

* auris ear
aurum gold
auscultāre listen
auxilium aid, reinforcements
avārus greedy
avidus eager
avunculus uncle

B

baca (or bacca) berry
baculum stick, staff
barba beard
* beātus happy, blessed
* bellum war
bellus pretty, handsome
* bene well (see bonus)
bestia beast
bibere drink
* bonus good
    melior better
    optimus best
bos, BOV- ox, bull, cow
* brevis short
bucca cheek
bulla bubble, seal

C

caballus horse (vulgar Latin)
* cado: CADere/CASum fall (-cidere)
* caedo: CAEDere/CAESum cut, strike (-cidere, -cisum)
caelebs unmarried
caelum sky
caleo: CALēre be warm, glow
callum hard skin
calx, CALC- pebble
campus open field
cancer crab
* candeo: CANDēre glow, be white
* cano: CANere/CANTum sing
canis dog
caper he-goat
* capio: CAPere/CAPTum take, seize (-cipere, -ceptum)
capsa box
* caput, CAPIT- head
cardo, CARDIN- hinge
* caro, CARN- flesh
* castra (n. pl.) camp
castus pure, chaste
* causa cause, reason case
cavus hollow

* cedo: CEDere, CESSum go, yield
* celeber, CELEBR- crowded, honored
* censeo: CENSēre/CENSum assess, rate, estimate
* cerno: CERNere/CRETum sift, separate, decide
* cella storeroom
* cerēbrum brain
* cieo: CIēre, CITum move, stir, rouse, call
* civis citizen
* clamo: CLAMāre/CLAMĀTum [-claim] shout
* clarus bright, clear, famous
classis fleet, class (first class)
* claudo: CLAUDere/CLAUSum close (-cludere, -clusum)
* clavis key
clavus nail (cf. clava club)
* -clino: CLINare/CLINĀTum turn, bend
* codex, CODIC- trunk (of a tree), book
cogito: COGITāre/COGITĀTum think
cogo: COGere/coactum drive together, compel (from agere)
* colo: COLere/CULTum till, cultivate, honor, dwell
comis courteous, friendly
* condo: CONDere/CONDITum build, store, hide
contumēlia insult, invective
* copia abundance
copula bond, tie, link
* cor, CORD- heart
* corōna crown
* corpus, CORPOR- body
* creo: CREāre/CREĀTum create
      cresco: CRESCere/CRETum grow, increase
* credo: CREDere/CREDITum believe
creta chalk
crimen, CRIMIN- accusation, charge
* culpa fault, blame, guilt
* cura care
* curro: CURRere/CURSum run
cutis skin

D
dare see under DO
debeo: DEBēre/DEBITum owe
debilis weak
dexter (dexteri/dextri) right, on the right side, right hand
* dico: DICere/DICTum say, speak
* diēs, diei day
* difficilis difficult (cf. facilis)
* dignus worthy
diluvium blood
discipulus student (cf. discere: learn)
* divus godly, of God

315

* do: DAre/DATum give
* doceo: DOCēre/DOCTum teach
doleo: DOLēre/DOLITum be in pain, grieve
* domus home, house
donum gift
dorsum back
dos: DOT- dowry
* duco: DUCere/DUCTum lead
* duo two

E
efficax, efficāc- accomplishing (cf. facere)
* emo: EMere/EMPTum buy, procure
eo, ire/itum go: see under IRE
equus horse
* erro: ERRāre/ERRĀTum wander, go astray, make a mistake
* ESSE, FUTŪRus (-ent-) be
exterior outer
externus outward

F
* facilis easy
* facio: FACere/FACTum (-ficere/-fectum) do, make
fama talk, rumor, reputation
* fanum temple
* FĀri/FĀTum speak
* fateor: FATēri/FASSum (-fiteri/fessum) confess, acknowledge
* fatum the thing said (cf. fari), fate
* fatuus silly
fecundus fertile
felix, FELIC- happy
* femina woman
-fendo: FENDere/FENSUM strike, hurt
* fero: FERre/LATum carry, bear
* ferveo: FERVēre boil, ferment
* fido: FIDere/FISum trust, rely on, confide
findo: FINDere/FISSum split, divide, burst
fingo: FINGere/FICTum (FIG-) form, shape, mold
* finis end
firmus firm, strong
flatus blowing, breeze
* flecto: FLECTere/FLEXum bend, turn
* flos, FLOR- flower
     FLORēre thrive
* fluo: FLUere/FLUXum flow
foedus, FOEDER- treaty, league
* forma shape, beauty
* fortis strong, brave
* frango: FRANGere (FRAG-)/FRACTum break
frater, FRATR- brother

fraus, FRAUD- deceit
* fugio: FUGere/FUGITum   flee, escape
* fundo: FUNDere/FUSum   pour, shed, scatter
fungor: FUNGi/FUNCTum   perform, do, discharge
* funus, FUNER- funeral, death
furo: FURere   rave, rage

G
gaudeo: GAUDēre   rejoice
* genus, GENER- birth, race, kind
* gero: GERere/GESTum   carry, wear, wage
* gladius   sword
* globus   ball, sphere
* gradior: GRADI/GRESSum (-gredi)   walk, step
      gradus   step
* granum   grain
* gratia   favor, grace
* gratus   pleasing, beloved, favorable, thankful
* gravis   heavy, serious
grex, GREG- flock, herd

H
* heres, HERED- heir
* habeo: HABēre/HABITUM   have, hold, keep
haereo: HAERēre/HAESum   cling, stick
* homo: HOMIN- man, human being
* horreo: HORRēre   shudder, stand stiff
* hostis   enemy
* humānus   of mankind
humeo: HUMēre   be moist/damp
* humilis   lowly

I
* ignis   fire
ille   that
imitor: IMITāri/IMITATum   copy
* immūnis   tax-exempt
infernus   beneath
injuria   injustice, wrong
insidiae (f. pl.)   ambush, trap
* Īre, ĪTum   go
iter, ITINER- journey

J
* jaceo: JACēre   lie
* jacio: JACere/JACTum (-icere, -jectum)   throw
Janus   god of doors
joculus   a little joke
* jocus   joke
judicium   judgment

judex, JUDIC- judge
* jungo: JUNGere/JUNCTum join
* jus, JUR- right, law

L
labor: LABi/LAPSum slide, slip, fall
labor work, exertion
lacrima (Late Latin: lachryma) a tear
laevus left
lassus tired
* latus, LATER- side
* latus wide
-LATum 'carried' (see under fero)
legāre to depute, commission
* lego: LEGere/LECTum collect, speak, choose, read
* levis light
* lex, LEG- law
* līber free
liber, LIBR- book
libertus freedman
lino: LINere/LITum smear
* linquo: LINQUere/-LICTum leave, quit
* liqueo, LIQUēre be fluid, be clear
littera (in Eng. liter-) letter
liveo: LIVere be black and blue
* locus place
* longus long
loquax, LOQUAC- talkative
* loquor: LOQUi/LOCUTum speak
* luceo: LUCēre shine, be light
* ludo: LUDere/LUSum play
* luna moon
lupus wolf
lympha water

M
* magister, MAGISTR- teacher, master
* magnus big, great, large
    major greater, bigger, larger, older
    maximus greatest, biggest, largest
* maneo: MANēre/MANSum remain, dwell
* malus bad
    pejor worse
    pessimus worst
* manus hand
* mare sea
* mater: MATR- mother
medius middle
melior better, see bonus
* memini: MEMINisse remember

318

memor mindful
mendax, MENDĀC- lying, false
merx, MERC- goods, wares merces, merced- pay, wages
* metus fear
* migro: MIGRāre/MIGRĀTum move, change one's place of
* miles, MILIT- soldier
minae projecting points, threats
* minister, MINISTR- attendant, servant, helper
minor smaller, less
mimimus smallest, least
* miser wretched, unhappy
* mitto: MITTere/MISSum send
* modus manner, means, limit
* moles mass, bulk, pile
* moneo: MONēre/MONITum warn, advise, remind
mons, MONT- mountain
* mordeo: MORDēre/MORSum bite
* mors, MORT- death
* mos, MOR- manner, custom
* moveo: MOVēre/MOTum move
mundus world
* murus wall
* mus, MUR- mouse

N
* nascor: NASCi/NATum be born
* navis ship
* necesse unavoidable
nemus, NEMOR- wood, grove
* nervus tendon, sinew
* nomen, NOMIN- name
* (g)nosco: NOSCere/NOTum know
* novus new
* nox, NOCT- night
* numerus number
nuntius messenger, message
* nux, NUC- nut

O
* oculus eye
* odium hatred
* omnis all
* onus, ONER- burden
ops, OP- means, resources
optimus best (see under bonus)
* opus, OPER- work
* ordo, ORDIN- rank, row
* orior: ORĪri/ORTum rise
* os, OSS- [ossu-] bone
otium leisure

319

P

paene almost [PEN-]
* paenitet: PAENITēre repent
pagus village, country district
palleo: PALLēre be pale/yellow/faded
palus stake
panis bread
* par equal
pareo: PARēre show
* paro: PARāre, PARĀTum prepare, get ready, get
* pars, PART- part
parcus sparing, stingy
pasco: PASCere, PASTum feed, protect
* pater, PATR- father
* patior: PATi/PASSum suffer
* pauci (pl.) few
pauper poor
* pax, PAC- peace
peculātor embezzler
pejor worse (see malus)
* pello: PELLere/PULSum push
* pendo: PENDere/PENSum hang
perfidia faithlessness, treachery (see fido)
* pes, PED- foot
pessimus worst (see malus)
* pestis plague
* peto: PETere/PETĪTum aim at, seek, attack
pingo: PINGere/PICTum paint, tatoo
* pius devoted to duty, godly
* placeo: PLACēre/PLACITum please, be agreeable
planus flat, even, level
plaudo: PLAUDere/PLAUSum (-plodere/-plosum) beat, clap
        approve
plecto: PLECTere/PLEXum weave, plait
* plenus full
plicāre plait
* pono: PONere/POSITum place, put
* populus people
* porto: PORTāre/PORTĀTum carry
portus harbor
* possum: POT- be able
* posterus next, following
praeda booty
* prehendo: PREHENDere/PREHENSum seize, grasp
* premo: PREMere/PRESSum squeeze
* primus first
prodigium portent, unnatural deed
prodigus wasteful
proles offspring
* proprius one's own, peculiar

320

puer boy, child
pugno: PUGNāre fight
pungo: PUNGere/PUNCTum prick, sting
* pulcher, PULCHR- _beautiful
* puto: PUTāre/PUTĀTum think, reflect, consider (orig. 'prune, clean')

Q
* quaero: QUAERere/QUAESITum (-quirere/-quisitum) ask, seek
* qualis of what sort, what kind of
* quantus how great, how much
* quattuor four
quiētus at rest
quis, quid who? what?
quotus how many

R
* radius ray, rod, beam
* radix, RADIC- root
ramus branch
ranceo: RANCēre stink
* rapio: RAPere/RAPTum (-ripere, -reptum(snatch
* ratio, RATION- reckonong, account, reason
* rego: REGere/RECTum move in a straight line, rule, direct
* reor: Rēri/RĀTum think, suppose, consider
* rete net
* rex, REG- king
rigeo: RIGēre be stiff
ripa bank
* rogo: ROGāre/ROGĀTum ask, stretch out the hand
* rota wheel
ruga wrinkle
* rumpo: RUMPere/RUPTUM break
* rus, RUR- country

S
* saeculum generation, age, the times
* salio: SALĪre/SALTum leap, jump [later Latin -sultare]
* salus, SALŪT- health, safety
* sanctus holy
* sanguis, SANGUIN- blood
* sanus sound
* satis enough
scalprum knife
* scando: SCANDere (-scendere, -scensum) climb
* scio: SCĪre/SCĪTum know
* scribo: SCRIBere/SCRIPTum write, incise, scratch
* scrupus sharp stone
* seco: SECāre/SECTum cut
secūrus untroubled, free from care (cf. cura)

321

* sedeo, SEDēre/SESSum sit
semen, SEMIN- seed
* senex, SEN- old man
sensus SENSU- _feeling
* sentio: SENTīre/SENSum feel
* sequor: SEQUi/SECUTum follow
* servo: SERVāre/SERVĀTum save
* servus slave
signum mark, sign
simplex, SIMPLIC- single, simple
singuli (pl.) one at a time
silva woods, forest
* similis like
* sisto: SISTere set, place, stop, stand
sobrius sober, moderate
* socius companion, ally; follower
* sol sun
* soleo: SOLēre/SOLITum be accustomed
solidus solid
sollicitus anxious, worried
* solvo: SOLVere/SOLŪTum loosen, release, undo
* somnus sleep
species sight, appearance
* specio (spicio): SPECere/SPECTum look, look at
spiro: SPIRāre/SPIRĀTum breathe
sponte of on's own accord
squaleo: SQUALēre be rough, be stiff, be clotted
* sto: STĀre/STĀTum stand
sterno: STERNere/STRATum spread
* stinguo: STINGUere/-STINCTum extinguish, quench
* stringo: STRINGere/STRICTum draw tight, press together
* struo: STRUere/STRUCTum construct (spread)
* studeo: STUDēre be diligent, be zealous for, apply oneself to;
    study
* studium eagerness, zeal, study
stupeo: STUPēre be stunned
* sumo: SUMere/SUMPTum take, use, spend
sumptus (sumptu-) expense, cost (cf. sumere)

T
* tango: TANGere/TACTum touch (-tingere)
tego: TEGere/TECTum cover, hide, defend
temno: TEMNere/-TEMPTum slight, despise
templum sanctuary
* tempus, TEMPOR- time
* tendo: TENDere/TENTum, TENSum stretch, spread, aim
* teneo: TENēre/TENTum hold, keep
tenuis thin, stretched
* terminus boundary, end
tero: TERere/TRITum rub away, thresh, tread, wear out

322

* terra land, earth
* terreo: TERRēre/TERRITum frighten
* testis witness
* texo: TEXere/TEXTum weave, build
* timeo: TIMēre fear
* tingo: TINGere/TINCTum dip, soak, moisten, dye
tondeo: TONDēre/TONSum shear, clip, shave
torpeo: TORPēre be stiff, be numb
* torqueo: TORQUēre/TORTum twist, turn
torreo: TORRēre parch, scorch
* traho: TRAHere/TRACTum draw, drag
tremo: TREMere quake, quiver
trux, TRUC- wild, rough
tumeo: TUMēre swell, be swollen
turba uproar, disturbance

U
* ultimus last
universus all together
* unus one
* urbs, URB- city
* utor: UTi/USum use

V
vacuus empty
* vado: VADere/-VASum
* valeo: VALēre/VALITum be well
* varius colored, diverse
* vello: VELLere/VULSum pluck, pull, pick
* vendo: VENDere/VENDITum sell
* venio: VENĪre/VENTum come
* venter, VENTR- stomach
venum sale
ver spring
* verbum word
* vermis worm
* verus true
* verto: VERTere/VERSum turn
vestigium track, footprint
vestis clothes
vexo: VEXāre/VEXĀTum shake, toss, trouble, distress
* via way, road
victoria victory see vincere
* vicus quarter of a city, street, village, estate
* video: VIDēre/VISum see
vigeo: VIGēre thrive, flourish
* vinco: VINCere/VICTum conquer, win
* vinum wine
* vir man
* virus slime, poison

vis   force, power, strength
* vitium   fault, flaw, offence
* vivo: VIVere/VICTum   live
* voco: VOCāre/VOCĀTum   call (cf. vox)
* vorāre   eat   -vorous 'eating' -vore 'that which eats'
* vox, VOC-   voice
voveo: VOVēre/VOTum   vow, dedicate, promise, wish
vulgus   the mass of the people, the crowd, rabble

GLOSSARY OF BASE WORDS: GREEK

A

adēn gland
aeidein sing
aeirein lift, raise up
aēr air (lower air)
agein lead, bring
agōn contest, struggle
agora market-place, gathering place
agros field agrios living in the fields, wild
ainigma riddle
aitia cause, responsibility
aiōn age
aisthanesthai [AISTH-] feel, perceive
aithēr upper air (bright air)
Akadēmos a legendary Attic hero
akos remedy
akouein hear
akros topmost, extreme
algos pain -algia pain
allos another
anemos wind
angelos messenger
angos vessel
anthos blossom, flower
anthrōpos human being
anēr, ANDR- man (male)
ariston breakfast
aristos best (most fit)
arithmos number
arktos bear: the north
archein begin, rule (be first)
　　archē beginning, rule
　　archaios from the beginning, ancient
arthron joint
askein exercise
aspis, ASPID- shield, asp
astēr star
atmos steam, vapor
autos self
axios worthy

B

bainein go, walk, step
baktērion staff, cane
ballein, BLE-, BOL- throw
baptein dip
barbaros foreign, barbarian (imitative of sound of birds)
barus heavy

325

basileus   king
bathus   deep   bathos   depth
biblos   papyrus, book   biblion   book
bios   life
botanē   pasture, herb, grass
bous   bull, ox, cow
brachiōn   arm
brachus   short
bronchos   windpipe
brotos   mortal man
bruein   grow
bursa   the hide, wineskin: pouch, sac

Ch

chaos   empty sapce
charis   grace, favor
charasmein, charak-   engrave, mark
cheilos   lip
cheir   hand
chemeia   art of alloying metals
Chimaira   she-goat
chilioi   thousand
chloros   light green
cholē   gall, bile
chondros   cartilage, grain
chōrein   move   -chore indicates a plant distributed by specific
      means
choros   dance
chrēstos   useful
chriein   anoint
chrōma, CHROMAT-   color
chronos   time
chrusos   gold
chthōn   earth

D

daimōn   deity, divinity
daktulos   finger
deiknunai (DEIK- DEIG-)   show
dein   bind, tie
deinos   terrible
deka   ten
dēmos   the people
dendron   tree
derma, DERMAT-   skin
despotēs   master of the house, lord
diaita   way of living
diakonos   servant, attendant ('one thoroughly active')
dicha   in two
didaskein (DIDAK-)   teach

didonai (DO-) give
dikē right, law
diploos twofold
dis, di- twice
diskos 'something thrown', a plate
dokein (dok-, dog-, dox-) seem, think
    doxa glory, reputation
doulos slave
drakōn serpent
dramein (drom-) run
dran do, act, perform
dunasthai be able

E
echein [hek-, schē-, och-) hold
ēchō a reverberated sound
eidos form, shape, thing that is seen
eikōn image
einai (ONT-) be
eirōn dissembler: one who says less than he thinks
eisō inside
elaunein (ELA-) drive
ēlektron amber
eleos pity, mercy
elthein come
enantios opposite
endon inward
enkephalos brain
ennea nine
enteron intestine
eran love
erēmos lonely, desert
ergon work, deed
ethnos nation, people
ēthos custom, moral character
epos word
etumos true
eu well
eunē bed
eurus wide
exō outside

G
gala, GALAKT- milk
gamos marriage, sexual union
gastēr, GASTR- belly, stomach
gē earth
genos birth, race, kind (GON-)
genus cheek
gignōskein GNŌ- know

327

glōtta, glōssa tongue
glukus sweet
gluphein carve
gnathos jaw
gōnia angle, corner
gonu knee
graphein (GRAPT-, GRAM-) write, draw, scratch
gumnos naked
gunē, gunaik- woman

H (rough breathing)
haima, HAIMAT- blood
hairein take, grasp, choose
harmozein fit together, join
hēdonē pleasure
hedra seat, chair; surface
heis, mia, HEN one
hēlios sun
hēlix, HELIC- spiral
hēmera day
hēmisus, HEMI- half
hēpar, HEPAT- liver
hepta seven
hērōs hero, protector
heteros one of two, other, different
heuriskein find, discover
hex six
hienai (HE-) send, throw
hieros holy, sacred
hippos horse
histanai (STA-/STE-) stand
histōr learned
histos web, beam, mast (that which is set up)
hodos road, way
holos whole
homoios like
homos one and the same
hoplon implement, armor
hōra period of time, hour
horan see
horkos oath
horos boundary
hudōr; HUDAT-; HUDRO- water
hugiēs healthy
hugros wet, moist
hulē forest, material, matter (suffix: -YL)
humēn membrane
humnos song
hupnos sleep
hupsos height, summit

328

hustera   womb
husteros   later, behind

I

iasthai   heal, cure
    iatros   physician
ichthus   fish
idios   one's own, peculiar
ienai   (I-)   go
iris, IRID-   rainbow, iris
ischion   hip, thigh
isos   equal

K

kaiein, KAU-   kindle, burn
kainos   new (ceno-, -cene)
kakos   bad
kalein, KLE-   call
kalos   beautiful
kaluptein   hide
kamara   vaulted chamber
kanōn   rod, rule, standard
kapnos   smoke
kardia   heart
karpos   fruit
karpos   wrist
katharos   clean, pure
kenos   empty
kentein   stab, pierce
kephalē   head
kerannunai, KRA-   mix
keras   horn
kinein   move, set in motion
klan, KLĒ-   break
kleptein   steal
klēros   lot, legacy (that which is cut off)
klinein   bend, make to slope, recline
kluzein   wash away
koinos   common (cen- coen-; -cene)
kolla   glue
kolossos   120 foot statue of Apollo
kolpos   bosom, womb, vagina
kondulos   knuckle
koptein, kom-   cut
kosmos   order, universe, ornament
kōma, kōmat-   deep sleep
kranion   skull
kratein   rule [kratos   strength]
kreas   flesh
krinein   separate, decide, judge

329

kruos   frost
kruptein   hide
kubernan   steer
kuein   swell   kuma, kumat-   anything swollen, wave (-cyme)
kuklos   ring, circle
kuōn, kun-   dog
kurios   swollen, strong, powerful: Lord
kustis   pouch, bladder
kutos   hollow vessel (indicates <u>cell</u>)

L
labrus   'double axe'
Lakōn   native of Laconia, Spartan
lambanein LAB-, LEP-, LEM-   take seize
laos   the people
latris   servant   -latry   worship
legein   speak, choose
leipein   LIP-   leave, be wanting
leōn   lion
lēthē   forgetfulness
leukos   white
lithos   stone
logos   speech, word, reason
luein   loose, break
lukos   wolf
lura   lyre

M
Magnētis (lithos)   (stone) of Magnesia
magos   enchanter, wizard (of Persian origin: mighty one)
mainesthai, MAN-   rage, be mad
        mania   madness
        mantis   seer
makros   long
martur   witness
mastos   breast
mathein   learn
mēchanē   contrivance, machine
megas, MEGA-, MEGAL-   big, large, great
melas, MELAN-   black
meros   part
mētēr   mother   METR-
metōpon   forehead
metron   measure
mikros   small, little
mimos   imitator
misos   hatred
mitos   thread
mnasthai, MNE-   remember
monos   alone, sole, only, single

330

mōros   foolish, dull
morphē   form, shape, beauty, outward appearance
Mousa   Muse
muein   close, be shut
murios   countless, ten thousand
mus, MU-   mouse; muscle
muthos   speech, story
muxa   mucus, slime

N

narkē   numbness, cramp
naus   ship
nekros   corpse
nektar   the drink of the gods ('overcoming death')
nemein   assign, allot
      nomos   portion, custom, law
neos   new
nephos, nephele   cloud
nephros   kidney
neuron   sinew; pl. nerves
nomos   see under nemein
nous   mind
nux, nukt-   night

O

ochlos   crowd
ōdē   song (cf. aeidein)
odous (odon)   ODONT-   tooth
oikos   house
oktō   eight
oligos   few, little
omma, ommat-   eye
ōmos   shoulder
onoma, ONOMAT-; -ONUM-   name
ōon   egg
ophthalmos   eye
ōps   eye, face
opsis   sight, view, face
organon   tool, instrument (cf. ergon)
ornis, ORNITH-   bird
oros   mountain
orthos   straight, right, correct
osteon   bone
ostrakon   shell, potsherd
oura   tail
oxus   sharp, keen; (acid)

P, PH, PS

Paian (title of Apollo as physician of the gods)   cry of joy
pais, PAID-   child

palai long ago
palin again
Pallas title of Athene
Pan woodland deity (who arouses terror in lonely places)
papuros papyrus
pas, PAN-, PANT- all, entire, every
patēr, PATR- father
pathein suffer, experience _pathos_ suffering
pauein cease, stop
pedon soil, gound
peira attempt
pelagos sea
pempein send _pompē_ procession
pente five
peran pass through _poros_ ford
petesthai PT- fly
    pteron feather, wing
petra rock
phagein eat
phainein PHAN- show, make appear
phanai PHA-, PHĒ- speak
    phēmē saying
pharunx throat
pherein, PHER-, PHOR- bear, carry
phialē vessel, bowl
philos loving, dear
phlegein burn
phobos fear, flight
phrazein show, tell
phuein make to grow
    phyton plant
phōnē voice, sound
phōs, PHŌT- light
phrēn diaphragm, midriff, mind
phulax, PHULAKT- guard
phulē tribe
phullon leaf
piptein PTŌ- fall
planasthai PLAN- wander
plassein mold (spread out)
platus wide, broad
plessein beat, strike (-_plegia_ paralysis)
pleura ribs, side
ploutos wealth
pnein breathe
    pneuma, pneumat- wind, spirit
    pneumon lung
poiein make, do
pōlein sell
polemos war

332

polis   city-state
polus   much, many
posis   a drink
potamos   river
pous, POD-   foot
prattein, PRAG-, PRAK-   do
presbus   old
prōktos   anus
prōtos   first
psallein   pluck, play the harp
pseudēs   false
psilos   bare, plain
psuchē   breath, life, soul
pur   fire
puxos   box-tree: box

R(H)
rhaptein   sew together, unite
rhēgnunai, RHAG-   break
rhein, RHEU-, RHU-, RHO-   flow
rhētōr   speaker
rhis, RHIN-   nose
rhiza   root
rhodon   rose

S
sarx, SARK-   flesh
sauros   lizard
sbennunai, SBE-   quench, extinquish
schizein   split
scholē   leisure
sēma, sēmat-   sign, signal, thing seen
sēpein   make rotten
sitos   grain, food
skandalon   trap, snare, stumbling block
skelos   leg
skēnē   tent, hut: scene
skia   shadow
sklēros   hard
skeptesthai   examine
skopein   see
sōma, sōmat-   body
sophos   wise, clever
sōzein   save
sperma, SPERMAT-   seed
sphaira   globe
sphuron   ankle
stalassein   stalak-, stalag-   drip
stenos   narrow
stear   fat

333

stellein STOL-, STAL- make ready, send
stereos firm, solid
sternon breast-bone
stēthos chest
sthenos strength
stichos line, verse
stizein, STIG- tattoo, mark
stoa porch
stoma, STOMAT- mouth
stratos army
strephein STROPH-, STREPT- turn, twist
stulos column, pillar
sukon fig

T, TH
taphos tombtattein, TAK- arrange, array, assess, assign
tektōn worker, builder, carpenter
technē art, craft, skill
teinein, TEN-, TA-, TON- stretch out, strain (cf. tonos)
tēle far away
telos end
temnein, TOM- cut (TM-)
tettares, tessares, tetra- four
teuchos tool, papyrus roll, volume
thanatos death
theasthai behold, view
theos God
therapōn (or theraps) attendant
thermos warm, hot
thēsauros store, treasure
thōrax, thōrak- thorax
thrix, TRICH- hair
thronos seat
tithenai, THE- put, place
tokos birth
tonos accent, tone
topos place, position
toxon bow, pl. bow and arrows (poison)
tracheia windpipe
trachus rugged, harsh
treis, tri- three
trephein TROPH- feed, nourish
trepein TROP(H)- turn
tupos blow, mark
turannos tyrant

X
xenos stranger
xēros dry, harsh
xulon wood

Z
zēlos   eagerness
zōnē   belt, girdle
zōon   living thing, animal
zumē   leaven, yeast

Note:
Prefixes from Greek will be found in CHAPTER SIX of the Greek section.
Suffixes from Greek will be found CHAPTER FIVE of the Greek